With best wishes —

The Forgotten Giant of Bletchley Park

Enjoy this account of an extraordinary codebreaker and diplomat of integrity.

Harold Gilbertly

Brigadier John Hessell Tiltman CMG MC, codebreaker extraordinary. (*Photograph, Clabby 2007*)

The Forgotten Giant of Bletchley Park

Harold Liberty

Pen & Sword
MILITARY

First published in Great Britain in 2022 by
Pen & Sword Military
An imprint of
Pen & Sword Books Ltd
Yorkshire – Philadelphia

ISBN 978 1 39908 961 6

A CIP catalogue record for this book is available from the British Library.

Typeset by Mac Style
Printed and bound in the UK by CPI Group (UK) Ltd,
Croydon, CR0 4YY.

Pen & Sword Books Limited incorporates the imprints of Atlas, Archaeology, Aviation, Discovery, Family History, Fiction, History, Maritime, Military, Military Classics, Politics, Select, Transport, True Crime, Air World, Frontline Publishing, Leo Cooper, Remember When, Seaforth Publishing, The Praetorian Press, Wharncliffe Local History, Wharncliffe Transport, Wharncliffe True Crime and White Owl.

For a complete list of Pen & Sword titles please contact

PEN & SWORD BOOKS LIMITED
47 Church Street, Barnsley, South Yorkshire, S70 2AS, England
E-mail: enquiries@pen-and-sword.co.uk
Website: www.pen-and-sword.co.uk

Or

PEN AND SWORD BOOKS
1950 Lawrence Rd, Havertown, PA 19083, USA
E-mail: Uspen-and-sword@casematepublishers.com
Website: www.penandswordbooks.com

To

Tempe Denzer (1928–2020), daughter of Brigadier John Tiltman
and one of the 'greatest generation'

and

Alan Harris, formerly Chief Steward at Bletchley Park,
who inducted this writer into the work of stewarding at BP in 2014
and has been a stalwart among colleagues there.

Contents

Introduction

John Tiltman – 'The Brig' – is the 'forgotten giant' of the Bletchley Park story.

His code-breaking skills were held in awe by his colleagues; he became the Senior Cryptanalyst at Bletchley Park, effectively from 1941 onwards when Dilly Knox was increasingly incapacitated through ill-health, and officially from 1943; he was the one others turned to when they needed help; he was so able that, even when well past retirement age, both the UK and the USA wanted to make use of his talents.

As a man (apart from being a codebreaker) he was liked, admired, even loved by those around him. A military man who was nevertheless relaxed about matters others were unnecessarily pernickety about, he would do what was good, or kind, and it is hard to find anyone who sincerely disliked him.

Yet he has none of the reputation of Turing, or the historical recognition that (belatedly) has come to Denniston or Welchman. He did not go on from Bletchley Park to be in the House of Lords like Baroness Trumpington, Hugh Trevor-Roper or Asa Briggs, nor play chess for England as Alexander did, nor help to found the science of computing like Turing or Peter Hilton. Instead he remained a man committed to his calling in cryptology, serving his country (and others) with quiet and professional competence unrivalled (perhaps a William Friedman would disagree, but only gently) by any of his time.

Part of the reason is that his name is not attached to the Enigma challenge – though he made a contribution there for longer than is sometimes remembered – and the holy twins of Bombe and Colossus have claimed so much of the limelight in the history.

This account seeks to redress the balance a little. Errors and omissions are solely this author's, and should not detract from the greatness of the man.

Foreword

'A biography of Tiltman is long overdue.'
Joel Greenberg, 2014

The genesis of this writing lies in a talk I gave to a gathering of Bletchley Park volunteers and staff at a meeting in 2016. There was a chance to outline briefly the life of 'The missing giant', which was the title of the talk. There were three themes:

a) that there was much more behind the man than the codebreaker,
b) that Bletchley Park could consider his role and that of the non-Enigma ciphers to deserve a higher profile,
c) that his role in US-UK relations is more important than has been generally recognized.

The discovery of the NSA declassified historical archives was a great encouragement for me to pursue the topic. But having prepared it over a number of weeks, I discovered, just under three weeks before delivery, that a detailed lecture on Tiltman's life had been given about three years before by Michael Smith, and probably been heard by some in the audience!

No matter; the talk was pleasantly received. But there was always a feeling that much more needed to be said and written, if the material could be found and assembled. The only attempt to do so (apart from a biography by Erskine and Freeman in 2003 in *Cryptologia* magazine) was a monograph by John Clabby, published in 2007 through the NSA. Over the next few years I returned spasmodically to the topic.

It was the onset of the coronavirus in 2020 that gave me the time to develop the writing. The closure of Bletchley Park to the public, and the consequent inactivity of volunteer guides and stewards, meant that there was time to explore the materials more fully.

Though much is made of material linked to Bletchley Park, and the trustees have been most helpful in permitting the use of documents and other materials, the opinions and ideas expressed in this writing are solely those of the author and are not necessarily those of Bletchley Park Trust or its officials.

Abbreviations

AFSA	Armed Forces Security – organisation to oversee US intelligence across all the armed forces, instead of separate organisations. Formed 1949, superseded 1952 by NSA.
Arlington Hall	Centre for the US Army codebreaking organisation during the war, a girls' school taken over in 1942.
BP	Bletchley Park, a country estate on the edge of Bletchley, Buckinghamshire, centre for the UK Government Code and Cypher School, Britain's codebreaking centre during the war.
BRUSA	**BR**itain and **USA** 'in concert' – especially: agreement in 1943 between Britain and the USA for continuing close cooperation on signals intelligence – developed by the UKUSA 1946 agreement; foundation of the 'special relationship' we think of today (2021).
Comintern	The Communist International, an organisation promoting world communism between the wars, overtly and covertly; its messages were the frequent targets of British codebreakers through the interwar years and beyond.
ECM	Electronic Code machine/Electric Cipher Machine – acronym for what became the standard US high-grade code machine (see also SIGABA and 888/889, or Mark II) in the USA.
FECB	Far East Combined Bureau: British signals intelligence listening station in Hong Kong, focussing on interception and analysis of Far Eastern signals.
FISH	Generic name given by BP to the German signals system using teleprinter coding (Baudot-Murray) and enciphering, notably on Lorenz and also Siemens machines..

Floradora	A system of double-enciphering messages, used particularly by German diplomats in the war.
FO	Foreign Office: in the UK, the department concerned with all foreign affairs (US equivalent: State Department).
FRUMEL	Fleet Radio Unit, codebreaking base in Australia (MELbourne), used by Australia and the USA in the course of the war.
G-2	US Army Intelligence section within a unit or base of the army.
GC&CS	Government Code and Cypher School – Britain's codebreaking centre 1919–46 (forerunner of GCHQ).
GCHQ	Government Communications Headquarters, the UK successor to GC&CS, monitoring signals intelligence, security and related issues.
JMA	Japanese Military Attaché (code).
JNA	Japanese Naval Attaché (code).
KOSB	King's Own Scottish Borderers, Tiltman's regiment in the First World War.
LSIB	London Signals Intelligence Board, counterpart of USCIB, the body in the UK scrutinising intelligence and cryptology etc post-war.
NSA	National Security Agency, USA security section of Defense Department, responsible for intelligence gathering, analysis etc.
OP-20-G	US navy codebreaking organisation in the war.
OTP	One-Time Pad, a system of coding where only sender and receiver have a single copy of the message key, which is used once and then destroyed; basically unbreakable if used properly.
SHAEF	Supreme Headquarters, Allied Expeditionary Force – top HQ for Normandy invasion in 1944.
SIGINT	American abbreviation, widely adopted, for Signals Intelligence, i.e. from messages, signals, codes etc, sent in some way (radio, telegram, cable etc) and intercepted, as opposed to 'human intelligence', the work of spies and agents.

SIS	1) The USA Army Signals Intelligence Service (from 1942 associated with Arlington Hall). 2) From the correct designation of MI6, Britain's Secret Intelligence Service – the 'Secret Service' with responsibility for international matters (MI5 being internal security); GC&CS came under its umbrella.
SOAS	School of Oriental and African Studies – centre for language and culture studies, London University.
TA	Traffic Analysis – the art of looking at the information coming from the actual transmission of a message (including direction-finding, call-signs, communication networks, as well as certain electronic features).
TICOM	Target Intelligence Committee – the Allied group organized at the end of the war to examine as much enemy scientific and intelligence material (papers and documents, machines and equipment) as could be found.
ULTRA	The term used in Britain in the war for all intelligence derived from codebreaking and related work at Bletchley Park – not only 'top secret' but 'beyond top secret'.
USCIB	United States Communications Intelligence Board – US organisation post-war for overseeing communications security, codes and intelligence matters.
WEC	Wireless Experimental Centre – cover name for a listening and monitoring station in India, with main base at Anand Parbat near Delhi, additional centre at Abbottabad; an outstation for BP.
WO	War Office – British government department in charge of Army service, comparable to the 'Admiralty' for the Royal Navy.
WT	Wireless Telegraphy – the sending of messages by radio.

Important Personnel

UK

Commander Alistair Denniston
In charge of GC&CS (under Director, MI6) from its foundation until 1942 (London, then BP 1939–42); moved to direct the Diplomatic section in London.

Captain Edward Hastings
British liaison officer to US navy 1941–45, linked to OP-20-G (navy codebreakers); later deputy director, GC&CS.

Captain (Colonel) Freddie Jacob
Codebreaker in India with Tiltman; his deputy in the Military Section 1930 onwards; Italian specialist; Tiltman's successor as head of Military Section and in US liaison.

Dilly Knox
Leading codebreaker in GC&CS (and before this navy codebreaker in 'Room 40') until forced by illness to step back in 1941 (died 1943); a main contributor to breaking the Enigma system.

Stewart Menzies
Director of MI6, under whose control GC&CS worked, 1939–52.

Admiral Hugh Sinclair
Director of SIS (British) 1923–39, having been director of Naval Intelligence. This included GC&CS. Obtained BP site for the SIS with codebreaking as a focus in 1938.

Geoffrey Stevens
British liaison officer for GC&CS with Arlington Hall (US army codebreakers) from July 1942.

Edward Travis

Deputy Director of GC&CS military section at Bletchley Park until 1942; Director at BP 1942 onwards.

Alan Turing

British mathematician and codebreaker; led Enigma work, especially Naval Enigma, Hut 8, 1940–42; worked on voice encodement; wrote fundamental paper in 1936 which began computer science.

William (Bill) Tutte

British scientist, Cambridge; joined Research group at BP in 1941 working on Hagelin machine; analysed coded material from Lorenz teleprinter cypher attachment to reveal how the machine worked (and could be mastered).

USA

Brigadier General Carter Clarke

Senior G-2 officer in War Department, US army.

William Friedman

Senior cryptanalyst, US army codebreakers in the US SIS, 1942, based at Arlington Hall.

George Marshall

Chief of Staff, US army 1941–45 (later Secretary of State).

Admiral Joseph Redman

Senior officer in Naval Communications in the US Navy in 1940, and then Director from February 1942 for most of the rest of the war; he represented the Navy in post-war US-UK negotiations. His brother John ('Jack') was a Captain in the US navy and served in OP-20-G, and became head of its Intelligence section February 1942.

Abraham Sinkov

US army codebreaker under Friedman; leader of 'Sinkov mission' February 1941 which began close cooperation over cryptography and intelligence later to become the 'special intelligence relationship'.

General George Strong

Deputy Chief of Staff in G-2, US military intelligence, US Army War Department.

Colonel (later General) Telford Taylor
US army, led US team in Hut 3, Bletchley Park, selecting and sending intelligence to USA from UK, 1943 onwards (part of US prosecution at Nuremberg 1946).

Admiral Joseph Wenger
Senior officer in US navy, expert in using automation in codebreaking work; became head of OP-20-G Cryptology in 1942, prominent in liaison with the UK.

FRANCE

Gustave Bertrand
Senior officer in Deuxième Bureau (French secret service); made initial contact with Hans-Thilo Schmidt who passed Enigma secrets to him; shared them with Poles, who he helped escape at start of war; served with Resistance.

Chapter 1

Youth and First World War

John Hessell Tiltman was born on 25 March 1894 in London to reasonably prosperous parents.[1]

His father Alfred was an architect. Alfred[2] was born in 1854 in Islington but the family settled in Sussex,[3] the county of his father Thomas's birth, according to census records – and was articled in 1872 to a firm of architects in Hastings.[4] His brother Henry Thomas was two years younger and became a Professor of Music. After a range of training activities, including a short time with the Royal Academy and two years with Roland Plumbe, Alfred was admitted to the Royal Institute of British Architects in 1880 and later became a Fellow. In the early 1880s he lived (with the family) in Guildford, Surrey, with his brother Thomas and now widowed mother Mary. Alfred's fortunes with various partnerships were varied but he had some successes with municipal design work (including Glasgow Royal Infirmary) and became a lecturer. He moved to 70 Torrington Square in London some time before 1888, having married Sarah (formerly Kerr) in 1885. It was here that John was born, by which time the family was earning enough to have three servants[5] and a nurse.

Torrington Square was to be purchased between the wars by the emerging London University, and most of the housing in it was demolished, apart from a few of the nineteenth century houses, numbers 27–30, which give some impression of what the area might have looked like at the time of Alfred's occupation – refined, tall brick-built homes with four storeys and railings. Christina Rosetti lived in number 30 until her death in the year of Tiltman's birth. Today the square features Senate House and other university buildings. The nearby School of Oriental and African Studies was to feature in Tiltman's career.

John was the youngest of three children, with an older brother and sister.[6]

Mary was the first, born in 1890.

His brother Alfred Hessell Tiltman[7] was born in 1891 and became known as Hessell. Hessell graduated from London University in engineering design in 1910 before joining the Daimler company as an apprentice. In 1916 he transferred to the fledgling De Havilland company, becoming a designer for them before joining Vickers Airship Guarantee Company, a name also associated with Barnes Wallis and Neville Shute Norway. Shute and Hessell set up the Airspeed Company (which was also connected with the renowned aviator Sir Alan Cobham), and Hessell played a vital role in designing the Horsa glider.

John went to Charterhouse school from 1907 until 1911. Charterhouse is a high-ranking English public school. The school, originally in London, moved to Godalming in 1872, with three boarding 'houses'. It has expanded steadily since, maintaining a reputation of excellence among the best in the country. Among Old Carthusians (as pupils are known) are Robert Graves (writer and poet), Ralph Vaughan Williams (composer), John Wesley (founder of Methodism), Hastings Ismay (Churchill's military assistant) and Lord Baden-Powell (founder of the Boy Scouts); more recent names at the time of this writing include politician Jeremy Hunt and broadcaster Jonathan Dimbleby.

The school's ethos left its mark on Tiltman's character. Here he won both junior and senior scholarships.[8] He excelled there to such an extent that he was offered a place at Oxford University at the age of 13. However his father died suddenly in 1910. John and his family were in what were euphemistically called 'reduced circumstances', so, though his brother was graduating at this time and entering an engineering career, University was out of the question then for him.

On leaving school at 17 he went into teaching. He worked in three schools before the First World War. Clabby in his account rightly maintains[9] that this inclination is reflected in later stages of his career – his interest in training and developing people in a range of skills, cryptological and linguistic particularly. Initially he taught in Fulham, then (perhaps drawn by family connections with the area) in Hastings.[10] The final post he held was at Northcliffe House School[11] in Bognor Regis. At this time Bognor had something of a reputation for both quality and numbers of schools and it seems that the school was housed in a fine Georgian building; the young teacher would have been fortunate to find such a post. The school itself does not exist today but some of the buildings survive as Chichester University accommodation.

When war broke out in 1914, Tiltman enlisted in the King's Own Scottish Borderers (KOSB), eventually being assigned to the 6th Battalion, 9th Division. It may be that his school's background affected his choice to serve, and that of others. Another Carthusian, who played an important role in the war linked to Tiltman's future but as yet unseen career, was Edward Russell Clarke, who went from Charterhouse to Pembroke College, Cambridge, and studied Mathematics and Mechanical Science; he was one of the leading radio 'hams' of his day and was co-opted by Naval Intelligence to intercept German signals and report them to Room 40. Three thousand five hundred Old Carthusians fought in the war and 698 were killed in it. The culture of loyalty and service seems significant in Tiltman's background.

Training took place at Salisbury, and the division was assembled near Bordon in Hampshire. It was delayed because of shortages of equipment, but was eventually completed in 1915 by which time the battalion had moved to nearby Bramshott. Kitchener himself saw the recruits at Ludshott on 5 May. Two days later the battalion was sent to embark (7 May 1915); the crossings were made between 9 and 12 May, landing at Boulogne.

The KOSB were involved in key battles, including Loos (1915, where their role was support rather than front-line), the Somme (Bazentin, Delville Wood and le Transloy, 1916) and Arras (1917). By the end of July 1916 Tiltman is listed[12] as having been wounded in action, probably in one of the Somme battles mentioned above.

It was at the Battle of Arras (not the Somme as DNB and others have said, but as Smith says in his lecture) that he was awarded his Military Cross.

Fighting at Arras began on 9 April 1917 and lasted for six weeks.[13] Its purpose, apart from the usual one of gaining ground, was to back the grand French plans for a major offensive near Reims at the Chemin des Dames. It was hoped to draw away German reserves northwards, giving greater opportunity for Nivelle to punch through. This would be harder to do now; German forces had withdrawn to a new, stronger defensive position (part of the Hindenburg line) and at Arras the salients intended for attack had been smoothed out.[14] This sequence of battles involved the heaviest concentration of Scottish battalions seen in the war and they took over 50,000 casualties. The offensive made initial gains (First Battle of the Scarpe) but became increasingly slowed and more costly. The

6 Battalion KOSB were used as a lead group on the left with the Royal Scots. Scottish divisions including the 15 Battalion were involved in the central area (under Allenby) and there was success east of Arras, capturing ground on the Gavrelle Road in the second phase of the campaign. The success of 9 Division was commemorated by a cairn set up in 1922 (now in the Point du Jour war cemetery, it remembers all the 9's service in the Great War).

It was in this area that the third wave again used Scottish forces (Third Battle of the Scarpe). By now the French efforts had faltered, and were to lead to a series of mutinies which threatened the integrity of their forces. Haig therefore had to pursue this phase to distract German pressure. The KOSB 6 Battalion was involved in the attack on 3 May near Gavrelle. They were selected to lead[15] on the left alongside 9 Cameronians (Scottish Rifles), supported by 11 Royal Scots regiment (Lothian). The Cameron Highlanders and the Black Watch led on the right. The attempt, described as 'hurriedly organized and against well-set defences' was unsuccessful – perhaps a consequence of it being a hasty response to failures elsewhere. During the attack the 6 KOSB were cut off overnight, and were assisted by 12 Battalion, the Royal Scots, in withdrawing, sustaining some 300 casualties in the process. The attack, it seems, was held by sustained artillery, and 6,000 lives were lost in the 15-hour action. Other efforts nearby to the south at Roeux and Bullecourt also had limited effect, and Haig called off all further action on 17 May.

The official citation indicates that Tiltman (a second lieutenant and since March an acting captain) led the charge and capture of two machine guns with few casualties. This fighting withdrawal was remarkable in keeping casualties down in Tiltman's specific area.

The wounds that Tiltman received were serious and had a lasting effect.[16] He was hit in the chest. Apparently it took him many hours to make his way back from no-man's land to the safety of his lines. The marks on his body left by the wounds were extensive even later in life, and the injury was to be the background to his illness after the war.

The Carthusian magazine dates the MC award as 26 July 1917. His award record survives, as does the despatch card (though dated 1921). His wounds sustained in the 1917 campaigns later shortened his service in Russia. *The Carthusian* states that Tiltman was wounded in action three times.

It may well be a further result of his war wounds that later in his career, as a codebreaker, Tiltman preferred to work not seated, as most would, but standing, at a specially made desk something like a lectern.

The year 1917 saw the name of Tiltman first associated with codebreaking and related secret work. However this was not the future 'Brig'. It was his sister Mary, who served with the Women's Army Auxiliary Corps (WAAC).

The WAAC was formed at the start of 1917, and between this date and the Armistice some 57,000 young women served in a range of roles. They were renamed 'Queen Mary's Army Auxiliary Corps' in 1918. The first to serve in France arrived at the end of March 1917 – about a dozen cooks and waitresses. Others served at headquarters with communications work. They were followed by a very different group[17] – a dozen serving with the Intelligence Corps (IC) as 'officers' ('assistant administrators'). They became known as 'Hushwaacs'. Their distinctive IC insignia created a stir. They arrived at St Omer and thereafter endured much of the discomfort shared by the men at the front or in reserve. Mary Tiltman was one of this group. It is probable that she was selected because of her language skills – German. She and the others were involved[18] with breaking of messages where the code systems were known, and examining others including the 'bookbuilding' work of compiling enemy code books from detailed analysis (see Chapter 4). Mary's record card[19] shows her entitlement to the award of the Victory Medal and the British War Medal, like her brother.

Thus far John Hessell Tiltman had served with honour but without anything to distinguish the greatness within him. His injuries too were not unusual for a conflict that took some 950,000 British lives and left wounds and scars, seen or unseen, on many more. But an opportunity was to emerge from the wreckage of Europe after the Armistice, of an apparently unexpected nature.

Chapter 2

Between the Wars – Entry into Cryptography

It all began as a two-week assignment.

In his twenty-fifth year, with war wounds still troubling him, Tiltman would have been rightly concerned about his future. He could hope to continue in the army despite injury, though many would be demobilised to return to civilian life – 'homes fit for heroes to live in' was the cry of government as planning for peace got under way. Would this be sufficient for his able and inquiring mind? We shall examine how the Russian dimension was to maintain his combat status in an entirely new way for him.

Russia had changed out of all recognition during the war. The Tsarist regime, remote from its people and showing increasing desperation against the German-led Central Powers, lost control. In February 1917 there was revolution and a new government under Prince Georgy Lvov and then Alexander Kerensky was formed based on the state Duma ('parliament') in Petrograd. Tsar Nicholas abdicated. The idea was that elections should be held for a constituent Assembly, but though a Republic was proclaimed in September there was multi-factional argument and no clear leadership. Worse, there was no sign of the government ending the war. Consequently local 'soviets', committees based on Communist ideas, moved to gain support of the army, factories and transport workers. In another revolution in November 1917 the Communists seized control, led by Lenin and Trotsky. Their political philosophy appeared to threaten all the ideals of Western countries, who supported counter-revolutionary forces termed 'White Russian' against the 'Red' Communist movement, units of which assassinated the former Tsar and his family in 1918 and ended Russia's role in the First World War.

At the Armistice in November 1918 the British Army was looking for forces to serve with the White Russians against the Communists in Russia. Tiltman, still recovering from his injuries, was involved in teaching officer cadets as the last shots were being fired, and has described the Russian experience:[1]

> *And I was accepted* [for Russian service] *and sent to Siberia... We didn't actually know when we left Liverpool what part of Russia we were going to. We did go to Siberia; I was there for a very short time.... I had learnt a little Russian before I went there. I had learnt it a little before the war – taught myself. And I was only in Siberia two and a half months. I was in Irkutsk for a bit, and I was in hospital in Vladivostok before being shipped home.*

The British military mission in Irkutsk was monitoring supplies intended for the tsarist forces, to keep them from the Communists.[2] Tiltman's war wounds were troublesome. Part of his work involved training White forces, in cold and sapping conditions. On one occasion a walk several miles in below-freezing temperatures on an assignment, and then back again after it, led to his hospitalisation in Vladivostok.

He goes on:

> *When I got back* [to Britain] *eventually, when I was passed... fit enough, I joined a regular battalion... But then, I took the opportunity offered and went on a Russian course to London...This was a fairly elementary course, and none of the other army officers who went on the course knew any Russian to start with. And they passed the preliminary examination, and I just scraped through the* [intermediate]... *second-class interpreter degree. And I was in the – quite by chance – in the War Office when they were looking for interpreters.*

Tiltman's linguistic skills thus played a role in his becoming involved with Russian work, and his wartime injury explains his early return from what might have been an arduous posting.

His task then became one of translating Russian diplomatic messages from intercepted traffic. The traffic had been worked on by the newly-formed Government Code and Cypher School (GC&CS). It was Tiltman's first encounter with the organisation which was to shape his life and career for the next fifty years.

Tiltman describes what happened next:[3]

> *During the summer of 1920, J was on a Russian language course in London. At the end of it, I was about to return to regimental duty, but the War Office intervened and on 1 August I went to work on temporary attachment for 2 weeks at the Government Code and Cipher School... which at the time had a growing backlog of untranslated Russian*

diplomatic messages. After a few days the War Office decided to hold me there for a year and, in fact, I never returned to my regiment.

GC&CS had been formed in 1919 when the army and navy codebreaking groups from MI1(b) and Room 40 were amalgamated into one organisation. While both groups had achieved success in various ways, Room 40 had been particularly celebrated as the breakers of the 'Zimmerman telegram', the message sent by Germany to Mexico encouraging the latter to act against the USA in 1917, while the Germans also reintroduced unlimited submarine warfare in the Atlantic in an effort to bring Britain to its knees. The decoding, passed to the USA and publicly disguised as a leak, contributed to bringing America into the First World War.

The immediate focus for GC&CS was to be on diplomatic traffic, and it was run by Alastair Denniston, under Admiral Hugh Sinclair who at the time was Director of Naval Intelligence. Sinclair's move to be Head of SIS/MI6 in 1923 coincided with GC&CS coming under the umbrella of the Foreign Office instead of the navy.

Working initially in the Strand, and then Knightsbridge, GC&CS later moved into No 54 Broadway where MI6 was based, taking the 'third floor', a phrase which grew to carry significant meaning. Denniston continued to lead; he had been a member of Room 40 in the First World War, and in 1919 was given the job of leading GC&CS when it was formed. His wife Dorothy had also been involved with Room 40.[4] It was Denniston who later saw the need for, and sought out, the 'dons' who were to be an essential part of the Bletchley Park story when the main codebreaking group moved to Bletchley just before the Second World War.

In its early days GC&CS was virtually all to do with diplomatic codes.[5] The three armed services regarded their own intelligence people as reliable enough and anything GC&CS could offer was to be subservient to their wishes and needs (a view that persisted in some quarters well into the Second World War). The only service section to be organized in the 1920s within GC&CS was the naval one (and that subject to navy requirements); the Military Section did not appear until 1930 and the Air Section in 1936. Interest in commerce-linked codes became formalized in 1938. GC&CS also lived off the intercepts from other sources – the Post Office, the Services' listening and interception posts, etc. It had no wireless interception of its own.

It was at GC&CS that Tiltman encountered Fetterlein. Ernst Fetterlein was born in St Petersburg in 1873, the son of a German language tutor. He studied languages at university and joined the Russian foreign ministry in 1896. He became the leading cryptographer to the Tsar, working on various codes (including British ones). In 1917, with the onset of the Russian Revolution, he fled with his wife to western Europe, coming to England where in 1918 he joined Room 40. Here he worked on Austrian and Bolshevik codes, transferring to GC&CS when it absorbed the navy and army organisations in 1919. His attention now went on Soviet messages. Tiltman continues:

> *At the time of my arrival, Fetterlein's small section was entirely occupied with the solution of the current Moscow-London and London-Moscow diplomatic traffic intercepted in the cable office. All messages were enciphered by simple columnar transposition of Russian plain text conventionally transliterated out of Cyrillic characters. As each message was transposed on a different key, all messages had to be individually solved.*

Fetterlein gave Tiltman some tuition – the only time, according to Tiltman, that Fetterlein ever taught someone directly.

And so it came to pass, almost casually, that Tiltman began to take notice of the original messages and not just the decoded ones:[6]

> *There were a great many messages. There was a great deal of correspondence. Some of the messages were quite long, and they weren't very difficult. The nature of the transliteration made it a fairly easy job. Letters which were single in Russian, were 2 letters in English – 'li' – 'ya', and the single Russian letter was 'shch', and this sort of thing, so it wasn't particularly difficult to put them together. This suited me very well. I was pretty quick at it… It was absolutely new to me. The Gold Bug* [story by Edgar Allen Poe] *was the highest* [I had been before].

The Poe story features a simple 'substitution code' (see Chapter 4), not unlike Sherlock Holmes and the 'Dancing Men'.

Tiltman has described some of these codes in outline (see also Chapter 4). His gentle ease of description belies the concentrated effort needed to bring out the decodes from a system that did not remain static for long:[7]

> *The Russian ciphers ... were using single columnar transposition or Russian transliterated into English characters and sent in English characters. The keys for the transposition were taken from English poetry and no key was used twice by intention and so each message had to be worked on separately.*

The subsequent tracking-down of the keys, from obscure English poets of the seventeenth and eighteenth centuries, took Tiltman much time and the connivance of several rare-book minders. Tiltman[8] says:

> *I went to the Director of the British Museum and said we wanted to borrow this book. I can still remember his saying, 'I know it's only a shilling edition, but you're asking me to break the law of the land.' However, we managed to get hold of the book.*

At the time, the British Library was housed in the British Museum, which was not permitted to loan out its copies; by law a copy of every British book published was to be deposited there. The poetry lines were used as a running key (Chapter 4).

In 1921 he was sent to India to work on Russian ciphers. His efforts, largely based at Simla lasted until 1929. From 1925 until the end of his India role he was a Foreign Office civilian, having retired – his first military retirement but by no means his last.

India was the symbolic height of the British Empire, and was also well-placed to monitor the Russian signals going to various Far Eastern embassies whose purpose was invariably that of spreading the Revolution. The continuation of the 'Great Game' in the Middle East and Asia, coupled with the instability of China at this time, made India a vital centre for gathering intelligence and breaking codes. The Indian Royal Engineer Signal Service was one of the oldest dedicated signals units, organized in 1910, and the Indian Signals Corps was founded a decade later, rapidly becoming one of the biggest.

At this time the whole area of radio communications and the use of interception for intelligence purposes was still in its infancy. The Royal Corps of Signals was formed in August 1920, and the 'Army Chain' which grew from it linked Aldershot with the Rhine, Sarafand in Palestine and Jubbulpore in India, with a range of smaller posts within the Empire.[9] Before this the Admiralty, with the need for advanced radio communications at sea and over long range, had begun creating a series of British intercept stations from 1914 with special attention to German traffic, and linking to 'Blinker' Hall's code team in room 40 (a hub of the navy's code-breaking effort at the Admiralty) and was intercepting around the world from its ships and bases. Coherent management of the material collected was not always present – the problems at the Battle of Jutland in 1916 were in part created when newly intercepted and decrypted information was not expedited to British commanders – and the separation of army and navy organisations could create duplication of effort or inhibit sharing. Tiltman was therefore becoming involved with an area still evolving and developing, adjusting to new technology and a world order recovering from a great war.

Tiltman says of this time:[10]

> *From 1921 thru* [sic] *1929 I was a member of a section of the General Staff at Army Headquarters in Simla, India, consisting of never more than 5 persons. We were employed almost entirely on one task, to read as currently as possible the Russian diplomatic cipher traffic between Moscow, Kabul in Afghanistan and Tashkent in Turkestan. From about 1925 onwards I found myself very frequently involved in all aspects of the work – directing the interception and encouraging the operators at our intercept stations on the North West Frontier of India, doing all the rudimentary traffic analysis that was necessary, diagnosing the cipher systems when the frequent changes occurred, stripping the long additive keys, recovering the codebooks, translating the messages and arguing their significance with the Intelligence Branch of the General Staff.*

That Tiltman was given an overview of all the stages of the process meant he had an appreciation of the needs and problems of each area, something that would enable him to understand others' difficulties as well as having the specific knowledge of technicalities himself. He says:

> *I realize that I was exceptionally lucky to have this opportunity and that very few others have had the chance of acquiring this kind of general working experience. Between 1921 and 1924 I paid three visits to the corresponding unit in Baghdad and on several occasions, sitting amongst the operators in the set-room of the Baghdad intercept station, worked directly on the red forms fresh off the sets, to the benefit not only of my own experience but also to the morale of the operators.*

The coded materials at this time came from two main sources. One was the intercepts provided by the listening stations, of the kind described by Tiltman in his experience in Simla and also on his visits to Baghdad. The other, in particular for materials worked on in Britain from 1925, was 'drop copy' obtained through the Post Office. At the time there was agreement between the Post Office (which managed traffic sent via cables) and the Intelligence Service that a copy of all traffic should be made and given to the service. The legality of this practice was sometimes questioned, as confidentiality was a 'given' for users of the cable system, but there was tacit acceptance of the position which was not openly questioned. The position was in part formalized by the insertion into the Official Secrets Act of 1920 an additional clause[11] requiring cable companies working in Britain to give copies of their messages to the authorities.

The value of the team in India grew as their hold on Russian signals and ciphers grew. Smith has opined[12] that the work of Tiltman and his team in 1923 gave the foreign secretary Lord Curzon the material he used in his protest memorandum to the Soviets of 8 May 1923 in which he quoted decrypts. The ultimatum[13] challenged Soviet activity against the British Empire, demanded withdrawal of certain diplomats, financial compensation for mistreated Britons and other concessions, and threatened cancellation of the new UK-Russian trade agreement. Fractious negotiations led to some minor concessions by Russia in due course.

One example of how careful Tiltman had to be comes from an incident in 1925. Tiltman recounts:

> *Stark, the Russian Ambassador in Afghanistan, sent a cipher telegram to Moscow in which he inquired what joint action was proposed between the Russian and Afghan governments 'in view of the occupation of Vaziristan (W Widu Okkupacii Waziristana)'. Our interpreter, who was quadrilingual in Russian, English, French and German, but not outstandingly literate in anyone of them, translated this as '<u>with a view to</u> the occupation of Vaziristann'. The intelligence branch of Army Headquarters was in Delhi, and we were in Simla, and there was a day of near crisis in Delhi before someone, realizing that it would take something like six months for Russians and Afghans to join forces over the Hindu Kush, queried the translation back to us. I well remember Colonel Jeffery* [sic] *saying: 'In future all startling statements of this nature will be viewed with the utmost suspicio'. The outcome was that I was told to check all our interpreters' translations before they went out.*

The mistake – a single Russian letter! – caused much alarm about possible conflict.

In 1925 Tiltman organized a cryptanalytical competition[14] in India, which was open to army officers and instigated by the Intelligence branch of the Indian army. It proved to be a useful way to identify potential codebreakers. A winner was Captain, later Colonel, Freddie Jacob. Jacob was to join the newly-formed GC&CS Military section in 1930 and to work through the Second World War at Bletchley Park, taking over from Tiltman as head of the Military Section (and following him as liaison officer in the USA when Tiltman retired in 1954).

Tiltman's India posting was ostensibly to relieve the incumbent Colonel Jeffrey. Mention of Jeffrey brings us to the more interpersonal problems Tiltman had when he went out to Simla, which he describes thus:[15]

> *We had a Colonel named Jeffery* [sic] *who was working in the Indian government, in Simla… He was a very good Chinese scholar. He broke a number of difficult Chinese… codebooks. Well then, China ceased to be a problem and he was asked to take up Russian. This was a considerable difficulty. He absolutely refused to learn Russian… The India Office descended on Colonel Jeffrey and said at the end of the war… that he would have to go back to regimental duty. This appalled him – he'd never been near a regiment in his life… So he decided to retire…*

He would be losing some rank (he held a 'brevet' rank, giving him seniority) unless he went to a regiment.

> *Then, while I was on the high seas, on my way to relieve him in September 1921, they changed their mind and said that he could stay, but they made a condition which was that he should go on a year's leave to recover his health and leave me with his job. Well, he had never met anybody who had broken ciphers at all. This was something he invented himself, as far as he knew. By this time, he and I were on nothing like speaking terms… He went off on his leave, leaving his beautiful job to me… I said, 'Sir, I would like to come down and see you off at the station,' and he said, 'No, you'd better not, we'd only quarrel on the way down.'*

After Jeffrey's return a year later however, the two gradually developed respect for each other.[16] Tiltman says:

I left India at the end of 1929, having been with Colonel Jeffery for eight and one half years during which I had learned how to parry his sharp wit or divert it on to others, and we had become firm friends.

When Jeffrey retired in 1935 with eye trouble, he was not forgotten; it was Tiltman who persuaded him to return to service (under Tiltman!) in 1938 (he had had surgery to improve his sight) and help in the oncoming crisis.

The National Archives has mention of Jeffrey, Walter Hugh (1878–1957), a colonel in the Indian Army, who has left travel notes of experience in the Far East before the First World War. In the records of the Imperial War Museum there is one Walter Hugh Jeffrey, major in the Indian Army from 1915 and a lieutenant colonel in 1924. On the Bletchley Park Roll of Honour is Walter Hugh Jeffrey, who served in Elmers school and then Berkeley Street, 1940–43, as Head of the Chinese section, working on diplomatic codes. His presence is noted[17] by William Friedman in May 1943 while on a visit to London: 'A retired officer of Indian Army, elderly but determined; ... Jeffery charming and witty gent but definitely a unique case.'

In the mid-1920s a new cipher machine made its appearance on the commercial market. Promoted by a company headed by Arthur Scherbius, it was named 'Enigma'. It included a typewriter-like keyboard, connected electrically to a series of three rotors each labelled on a moveable outer ring with the alphabet. Each rotor had internal wiring from one face to the other in apparently haphazard fashion, and contacts matching the alphabet spacing on the surfaces of each. When a key was pressed, electricity flowed through the wiring through each rotor in turn and from these to a set of lights for alphabet letters, illuminating the cipher letter. Every time a key was pressed, at least one rotor moved, changing the entire internal wiring configuration, meaning that, for example, 'T' was not always enciphered as 'D'. The illuminated letters were to be written down manually as they appeared (Enigma did not generally type out the coded message). The machine was later developed by adding a plugboard ('Steckerboard') to the electric circuit on the front, which switched letters both at the typing and the output stages of the circuit, adding astronomically to the possible 'states' of the machine (the number of possible ways to set up rotors and plugboard was roughly 103×10^{21}). Because the machine worked in a 'reciprocal' way (if for example A encodes as P, then P will encode as A at the same rotor positions), a person with a similar machine and knowing the starting rotor positions could decode the message just by typing in the coded version.

Enigma was intended for commercial use, providing security in business transactions. It did not sell well but was noted by the small German army then permitted by the Treaty of Versailles.

It was at Simla in 1926 that Tiltman married Tempe Monica Robinson (on April 7). Born in 1898, she was the daughter of Major General Oliver Robinson of the Army Medical Service. Their daughter, also called Tempe, was born in 1928.

The codebreaking situation for GC&CS in London was complicated in 1927 because of the 'ARCOS' affair.[18] The All-Russian Co-Operative Society was an organisation for channelling Russian business in the UK, and believed to be a front for espionage work. Codebreaking on Russian ciphers in London was then being led by 'Dilly' Knox.

Alfred Dilwyn Knox was a leading cryptologist in GC&CS. He had been part of the Room 40 setup in the navy during the First World War and his predilection for baths meant he apparently made frequent use of one installed near his Admiralty room (53, according to a limerick composed about it),[19] the better to think things out. A renowned classical scholar, his later contributions to breaking the Enigma system and the German secret service codes were of the first magnitude.

Knox was brought into decoding the Russian traffic in the 1920s and his section's decodes probably contributed to the ARCOS raid. By May 1927 an internal informant had passed enough material to MI6 to convince them of dark deeds, and a decision to raid the premises was made on 11 May; the raid took place the following day. Nothing incriminating was found although people were seen burning papers in the furnace. Key documents they hoped to find, such as a naval manual, were not discovered.

The outcome was disruption of MI6's operations against ARCOS and a public row in Parliament. The government, without much other evidence to present, quoted decrypted messages to back themselves up, and the Russians began to change their codes. In 1928, as Tiltman[20] says:

> *...I should think the end of '28 or '29, when the Russians introduced one-time pads. But we were able to deal with it in a... very small way, because they used the pads twice – once forwards and once backwards.*

A one-time pad (OTP) has only two copies (sender and receiver) and each page of random coding material is meant to be only used once, so comparisons with other messages cannot be found by the codebreaker. Tiltman managed to break some examples where the error of repeated use was made.

At the end of 1927 the first consideration was given[21] to forming a Military Section within GC&CS. The concern was that in the event of war suitably well-trained cryptographers in military codes could be available who in peace time would be able to assist with the examination of others' military codes as well as helping the diplomatic work which was then central to GC&CS's work. They would also liaise with Sarafand and Simla on intercepts. A handwritten document[22] dated December 1929 fills out more detail, indicating eight officers of whom five were to be in London. Against the list of personnel and duration of appointment, the name written in to be head is that of Tiltman.

Chapter 3

The 1930s – Prelude to the Second World War

The dawn of the 1930s saw the coming in Britain and Europe of economic depression, its origins in America but its repercussions widely spread. Together with an intellectual climate of discontent with the order of things (Spengler's *Decline of the West* had been a major focus of discussion in the 1920s), the situation persuaded many that some other way to organize human affairs would be preferable. Fascism and Communism, on the face of it polar opposites, offered possible political alternatives. The Establishment, in the Old and New World alike, viewed these trends with suspicion if not fear, and this was a main driving force of events during this time.

Tiltman retired from the army in 1925 after four years in the India role, but was rehired as a civil servant, effectively to continue the work for another four years as one of two War Office civilians. After 1929 the GC&CS needed someone to head up the new Military Section. Tiltman, with his regular service experience and his codebreaking experience, was to be the man for the task. In recognition of his services, by June 1930 his temporary rank of captain was gazetted for formal promotion. He was also awarded the OBE.

The Military Section had two primary objectives:[1] 'the training of officers to enable them to carry out cryptographic work in the field' and 'the study of all military ciphers in use by foreign countries'. Its staff were to prioritize these two targets by training the officers sent by the army for instruction, and by studying and recording foreign military ciphers and their development. An additional duty was to maintain contact with the army centres at Sarafand (No. 2 Wireless Company) and Army HQ in India. It was stated that, in the event of war, the section was to be available to move elsewhere at the army's direction. Military ciphers were to be a priority.

Some of these directives were to cause friction over the next few years. GC&CS was deriving much of its material from diplomatic sources and purely military work was comparatively less available; a wider range of ciphers also helped with training. The potential pull between GC&CS in London and military demands elsewhere was evident. The assigned officers were to be chosen by the army, not necessarily with regard to the qualities that GC&CS might or might not find in them; the section was to serve the army, not GC&CS.

The Military Section began with just Tiltman, Freddie Jacob, the successful competitor,[2] Dick Pritchard (French specialism) and Tony Dangerfield (Japanese), and trainees assigned for a while before being sent (usually to the Middle East) on assignment. Several of those recruited were linguists who translated rather than cryptanalysts. Clerical support was necessary, and this came from wives, including Tiltman's wife Tempe, who was still serving in 1939.

Russian codes continued to be a, if not the, prime focus for GC&CS in the early 1930s. The dangers of what was perceived as an international threat of spreading Communism, and the emergence of cells in Europe including the UK, prompted continued monitoring of their communications. According to Peterson (quoting Tiltman):[3]

> *Starting about 1929 the Communist International set up a world-wide clandestine radio network to carry the intercommunications of the various national Communist parties with Berlin (not Moscow) as control. During 1930 our intercept consisted almost exclusively of telegrams between:*
>
> *a. Kompartei, Berlin and Komintern* [sic] *Moscow and*
> *b. Kompartei, Berlin and Comparty, London, known by us as 'Komintern' and 'Company' respectively. Both classes of intercepts were sent in 5-figure groups and were shown to have concealed indicators.*

This was Comintern: an international Communist organisation which emerged at the end of the Great War dedicated to the spread of Communist thinking and action across the world. Its people worked to subvert other organisations in industry, society and politics. Its outward-looking and active nature was to be modified to some extent in the late 1920s when Stalin took full power and made as a main focus the defence of the USSR, but its influence was to continue and be of concern to liberal democracy throughout the interwar years.

There was some concerns that Tiltman, in a military post, was giving priority to 'civilian' or political code issues. He was asked,[4] 'Why don't you work on military codes'? His answer was, 'If you'd find us some, we'd work on it.' It was simply the case that little purely military traffic was available. Tiltman:

> *There was a certain amount of Italian. I had nothing to do with the Italian because the man who had been appointed as Number 2, who also became a War Office civilian, Freddie Jacob, do you remember – he was an Italian scholar – and he and anybody who knew Italian worked on it here and quite separate.*

Part of the problem may also have been the ambiguous nature of Tiltman's actual job; he was, and remained, a civilian until 1939, but was to have a reporting role through Colonel Lycett to the Director of Military Intelligence rather than through purely military channels to MI8 where he would report to Colonel Vernham (who in turn reported to Lycett). Further, the role of GC&CS was ambiguous at this stage; it was still seen by the services as a 'servant' rather than the independent body it became providing intelligence and guidance for the services.

Tiltman ascribed his rise within the organisation at GC&CS to the fact that in this partial vacuum Denniston would often come to him[5] with questions and problems over a range of ciphers, so Tiltman grew into a sort of general consultant across a range of codes. Nevertheless, it was as head of the Military section of GC&CS that he was now supposed to function. Tiltman says:[6]

> *I had a lot to do with* [Sinclair's] *man, Colonel Vivian, whom you may have seen mentioned in the correspondence. On three occasions between '31 and '34 I went to Berlin looking for books, key source books, which they were using and then I went - I was paid for by the chief you see - and I went on his orders. So I had quite a lot to do with Admiral Sinclair.*

Tiltman's work included taking on the main task of the Berlin-Moscow Comintern traffic. In his view Fetterlein, who had been doing this, was 'not getting on very well with it',[7] and Tiltman took over in 1931 and broke the system.

This work expanded into providing information on a worldwide network of Comintern signals, which in turn meant involvement with signals outside the diplomatic area – other organisations (including illicit ones) which needed to be pinpointed. Signal interception in the UK of this material began in the early '30s with the help of the Metropolitan Police and Harold Kenworthy at the Denmark Hill site (a police nursing home). It also involved Kenworthy and Leslie Lambert driving round with radio detection equipment and being occasionally stopped by suspicious police.

Kenworthy and Lambert are two largely unsung heroes of the work before 1939 and during the war. Kenworthy[8] had gained experience in signals during the First World War in the Naval Reserve as a port wireless officer serving in Gibraltar. Between the wars he joined the Metropolitan Police as a civilian worker and worked in Scotland Yard's intercept station, which subsequently moved to Denmark Hill. Equipment was in short supply and of dubious quality. Kenworthy wrote[9] in November 1939: 'The closest touch was kept with MI5 through the offices of Colonel Vivian and Mr Harker. It was recognized that the apparatus employed by myself was wanted. It was also stated that no funds were available.' Kenworthy subsequently patented a fresh design which worked better than the standard PO device at the time. His work was to increase further in importance during the war, when a new intercept site was established at Knockholt in Kent, very much targeted at the interception of the teleprinter-based 'Fish' traffic (Chapter 4).

Leslie Lambert[10] was a well-known figure to radio listeners between the wars, for he was a broadcaster of stories under the pseudonym of A.J. Alan. A member of the Magic Circle, he was also a keen radio ham. He volunteered in the First World War as an interceptor based in Norfolk, but soon became involved with Room 40 and the Admiralty codebreakers. He transferred to GC&CS when that organisation was created and remained there until his death in 1941, being part of 'Captain Ridley's shooting party' when BP was first occupied for a time in 1938 during the Munich crisis, and working in the Naval section and Hut 8 at BP. According to Nigel West,[11] whose book on the 'Mask' operation provides complete texts as well as analysis, Lambert was also involved in codebreaking with Tiltman.

The monitoring of Comintern traffic, of which Tiltman was in charge, gained the operation codename of 'Mask', which applied particularly to the interception of traffic when it resumed in 1934. The work on the previous system had continued until 1933 when the monitoring was accidentally exposed,[12] but restarted when a new station went on air (with, of course, new ciphers to be broken). Operation Mask continued until 1937. The deciphered traffic revealed much about the organisation and working of the British Communists, as well as wider activities, and was useful for MI5 as it revealed opportunities to infiltrate or prevent actions. The public face of the Communist Party was not, of course, illegal or unacceptable as it stood, and in an age where various parties across Europe emerged and fought for expression its presence was not surprising; its official views were appealing to many intellectuals. But the covert side of the Communist movement, using the Party as a cover for its programmes of subversion and disruption both in the UK and in parts of the Empire – notably India – was a concern and it was this that 'Mask' revealed.

An early example[13] of an intercept from London to Moscow, dating from March 1934, shows the general areas of interest which are raised with the 'Central Committee' in Russia. They include fighting fascism in urban and rural middle classes, and promoting Russia, much as one would expect. Also mentioned are trades unions, revealing armament policy and opposition to 'Social Democracy', which was not considered sufficiently revolutionary.

The focus on organized labour and gaining support here is much in the minds of the Moscow advisors. The message to London on 21 August 1934 advises[14] the Communists to focus their attention on organized railwaymen, getting publicity out and influencing in particular those linked to the main ports. Port workers and their organisations should be targets, and attention should be given to any movements of goods associated with arms and munitions, with a view to possible disruption. And on 29 January 1935 the secretary of the Communist Party in Britain Harry Pollitt[15] received the advice for those working within trades unions to emphasize the issues of class struggle and democracy and try to get unity across unions for their aims. The National Unemployed Workers' Movement is also to be mobilized, in a message from 28 November 1934, to link with the Trades Union Congress and Labour supporters in big cities and create united opinion.

The financial support given by Russia to Communist organisations is shown clearly by Tiltman's group – as is the level of micro-management of the funds – in the 'Mask' messages. On 31 December 1934 London is advised of 43,000 Swiss francs and 35 Dutch gulden going to Sweden, from which they must pay specific sums to the English and Irish parties, and to Pollitt himself. A similar message, of 4 February 1935, shows money going to the same source for payment to English and Irish organisations, Pollitt, an Irish youth organisation, and students at a 'Lenin school', a training college for Communists in Russia.

Pollitt's direction by Moscow comes across in the decodes. A terse message of 9 April 1934 states that Pollitt should go to Moscow for several days for immediate discussions, including which people are to be delegates for meetings. And on 22 February 1935 Pollitt was told to organize a courier for 'Gordon' to go to Russia, and to expect orders on what he should bring. Direct influence and control within *The Daily Worker* is also apparent. On 26 February 1936 Moscow expressed its anger at the paper's improper representation of Stalin and incorrect reporting. A message was urgently sent in reply (showing the editors' subservience to Moscow). They are severely criticized again on 28 May for omissions and inaccuracies; the Comintern clearly expected value for their funding.

The messages occasionally reveal other interesting names or groups. A young Jomo Kenyatta is attested 'in Schooling' on 16 February 1934 – thirty years later he was to become the leader of newly-independent Kenya. On 28 December 1934, as the extradition trials in Switzerland of left-wingers Heinz Neumann and Ernst Thaelmann were approaching, Pollitt was to try to influence the MPs George Lansbury and future minister Stafford Cripps with a view to British opposition to the possible Swiss action of returning them to Germany. Percy Glading is a signatory of a message of 5 June 1934 from London (recommending an Indian student for Moscow training); he was to be arrested in 1938 as part of the Woolwich Arsenal group removing secret military plans and the 'Mask' material confirmed his direct links with the Comintern.

Promotion of Indian communism features in other messages, as well as the Glading one – another example is the Moscow message of 21 November 1934 telling Pollitt to organize and send at once to Moscow 'reliable Indian YAVKAS [delegates]' with a view to influencing the Indian Trade Union movement; and another ethnic group is targeted in the message of October 1934 requesting the selection of half a dozen 'negro comrades for school' – these were to be from a Welfare Association and to have retained links with their home country; the Communists were very interested in taking control of the West Indian workers.

Much of the concern within the security services focussed on essential British industries and military centres. Naval security was high on the list (West suggests that seamen and ports were a target following the effect of the 1931 Invergordon Mutiny). The labour movement and trades unions being also targets for the Comintern, the monitoring of individuals and communications linked to these became increasingly important.

Tiltman's role as leader of the 'Mask' team is thus of importance for the authorities in the unstable 1930s, with the economic downturns leading to the rise of Fascism on the continent (and possibility in the UK), the troubles (as the British saw them) in India under Gandhi's leadership, the memory of the General Strike less than a decade before and the tensions around the National Government of the day.

According to Mavis Batey[16] (who worked at Bletchley Park as Mavis Lever), the Russian and 'Mask' traffic brought Tiltman into involvement with 'Dilly' Knox. When the illicit signals emerged in the 1930s Knox and Tiltman worked together on them (with others). Mavis Batey says, 'The military man with his highly efficient methods' was probably not going to get 'close' to Knox in codebreaking, 'given the latter's penchant for Carrollian chopped logic,' but in spite of their different approaches they made an effective team.

The interest in Russian ciphers had taken Tiltman to France in 1932 (Tiltman says 1933 but other sources indicate a slightly earlier date and are probably right). Here he met with Gustave Bertrand, the French secret service officer who had made the all-important contacts with 'Asche', the agent Hans-Thilo Schmidt who passed him documents about early German Enigma use, and with the Poles to whom he forwarded this information, leading to the work of Marian Rejewski and his colleagues in breaking into Enigma in the mid-30s. According to Dermot Turing,[17] Tiltman took an incomplete 'book' on Russian codes and was hopeful that the French could fill in some of the missing parts. Though unsuccessful, the visit was an ice-breaker and established a line of communication. According to Tiltman:[18]

General Menzies took me over to Paris to talk to the French about what we were doing about Russian ciphers, and I flew over to Paris and I spent one day with Bertrand and two other French officers… I had very definite instructions that if I found the French were unaware of Russian additive ciphers, and particularly the one-time pad, which had been introduced by them, I wasn't to talk about it… [Bertrand] *started off (he didn't speak English – it had to be done through an interpreter, because my French wasn't good enough)… He started off by saying, 'I realize that you have probably been instructed not to tell us everything you know, so we put down on paper everything we know about Russian ciphers', which made it easy for me.*

By no means was everything in the garden rosy however. Paul Ferris has pointed out[19] that GC&CS did not put enough emphasis on 'defence'. There was over-confidence in super-enciphered codes (where a code has two parts, a codebook to encode the plaintext, and then something 'added' on top to disguise the message further) and a lack of 'stress-testing'. Tiltman was one of four senior officers who could advise on communications security, along with Travis, Josh Cooper and Denniston – but according to Captain Wilson these four never met to consider the issues together. More could have been done, by Tiltman and others, to underline the weaknesses in British codes; Tiltman's work with the army codemakers was not extensive. Wilson (Ferris thinks) believed that attacking the enemy codes was considered more 'exciting' than checking one's own defences.

Nominally Edward Travis was in charge of the security of British codes (it was one of his roles as Denniston's right-hand man). Oliver Strachey was (Tiltman says) also senior cryptographer for a time and as such could have taken an initiative. Tiltman was not to take up this role until half way through the war. But Tiltman's experience in the Military Section placed him in a good position to warn and advise; he was aware of some issues and perhaps he should have pushed harder.

An area where he did push to raise standards was in the training of military cryptographers. In a lengthy memorandum of February 1935[20] he outlines his concerns:

I believe the intellectual and psychological qualities requisite for a first class cryptographer to be very similar to those necessary for successful scientific research… [they] *are not necessarily exceptional linguists, but are prepared to take any unknown language in their stride… If a military cryptographer is to inspire confidence, it is impossible to restrict*

> *his experience to the solutions of certain classes of cipher, grouped loosely together under such a title as 'ciphers likely to be used in the field'... As regards the syllabus attached to the draft under review, I do not agree with its division in time. Six months' attachment to 'own language' section in GC&CS is too rigid a rule... two or three months of this type of work is quite long enough.*

Tiltman explains how he had prepared exercises for training, that some were better than others, and that once a cipher was broken it was not necessary for the trainee to decode all the messages himself. Tiltman wanted to see non-military ciphers used where they were appropriate in training. He advocated a 'probationary' time to assess long-term prospects before continuing with the full course, which at the time took up to three years, with potentially wasted resources on those not up to standard. Tiltman's comments were partly endorsed by Denniston[21] in a covering letter.

The memorandum on training was submitted as part of a review of the Military Section taking place in 1935. At a conference[22] on 11 April Tiltman was present with Jacob and Denniston, as well as Carr and other WO personnel. Amendments to the Military Section charter were agreed, accepting Tiltman's desire for more flexibility on lengths of time for course units, though not agreeing to his suggestion of 'probationary' time. The revised charter confirms Tiltman's duties as including half- and quarter-yearly reports to the WO on foreign ciphers and the progress of seconded officers. For trainees, a 2–3-month course at the WO would see if an officer was suited to the full training.

Interest in Japanese activity became a higher priority as Japanese militarism grew; its activity against China from 1931 and its interest in resources in the Far East looked like a threat to British interests. Tiltman broke[23] the Japanese Military Attaché (JMA) cipher in 1933 (see Chapter 4), and from 1935 worked for the establishment of a small military unit in Hong Kong to supplement navy personnel already there.

The importance of Tiltman's break of the JMA code was that, combined with other information, it enabled the recognition of Japanese foreign policy in particular relating to Germany.[24] Japan's 1933 withdrawal from the League of Nations, following its invasion in 1931 of Manchuria and its continuing anger at the Washington naval agreement (1922–23) which limited the size and nature of its fleet, led to increasing isolation and consequent distrust of other nations. This is reflected in some of the decoded messages which survive; an example[25] can be found in a signal to Buenos Aires, from April 1935, where the Japanese Foreign Ministry asks the Japanese minister there to investigate why there is 'a very marked tendency in the countries of South America to place obstacles in the way of the importation of Japanese goods'. The government in Tokyo felt that some of the 'big powers' were behind this. In another message the topic of naval visits and reciprocity of them was raised by the British, apparently concerned with more Japanese officers being able to 'inspect' British naval properties than British personnel were (frequently limited to just the attaché and assistant). The Japanese in London reported this back to Tokyo, and it reflects sensitivity: the comment in the message that 'the fact that the atmosphere has steadily been worsening should be well-known to you.' Japan's *rapprochement* with Germany, similarly isolated, gained from the presence of representative Oshima Hiroshi from 1934 in Berlin, originally as an attaché but during the war as ambassador. A fervent supporter of the Nazis, his communiqués to Tokyo, read by the codebreakers, were informative before and especially during the war.

The Far East Combined Bureau (FECB) was the British centre for intelligence gathering and was housed in office blocks on the Hong Kong naval dockyard. The centre included the Chief of Intelligence Staff. All sorts of material from a wide range of sources was handled here. The Hong Kong Y-station interception unit was based at Stonecutters Island and was initially mainly staffed by navy personnel, though there were a few RAF staff attached. Codebreakers (confusingly also called 'Y' here) were in a 'Special Intelligence' section.[26]

It took some time for the FECB to be effectively established. Smith explains[27] that relations between the sections were fraught at times, intelligence seeing itself as having the power over codebreakers regarding how to handle the latter's output. The army also, having no representation in the interception area, was felt to be unimportant in the distribution of intelligence. In 1936 therefore, four army intercept personnel were sent to Stonecutters to help in the work. Material relevant was then sent to London to be worked on, as there were no Japanese-skilled army staff available to work on it.

The position in London was also limited regarding Japanese experts. Tiltman took a personal initiative: he began to study Japanese:[28]

I learned what little I know of the written form of Japanese the hard way! We had a British Army intercept station at Hong Kong which from about 1935 forwarded to us considerable quantities of Japanese military intercept… I myself have never been able to memorize more than a very small number of the very simplest characters. I suffer from a sort of mental block which wipes out the memory of a character as soon as I take my eyes off it… During this period the cipher systems used seemed to be changed quite drastically about every 9 months, and I had a hard time keeping up with the changes. I had no Japanese interpreter attached to me and the other members of my military section were otherwise engaged, part of the time on Italian ciphers during the Abyssinian War.

The addressing of Japanese material introduced another element of personal relationships for Tiltman. He describes[29] some work done on the military codes:

There were at the time two very distinguished Japanese scholars in the office, who had each retired as British Consul General in Japan. One of them partially reconstructed the code-chart for me from the material in one of the 40 keys, and I set about recovering the other keys. Shortly afterwards the other expert came and said he had heard I had some interesting work in progress and that he would like to help so I gave him the material in one of the keys in which I had recovered most of the syllabic values, numbers and so forth. He returned it to me 3 weeks later unchanged, saying my solution was 'plausible'. This should have warned me that I was treading on hallowed ground.

Tiltman discreetly does not name these scholars, but they appear to be[30] Sir Harold Parlett and Ernest Hobart-Hampden, both very experienced eastern diplomats and experts in the language who perhaps were concerned that a 'new' person with little in the way of Japanese credentials was showing an interest in their area (not unlike Colonel Jeffrey a decade earlier). Parlett was later to serve with his skills at Bletchley from 1941.

In his draft half-yearly report[31] to the WO, Tiltman shows his concern that

[the Italian situation]… *has coincided with the interception of a great body of Japanese material emanating from China; such an opportunity of bringing our knowledge of Japanese military ciphers up to date may*

> *not recur. We have consequently been obliged to undertake two major operations without any increase in staff.*

It is perhaps no surprise that the summons for two of Tiltman's military personnel (Jennings and Dangerfield) to serve on WO exercises in July was cancelled given the strain on the Military Section at the time. Tiltman was able to get temporary support for six months from the WO in Captains Taylor and Thompson, but their return to normal duties early in 1936 was insisted on, despite pleas, by the WO. A report[32] which looks like Tiltman's states baldly: 'Owing to pressure of work in the Italian military field, it is regretted that no work has been possible on French military ciphers.'

Tiltman's account reflects the lower priority being felt about things Japanese during some of these years (among the reasons being shortage of resources and personnel generally). Though Hugh Foss, Tiltman and others had done valuable work on Japanese materials, the Middle East and particularly Italy, as well as the Communist threat, took attention away from the Far East in the mid-1930s. As late as 1938 Tiltman was to be concerned about lack of resources at GC&CS to cope with general progress. He complained[33] that there were not enough resources to deal with the traffic being intercepted by Chatham at home and by Sarafand in Palestine. It is not surprising if the Japanese material seemed less important. The eruption of war in China in 1937 began to change things.

The Japanese section was not the only area needing more support. Even the Italian codebreakers, a higher priority since Mussolini's campaigns in Africa, were under pressure. Back in 1935 an annex[34] to the description of the Military Section's functions showed that the peacetime establishment was three civilian staff (one being Tiltman, the head) and five seconded officers, two of whom were with no. 2 Wireless Company (in the Middle East). The description of the Italian code work surviving[35] from late in 1935 also highlights Tiltman's limited resources:

> [The code A-2] *gives all the moves of the Italian Expeditionary Forces from Italy to Eritrea and Somalia. Had it been possible to start work on this earlier… the whole organisation and order of battle… would now be available. It is impossible at the moment to deal with the back material, and work, owing to lack of* <u>*Italian speaking*</u> *staff* [emphasis in the original].

They were even using one of their secretaries in a part-time codebreaker role – Miss Sercombe.

The difficulties of some of the WO requirements in training when matched with practical military problems are brought out in Tiltman's report[36] to the WO. Given the Italian crisis all permanent staff in the section were tackling Italian ciphers except Tiltman and one clerk, who worked on Japanese materials. Italian ciphers were not the best for training purposes, but Tiltman had changed his view and now felt it right under present conditions to prioritize Italian codes. Both French and Russian codes were, in consequence of other priorities, at a standstill, but Tiltman was proposing 'when opportunity offers' to do a theoretical study, though not with great hope of success. He also urged an additional officer (Pritchard, recently retired from the army, was his choice) to be recruited. His report prompted a reply[37] from the WO querying various matters – they were under the impression that Italian codes were well in hand, they were dubious about the standard of field cryptographers needing to be so high, and they were not convinced by the argument for additional staff. A meeting with Tiltman was requested.

Evidently such a meeting took place, perhaps on 8 July for Tiltman has left a letter (surviving in hand draft) in which[38] he reviewed the discussion and sought to explain. Tiltman felt he 'was not thinking very clearly' and 'the staff is inadequate not so much in quantity as in quality. What is wanted is someone to relieve me of part of the heavy strain of doing practically all the thinking and higher scientific cryptography for the section.'

This is a striking, direct and vivid document, illuminating the immense pressure under which Tiltman was working at the time. Such personal expressions are not common from him. It shows his frustration at the army's lack of appreciation and underestimation of the demands, and of the skills needed to do the work. He alone, it seems, had the technical competence for the 'scientific' – technical and analytic – skills needed, and he is having to drop one thing to assist on another. Tiltman stressed 'the limitations in quality of the section as constituted'. The effect on his efficiency is clear; a simple example given in the letter is his failure to keep up with the demand for half-yearly reports.

Tiltman seems to have eventually been persuasive. Later in 1936 he, Colonel Allen and Freddie Jacob discussed further appointments, and (in consultation with Denniston) agreements were reached[39] on staffing readjustments, to include Pritchard.

In 1937 Tiltman went to the Far East to establish more securely the treatment of Japanese work. He reported:[40]

> *I went to Hong Kong in 1937 to try to handover; there was a Naval Officer, Commander Keith, who was prepared, at that time, to retire and take on the military Japanese in Hong Kong. I went over to hand over to him and it was quite clear that he had no confidence that he could do the job at all. So I brought it back again and I flew out in January 1939 and by this time... we had the Japanese military and air and they had taken on long additives that they used, 10,000 group additives. I briefed two of my officers, Marr Johnson and Stevens, who followed me out by sea... From that time onwards, the Japanese problem, apart from the military attaché, was a Hong Kong job in parallel with the naval job there.*

In June 1938 Jacob compiled a report for additional clerking in the section, outlining many problems given the changes in codes and increase in traffic. In endorsing the report, Tiltman[41] wrote:

> *I consider the need for one more temporary clerk is clearly shown. As regards the second I agree that it is at the moment unfortunately necessary to cover as far as possible the whole material intercepted in order to obtain intelligence which is really contained in quite a small number of messages. I think a case could be made for a further clerk provided the FO really insists on obtaining the maximum amount of intelligence from this source.*

Apart from the frustrations of getting things done administratively, there was a personal issue which rankled somewhat: Tiltman's own position and salary. In 1938 he wrote (for him, it seems) an extended letter[42] to Lieutenant Colonel Thomas at the WO outlining his concern, which linked to the issue of whether people in the Military Section would be called up in time of war. His view was that they should be but should continue to serve in their current role, and this would be more efficient than if they were mixed military and civilian particularly in the event of going overseas (see below, Chapter 8, for Henry Dryden's problems in this context). Leading the Military Section as a 'covenanted civil servant' had resulted in limiting and reducing his salary, he estimated by £30–50 per year:

> *I still do not consider that I am adequately paid for the duties expected of me, but I particularly dislike being regarded as a man with a grouse – so I have allowed the matter to drop. I felt however that I should like you to know something of the history of my appointment.*

The war was to see this change.

At the end of April Tiltman attended a meeting concerning the interception of military messages (GC&CS relied on established Forces intercept stations for material). Denniston chaired the meeting, with his deputy Edward Travis, heads of the Naval, Air and Military sections at GC&CS (Clarke, Cooper and Tiltman) and WO representative also present. The focus of attention was the shortage of intercept sites and the need for more in the worsening political situation. Tiltman's experience in India and the Middle East had shown him how important co-ordination was between interception, traffic analysis, cryptology and intelligence; the issue was to continue to involve Tiltman throughout the war. The following year was to see some modest expansion of interception capacity.

Tiltman now decided (June 1938) to initiate more regular reports to the War Office on the Military Section. The first of these[43] is dated 1 July. Tiltman addresses Colonel Allen, who had taken over from Thomas at the WO. He explains the background to the section's establishment and how the priority of training had been overtaken by the Italo-Abyssinian war and the need for sheer cryptography. Tiltman proposes a series of weekly lectures to compensate. Recruitment had tended to come from military linguists, who fortunately had some ability in codes at that time, but Tiltman felt that turning to the universities would now help to get the right sort of people. Japanese work was being limited by available expertise (Tiltman was training Geoffrey Stevens and Marr-Johnson to serve in the Far East); new codes remained unbroken though work on older ones showed progress. The Italian staffing issues were underlined, and the potential loss of Major Thompson (who like Tiltman seems to have had issues with pay) was a matter of regret.

There survives a scrawled note[44] from Colonel Allen indicating that there was indeed to be an increase in clerking at GC&CS, and 'I think Tiltman knows all about it.'

In spite of the problems with staffing, this was also the time when Tiltman made his break into the Japanese military code. The additive structure, a new feature on this system, was revealed and the building of code books and additives could begin. The work on this was refined and by the end of the year was handed over to the newly-established group in the Far East.[45]

Meanwhile the British had taken little notice of the central German high-grade machine Enigma, which had been known to them for more than a decade but dismissed as not being secure enough and then set aside because of higher priorities (Russian codes especially), or regarded by some (though not by Hugh Foss who wrote the early report on the system in the 1920s) as too tough. In 1936[46] the Military Section had expressed concern about the lack of attention being given to German ciphers generally. According to Mavis Lever[47] it was Tiltman who in 1936 identified features of the message indicators being used in the Enigma system employed in the Spanish Civil War (1936–9) – the pattern of encoding twice the three-letter starting-point for the rotor wheels for that message.

The *Anschluss* (annexation of Austria) in March 1938 sharpened attention on Germany and its capabilities. Tiltman requested in September 1938[48] that the French be asked to provide more information about various aspects of Enigma. All this shows that at that time he was involved in initial analysis of the machine (and was to continue to do so for a while at least). In a memo[49] of September 9 he comments:

> *The photographs show an attachment on the front of the machine* [the Stecker or plug-board] *which does not appear on the model available to the public. The directions given do not fully explain the function of this attachment… Can the French be asked to give us* <u>*all*</u> *the information they have?*

Tiltman lists a number of Enigma technical aspects:

> *Full details of all devices additional to or differing from the market model:*
>
> *i]* *fitting new drums;*
> *ii]* *changing the order of drums;*
> *iii]* *moving the tyres (bands) on the drums* [these were the lettered – numbered for the army – 'rings' which could be moved around the main drum, thereby changing the position of letters with respect to wiring inside];
> *iv]* *periodical alteration or resetting of any device or devices referred to.*

By September 1938 there was expectation of war; the consequences of the Anschluss and the Czechoslovakian situation were generating a crisis as Hitler pressed for Czech territorial concessions. Bletchley Park, acquired by the government that year, became the destination of what was later called 'Captain Ridley's shooting party' – perhaps it was called simply a 'shooting party' at the time. Ridley was an organizer and logistics man for this, the move to the Bletchley war station of the codebreakers of GC&CS (and others of MI6). Tiltman was among those who made this trip. The urgency of the belated enquiries about Enigma is pointed: the date is less than two weeks before the Munich crisis, when Chamberlain flew to Germany to try to prevent Hitler from occupying Czechoslovakia, only to appease him by suggesting the surrender of the western part.

The crisis was averted and the 'shooting party' went back. The return to London did not mean all was well. MI6 and the codebreakers in their midst were on the lookout for anything that might help their German knowledge, especially as Germany's military might and territorial ambitions were now clear. Tiltman, as well as the points listed regarding Enigma, also asked for information on other German ciphers.

There seems to have been some response to Tiltman's questions and requests, for another paper[50] dated 2 November 1938 shows him (the document is unsigned but 'Captain' is at the end, suggesting Tiltman) aware of new information about other German ciphers from the French, where he suggests that 'French cryptography does not appear to be of the highest class.'

This may be somewhat harsh on the work of the French. Bertrand says[51] that in the year before the war the French sent to Britain 925 intelligence reports; perhaps they were not all code-related, but clearly they were getting results. On 2 November Bertrand handed over 100 or so photographs of code material of sufficient quality to prompt Denniston to ask Admiral Sinclair permission to return the compliment with British material. Tiltman attended a conference the following day (with Bertrand, Knox and Denniston) at which Tiltman and Knox outlined their work to Bertrand. This laid the foundations for bringing in the Polish experts the following year. Things had become urgent, as the Germans modified their Enigma machine and procedures late in 1938.

It had been the Polish codebreakers, Rejewski, Zygalski and Rozycki, who made the first breaks into Enigma secretly in 1933–4, after receiving information from Bertrand (who remained in touch with and receiving information from 'Asche', German agent Hans-Thilo Schmidt) on how it worked. But at the end of 1938, when the Germans altered the Enigma system by increasing the number of 'steckers' used on the plug board to swap letters, and increased the available rotors from three to five, the Polish cryptographers – who thanks to persistence, brilliant mathematics and a little luck had been able to read some material – were shut out. They therefore again made contact with the French and British secret services (who might, they hoped, have superior resources), which resulted in a meeting in January 1939 in Paris. Tiltman was one of the British party, along with Denniston, Dilly Knox and Hugh Foss. The meeting however was unproductive, both sides being wary of revealing too much information. It was not until July 1939 that the Poles showed their hand (in the Pyry Forest near Warsaw), but this time Tiltman was absent, committed with other duties.

Hugh Foss has left some interesting comment[52] on the January meeting with them. He says: 'The Poles were mainly silent but one of them gave a lengthy description in German of the recovery of throw-on indicators when the operator used pronounceable settings. During the exposition Knox kept muttering to Denniston, 'But this is what Tiltman did', while Denniston hushed him and told him to listen politely' – evidently a reference to the work on the indicators Tiltman had done.

It would appear that Tiltman was a little modest when he insisted later that he knew little of the Enigma.

Tiltman was to be further involved in the training of potential new recruits in 1939. Denniston had made discreet enquiries at university level for possible new blood, including 'men of the professor type', by which he included some science- or maths-based people. The result was a list of potential recruits to be inducted into the work. In January 1939 a training course[53] was organized with several university luminaries, among them Hugh Last (an Oxford ancient history professor who was to serve with the Air Section on Italian codes and in research), Martin Charlesworth (classical scholar and Cambridge don, who subsequently recruited a number of BP people), Patrick Wilkinson (who became important in Italian naval codes), and a certain Alan Turing. Tiltman taught the bookbuilding section, and there was practical work organized. Another of those trained was Gordon Welchman, who presented himself in London in March 1939, along with, at various times, Turing, Denis Babbage and John Jeffreys – all of whom played vital roles in wartime codebreaking. Welchman[54] recalls Tiltman being involved on 21 and 28 March with the training, his subject being 'book-building' – a skill which was to be important especially in Japanese codes. Welchman was one of the first 'men of the professor type', i.e. from a science or mathematics background, to be recruited to GC&CS by Denniston. In 1940 he drew up the organisation plan which was the foundation of the Enigma army and air work in 'Huts' Six and Three, and for the Hut Four Naval codebreaking; he improved the electrical design of the Turing 'Bombe' machine with the concept of the 'diagonal board', additional circuitry which eliminated many false stops on the Bombe's searches for enigma message settings. Welchman was to be one of the most important figures at BP during the war.

Tiltman submitted a discussion paper[55] about his proposed move of a section to the Far East in January 1939. There were real concerns about changes to the Japanese code systems, and Tiltman was confident he could speed up the work if he were on the scene. Jacob was fully able to handle the Italian material, and the Military Section had functioned well in his previous absence.

In 1939 Tiltman visited India as well as Hong Kong. He was to return to France in September 1939, promoted to lieutenant colonel.[56] For now the whole scene had changed: war with Germany had been declared.

Chapter 4

The Codes – Tiltman Breaking and Making

This section is included to reveal the extraordinary scope and range of Tiltman's ability, as well as his interest in the nature of codes. The sheer variety of his expertise is striking. Tiltman's range of success over the years in codebreaking makes interesting reading not just for the quantity but also for the significance of his discoveries on the course of British history. A list of some leading achievements would include:

- 1920–21: Russian keys (new diplomatic substitution key; Russian diplomatic additive keys); DELEGAT; AZIYA
- 1924: Russian additive system
- 1931: Comintern ciphers and Mask
- 1933: Japanese military attaché code
- 1938: Japanese military code
- 1939–41: German Police codes
- 1939: New version of JN-25
- 1940: Barbarameldungen army artillery code
- 1940–2: Railway Enigma
- 1941: Research Section and Hagelin; Italian C-38M
- 1941: First break into Tunny
- 1942: JMA additive code (assists in break)
- 1942–3: German-Spanish Kryha code
- 1943: Japanese Army Air code 3366

This list does not reflect the subsequent work of using the understanding of the first breaks to continue to break daily into messages thereafter.

A **cipher** and a **code** are not quite the same. In a cipher, each individual letter/symbol is represented in the enciphered message by another letter/symbol. Thus on a Caesar wheel each letter is enciphered by another letter a set number of places on (e.g. CAT becomes DBU or FDW). Using the

Enigma machine, one letter is replaced by another. But in a code a whole word or phrase may be represented differently – by another word (as in some US Civil War messages), or perhaps a group of numbers (as with Japanese book codes of the Second World War), from a **codebook** which tells the sender and receiver the meaning of each codeword or group.

Tiltman was involved in a variety of codes and ciphers between the wars. A document[1] shows notes from him regarding codes from Germany, Iraq, China, the Vatican (!), Finland, Russia, Spain, Portugal, the Balkans, Romania, Hungary and Turkey. The document is annotated by its writer, showing Tiltman referenced in the third person, i.e. the notes seem to come from Tiltman's information. The handwriting looks like that of Friedman.

1920–21: Russian keys

Tiltman has described these early ciphers. The early Russian codes were based on simple **transposition**. They used a grid where the plaintext is written out across a grid, and the letters are then sent column by column. An experienced eye can begin to see language patterns when writing out the letters in grids of various sizes until the correct one appears. Where the columns rely on a key word or phrase (Tiltman gives the example of English poetry being used) then methods will be used such as filling the columns in the alphabetical order of the letters in the key word/phrase, the phrase dictating the number of columns to be used.

A simple example might be:

The message is '*Expect an attack from the East with tanks and gas*'.

The Message key is Shakespeare's 'ALL THE WORLDS A STAGE' (leaving out the apostrophe); the section used is 'THEWORLDS', which conveniently has no duplicate letters.

The key phrase has nine letters, so the message is written in rows of nine letters:

E	X	P	E	C	T	A	N	A
T	T	A	C	K	F	R	O	M
T	H	E	E	A	S	T	W	I
T	H	T	A	N	K	S	A	N
D	G	A	S	V	Q	W	F	X

1 2 3 4 5 6 7 8 9

The letters of the key phrase are now numbered in their alphabetical order:

T H E W O R L D S

Order of letters in alphabet:

8 3 2 9 5 6 4 1 7

Column 1 (ETTTD) is now written under letter 1 (D), column 2 (XTHHG) is written under letter 2 (E), and so on until all are done:

N	P	X	A	C	T	E	E	A
O	A	T	M	K	F	C	T	R
W	E	H	I	A	S	E	T	T
A	T	H	N	N	K	A	T	S
F	A	G	X	V	Q	S	D	W

The coded message can then be sent as NPXACTEEAOATMKFCTR... etc., though other changes can also be made (see below). Note that dummy letters are used at the end of the plaintext, to complete the number in the final row.

Tiltman says:[2]

> *There was a great deal of correspondence. Some of the messages were quite long, and they weren't very difficult. The nature of the transliteration made it a fairly easy job... I was pretty quick at it.*

Matters become more complicated if transposition is preceded by **substitution.** Here each letter (if a cipher) or word/phrase (if a code) is replaced by some other letter, group or phrase. For this a code book or substitution table is needed, one for the sender and an identical one for receiver. The code book can rapidly become large if numerous phrases are required (e.g. compass-points alone might need 16). For key letters or words, there would need to be more than one possible substitution, or the system would be vulnerable to **frequency analysis**, where counting the number of occurrences can indicate what is hidden (e.g. in English E is the commonest letter, followed by T and A, and pairings like TH are frequent; words like the German 'der' or 'die' are common).

Soon after Tiltman's first success the Russians changed the system:

> *After I had been going for I suppose a couple of months, they changed the cipher and they substituted 2 figures for each letter and then they did transposition on top – and there were variants for the common letters, for instance there were seven variant dinomes* [pairs of digits, starting 00] *for the vowel 'o' which is the commonest vowel in Russian, and so on. The whole 100 pairs from 00–99 were used and we were lucky… they used one key in the new cipher that they'd used in the old one… and eventually we built up the whole table.*

This kind of cipher needs to be analysed for frequency of use according to the features of the language (the most common dinomes, and especially small groups of dinomes, represent the common letters or letter-groups, such as 'th' or 'in' in English, or 'ski' or 'vitch' in Russian, perhaps), to build up the substitution book by trial and error.

This was how the 'Delegat' system was found to work. Tiltman again:

> *Then sometime very early in* [1921] *they changed again and brought in this new cipher Delegat… the only chance we had was to find a message that was in which* [sic] *the variants had been very badly used so that we would get recognisable repetitions in it, find the key length and put things together… I was lucky.*

He analysed a message where a Russian operator had repeated the same dinomes for a common word instead of a range of variants, and from this toe-hold was able to work things out, helped by Fetterlein. Tiltman observed that DELEGAT probably used keys (for transposing) from a

'running text', and suspected some lines of poetry were the source. With no success from Russian texts, he tried English and was successful. The poetry of George Wither, an obscure seventeenth century writer, proved to be the culprit; once located, this made solving future messages a much faster matter.

A 'running text' is similar to one way of using a keyword, in its use of a Vigenère square (see appendix for an example). But instead of using a single word repeated, the continuous passage of text would provide the system for using the Vigenère chart. The plaintext is lined up with the key 'running text', both having the same number of letters (there is no reason not to put in some deliberate garble or dummies in the plaintext, to try to throw a codebreaker off). So if the message is 'attack the town' and the running text is 'I wandered lonely as a…' you would write out:

I W A N D E R E D L O N E L Y A S A

and line up beneath it

A T T A C K T H E T O W N T O D A Y

Each plaintext letter is now enciphered by taking the Vigenère *row* that starts with that letter and looking along it to the *column* of the running text letter; the resultant letter is the ciphertext. From a normal Vigenère square the ciphertext of the above becomes

I p t n f o k l h e c j r e m d s y[3]

The system has weaknesses – for example an 'A' in either running text or plaintext leaves its opposite unchanged – but is more secure than using a single codeword as this can leave traces of frequency patterns more clearly than a running text. It can be further complicated by using a transposition system to shuffle the ciphertext again.

1924: Russian additive system

In an additive system a substitution table or codebook is first used to encode letters or words generally with groups of numbers (these might be 3– 4– or 5-figure numbers). Another set of similar numbers (from a separate 'additive' book) is then added to the coded numbers and the totals are sent. The addition is often done by Fibonacci system, i.e. not 'carrying' if the total exceeds nine – so 5 plus 3 is 8 but 5 plus 7 is 2 (the ten carried over is discounted). The starting place in the additive book would be defined by the day's instructions, or selected by the sender and concealed in various ways in the message. The additive numbers can be extracted in several ways: they might be as lines, or columns; they might be backwards instead of forwards.

So your codebook might tell you (using four-figure groups):

Advance	3125	North	6839	0600 hrs	9471
Retreat	4086	East	7741	0800 hrs	3167
Attack	9943	South	2218	1000 hrs	2467

If you order 'Advance East 1000 hrs' you will encode

3125 7741 2467

and your additive book might give you

6658 5312 4209.

You add

3125 7741 2467

plus

6658 5312 4209

giving

9773 2053 6666 as your ciphertext.

This kind of process was to underlie many of the Japanese book codes used in the 1930s and 1940s.

Tiltman writes:[4]

From 1924 to 1928 a succession of additive series, all of the same general form, were introduced, applied to a number of code-books widely differing in dimensions and form... The additives were all 1,000 5-figure groups long arranged in 100 lines of ten groups each and were applied 'boustrophedon', i.e., reading first line left to right, then the next right to left, etc. The starting point for a message was chosen by the operator and could be at any or the 1,000 groups of the additive. The construction of the additives was frequently far from random, exhibiting various personal idiosyncrasies, but was not often predictable and had to be solved figure by figure.

Several versions of this system were uncovered by Tiltman between 1924 and 1928.

Systems using similar principles continued to emerge, including 3-digit codes and dinomes for the letters of the Russian alphabet, until 1928 when one-time pads were introduced, making it very difficult to penetrate if they were used properly. The Russian switch to these probably owed much to the British government's publication of decoded messages, more than once in the 1920s but notably in 1927, in attempts to justify their actions against Communist front organisations operating in the UK.

1931: Comintern ciphers and Mask

Tiltman states (speaking of his setting up of the Military Section at GC&CS): 'We did all sorts of things. One of our main jobs was COMINTERN, the secret communications of the Communist International Centre in Moscow along [sic] Berlin.' He was involved in this from 1931 for much of the decade, thanks to his experience in the Far East (Chapter 3).

The Comintern codes being used in the early 1930s have been described by Tiltman, who says:[5]

During the years 1931 through 1934, I was almost entirely occupied with the study of KOMINTERN cipher systems, in all of which the cryptographic materials consisted of (a) a code or dictionary, (b) an alphabet consisting of a mixed sequence of dinomes to correspond to the letters of the alphabet (in whatever language was employed) used for converting running text to digits and (c) a book or books from which

> *to generate digital key* [running text]... *Complicated it certainly was, and yet we read virtually all of the messages. The system was used on the London-Berlin link starting in February 1934. Langenscheidt's Pocket English-German Dictionary, with an elaborate supplement, was used as the code. The alphabet was changed six times a month. The key source book was made up (two identical copies – one for each end of the link) by cutting up... five books into paragraphs, which were then completely shuffled and numbered consecutively... An indicator giving the number of the alphabet and the number of the paragraph (the paragraphs were never used twice)*[6] *was reciphered by addition of the sum of the first two textual groups and placed for London messages in the A3 position, for Berlin messages in the A1 position. Stereotyped preambles were buried in the text.*

So a combination of substitutions and transpositions with additive were used.

Tiltman, Lambert, Knox and the rest would use previous knowledge of cribs (guessed content, see below), trials of the dictionaries and cipher books, previous recovery of dinomes, and patience to strip off the additives and recover the plaintext. This all took time but within a week of transmission seems to have been quite possible. The information was seldom 'tactical' but built up a long-term picture.

1933: Japanese military attaché code

The outline of this is given by Tiltman:[7]

> *In 1933 I solved the Japanese military attaché code which had been in use since 1927. There was a small basic code-chart of, I think, 240 units which meant that a large part of the plain text had to be spelt out in syllables. I don't remember the details of the system except that the code-chart had to be reconstructed and 40 different sets of line and column coordinates recovered.*

This meant that there were forty possible keys for each message, each needing its own 'book'.

The process would involve examination of frequency of particular groups of the 240 units, or combinations of groups, which could be matched with likely solutions from the nature of the message. As many of the units were *Kana* syllables, those known to be certain syllables could lead to others being identified and the 'book' would grow. In the following example, groups 1 and 3 are known. So a combination such as *KO* – XX – *MO* – YY ('XX' and 'YY' being 'unknown') might allow speculation that XX was '*RO*' and YY was '*BO*', the whole thing being *KO-RO-MO-BO* – Colombo – and the message context would indicate if this was plausible. If the code group for 'MA' is also known as RR, then PP – XX – QQ – RR can now be analysed as PP – *RO* – QQ – *MA*, and this might lead to the idea that PP is '*HI*' and QQ is '*SHI*' – the whole being *HI-RO-SHI-MA.* The new identifications would then need to be confirmed by finding them in other contexts.

The ability to read codes such as this enabled some perception of otherwise secret Japanese policy to be obtained. Smith underlines[8] the importance of this, for example, in recognising the growth of militarism and dominance of the army over the Japanese parliament. The desire of the Japanese leaders for enough raw materials and resources to fuel their aspirations became clear, as well as some of their thinking over the situation in China.

1938: Japanese military code

> *I was getting military intercepts back from Hong Kong which were not being worked on by anybody else and this was before they used additives. They had various systems… until September… 1938 when they began to use the kind of additives which they used all through the war and which I broke into* [Tiltman's account is a little muddled about the date]… *This indicating system they used usually, I think, the first four-digit group of a message, they had two figures of it – two figures of the first group of messages, led to one of a hundred additives which was added over the two indicator and put in the second place. They did the same thing for the end of the message and I eventually established that there was a connection between the beginning and the ends of messages which started and ended on the same page* [of indicators]. *From that point on, the additives were very badly used.*[9]

So a message would have four-figure numbers in a code book to represent stock phrases, or specific syllables to spell out words, and when these were written out an 'additive' book with grids of numbers would be used, adding a four-figure number to each coded number. The indicator numbers Tiltman refers to showed from where in the additive book the added numbers began (page, line and column). Decrypting meant subtracting the additives from the ciphertext to reveal the four-digit code numbers, which are looked up in the code book to show the message.

But the encoders used the books lazily. For example, if sending several messages they might just start the second message additives from the point where they stopped the first, and if enough messages were sent, a 'depth' could be found – Tiltman refers to this weakness.

A **depth** is where more than one message has been encoded using the same message key (starting-point on an Enigma machine, page and line of an additive book, running-text etc). If the codebreaker can detect that this may be the case in a group of messages (by examining the indicators within the message which tell the receiver where in the code-book to begin using it for decoding) then they can be written out under each other aligned in columns where the same key is thought to be used. Subtracting the same key element from each coded piece in the columns, if guessed correctly, should leave something which makes sense for each message – it might be coincidence for one message, but not for several lined up in this way.

Routine messages also often had stereotyped phrases in the same position each time (e.g. starting salutations), so this allowed the additives to be recovered. The process when followed through allowed 'book-building', recovery both of the code-book and the additive book.

Good examples of how this process can lead to breaks are given by Alan Stripp[10] and by Michael Smith.[11] The basic concept is valid for a range of Japanese codes, which at various stages changed the additive book, or the actual code book, but by not doing so simultaneously made it possible for the codebreakers to use their knowledge of the unchanged part to help reconstruct the new part.

1939: German Police codes

When the Germans attacked Poland, among other things a large number of police messages, audible in Britain, were heard. The police and the SS used a range of hand ciphers. Henry Dryden, recruited to BP 'in anticipation' before the war, describes what happened with one.[12] The letters were counted to analyse frequency, and this showed that there was a pattern of transposition being used. 'This gave John Tiltman… the opportunity to demonstrate his versatility and practical approach.' Various messages were written out and aligned in a depth. Tiltman did his own depth-building, Dryden says, because 'ideas came to him during the process'. The resultant texts were then cut into vertical columns, and with the aid of pins and a cork bathmat Tiltman shuffled these around, gradually perceiving patterns which eventually revealed clear text and from there the actual key. It became possible to make more durable templates afterwards from this analysis.

Tiltman was able to discuss the techniques for the codebreaking of these messages with Abraham Sinkov when the latter led the secret mission to BP in 1941. By this time other forms of code were being used by the police (as well as the SS), in particular Double Playfair (see below). But police codes continued to produce some useful information, and (according to Hinsley) were of value later in the war in assessing the impact of the strategic bombing campaign on German productivity and – importantly, it was thought – morale.

1939: New version of JN-25

On 1 June 1939[13] the Japanese introduced a new General Operational Code for the Imperial Navy, which was to be known later as JN-25. Tiltman was brought in to advise. He recognized that some of the features in the material were similar to the military (army) codes he had worked on before. He explained:[14]

> *Sometime just after when we were in the war in '39… we got some Naval intercepts in what was afterwards called JN-25, and I tried to see whether it had a similar indicating system to the military, and I found that it did. It indicated the beginning and the end of message on the tables – on the key.*

This, he says, was shared with Commander Burnett, who

> *was really the best of the Japanese Naval interpreters… he was sent out to Singapore and he took the indicating system with him.*

There is some question about whether the Americans, who became heavily involved with JN-25, broke into the system independently. David Duffy says,[15] writing of events in March 1941: '[The Americans] had so far been unable to crack the new naval code known as JN-25.' Burnett went to Singapore before the Japanese invasion to show the FECB (including their leading codebreaker Eric Nave) how to get into JN-25: 'And now Burnett was on Corregidor Island to teach the Americans how to do it.' However Tiltman is more guarded. He says:[16]

> *My guess is that they broke it independently. Burnett always swears they got it from him,... he went from Singapore to Corregidor. At the time, he* [Burnett] *says that he handed over the indicator system, that they didn't have at the time. I think he's probably wrong. I don't know the answer to that.*

But if Duffy is right, then Tiltman's original analysis of the system was crucial to the subsequent success of the Allies with the code.

This initial break was an important step, but only one of many needed. Tiltman demonstrated how it worked. Each key word or phrase, as well as individual syllables where a new word had to be spelled out, was given a five-figure code, and a five-figure additive was added to each group from a book of apparently random additives. The starting point in the additive book would be disguised embedded within the cipher number groups (see above for a simple example of how additives worked).

In theory therefore there could be nearly 100,000 possible 'codewords'. However, the British discovery revealed that, perhaps as a way to avoid some garbling of the text, the Japanese only used codebook numbers which were divisible by three. This convenient error-checker reduced by two-thirds the range of numbers the enemy had to examine.

Codebooks and additive keys were altered time and again, and each time a renewed effort to book-build was needed. But the understanding of the system was key to the continuing battle, where increasingly the Americans were in the forefront.

1940: Barbarameldungen army artillery code

This system was used in the early part of the war, in particular when France was attacked. It was used to provide reports (named after the patron saint of weather and artillerymen among other things) which were about weather conditions and 'special influences' with respect to German artillery and other armaments which might be affected.

Tiltman liaised with Gustave Bertrand over this. The French had made some headway against the messages. Tiltman described some of the work on this in a heavily-redacted paper. He says:

> *An Army transmitter somewhere in western Germany began broadcasting at 4-hour intervals* [redacted] *messages known as Barbarameldungen. These proved on solution to be corrections for weather conditions to artillery range-tables. Regularly 2 hours later than each of these* [redacted] *messages the same station sent out long general weather forecasts and these were enciphered in the Heftschluessel* [a transposition **grid** 26x26 with pairs of letters along the top of columns and down the side of lines, allowing a choice of digraph letters, and using a 'key' as well] *and, owing to the limitation of textual message-lengths to 130 letters, each of them was enciphered and transmitted in 5 or 6 (sometimes even 7) parts. This meant that we received between 30 and 40 messages a day.*

The Germans replaced this quite early in the war, and its successor also, using Double Playfair systems instead.

A **grid** (grille, or stencil) is a device that can be used in a range of ways. The basic concept is sometimes named after Girolamo Cardano who developed (but perhaps did not invent) the system. A square or rectangle has a number of small windows in it, equivalent to the size of a letter or letter-group. The message is written one group or letter at a time into the windows, and the grid is then removed, and other groups or letters randomly filled in to give a square or rectangle of gibberish. Individual words can also be written into the windows and the space is then filled with other words to make apparently meaningful sentences – a very simple version of this is illustrated in the Sherlock Holmes story *The adventure of the 'Gloria Scott'*. But using words is hard to make coherent, and letters, or letter groups which have been already encoded, are more effective.

The device can be manipulated in several ways. A grid in theory could be used in any one of eight orientations – four possible rotations for each of two sides. When the rectangle is complete the letters can be transposed, for example by taking them out in columns (cf. the Russian example above) instead of rows, or by using a key to transpose columns, before transmitting the ciphertext. The receiver (or cryptographer!) would then have to reconstruct the letter grid correctly before applying the stencil in the right position to read the essential part.

So a simple grid might look something like this:

The message might be 'Attack town', which would be written into the spaces:

			A	
	T			T
A		C		K
		T	O	
W		N		

and the remainder filled in with random letters:

W	E	P	A	L
D	T	X	G	T
A	R	C	S	K
B	N	T	O	V
W	J	N	U	W

The columns can then be extracted and even without further substitution or transposition it can look daunting:

WDABWETRNJPXCTNAGSOULTKVW

1940–41: with team, German Double Playfair

In 1941 Noel Currer-Briggs came to work at Bletchley and describes[17] how in rooms 1–3 'Tiltman and a small team of cryptographers, of which I was one, laboured to break German Double Playfair… ciphers.'

The Playfair system had originally been devised in the nineteenth century by the British and was used by them in the First World War. It involved the idea of a single substitution square which used a keyword which had just one of each alphabet letter, followed by the remaining ones in alphabetical order, in a 5x5 layout (amalgamating I and J) as in the following (keyword: BURGLED):

B	U	R	G	L
E	D	A	C	F
H	I	K	M	N
O	P	Q	S	T
V	W	X	Y	Z

The message would then be divided into bigrams and each pair encoded with its 'rectangular opposites' – for example the word COME would be divided CO and ME and encoded as SE CH. There were rules for encoding when letters were in the same row/column and/or at ends of lines.

If the keyword is used once only there is a modicum of security, but the weakness lies in the frequent similarity of most squares in their lower half where fewer letters (V, X, Y, Z, above them P, Q) get used in keywords and so the grid layout is partly predictable. The Germans found their way into the system and made use of the idea by creating a version using two grids and making both of these 'randomized'. Each pair of plaintext letters is encoded by a similar process but with the first of the pair using the first square, the second using the other. The process was also made more complex by re-enciphering this coded pair once more on the same squares. Encoding is thus more time-consuming but decryption (especially by the enemy!) is much harder. It involves having to recreate the enciphering squares from minute clues in formal documents (e.g. ones where there is some form of numbering, or repeated salutations)[18]. The system was known and is described in Friedman's manual on military cryptanalysis written for US codebreakers. Advice on it was also received by the British thanks to Tiltman's continuing connections with Bertrand.

Double Playfair – called *Doppelkastenschlussel* by the Germans – was in use in a range of areas during the war. Currer-Briggs gives a useful account of the process of breaking a day's key, written from personal experience. He speaks of its use by the SS on the Russian front to give details of the prisoners-of-war, both taken and those who escaped. He was also part of a team sent to North Africa to work on material there in 1942–43 in the final stages of the African campaign, providing details on enemy dispositions and activity, in particular the identification of locations and intentions of the Panzer divisions played. An example from later in the war is given by Charles David, who explains that in 1944 the breaking of the system revealed unexpected activity among German forces in mid-December. The information was passed back to headquarters but presumably not analysed effectively, for it was a precursor to the Battle of the Bulge (16 December). Continuing work on the code after checking the German attack enabled the US air force to pinpoint the retreating German forces in great detail and thereby target them effectively.[19]

This example is a good one of the routine and monotony that was the life of a codebreaker. Tiltman played his part in this – not simply a giver of orders but one who worked at it like the others.

1940–2: Railway Enigma

Tiltman (as he said) had 'little to do with Enigma', as he reminds the Americans in his interviews[20]: 'I handed over everything I could. The Enigma wasn't my job. It had an entirely separate staff and so on.'

But his work where he did do it on Enigma was significant; his preliminary involvement with analysis of the machine has been noted (Chapter 3) in 1936–39. On the Railway Enigma he helped to show in some detail the atrocities going on behind the German invasion of Russia in 1941. Tiltman refers only briefly to it:[21]

> *I got the first solution of the commercial Enigma for the German railroad control... but I only succeeded because the underlying plain texts were of a very stereotyped nature and... because* [they] *were subject to the limitation of Enigma-type rotor machines, i.e., that a plaintext letter can only be represented by a different letter in cipher.*

Tiltman seems to have used the tendency of such messages to have predictable patterns, especially of numbers as one might find in a timetable or sets of statistics, to give himself help. The railway machine itself was one apparently without a plugboard, which may have helped.

Stereotypical phrases are one type of **crib** which codebreakers could use. A crib is a likely 'guess' of a word, phrase or group of letters in a message. It can be used, when compared with the ciphertext, to work out possible settings of the message key. Cribs were especially important in Enigma decoding, and were the foundation of the concept of the Bombe machine used with effect from October 1940 against Enigma itself (the machine rapidly tried out a given crib against a range of rotor starting positions to see if possible rotor settings could generate the crib from the ciphertext). But the principle of the crib was valuable in many other areas of both codes and ciphers. On the Railway system the cribs were often numbers which had to be spelled out as words, as the basic Enigma machine did not have numerical keys.

So if you use the crib (guess that your message has) EINSX ZWO at the start ('1, 2'; the 'X' is a word divider), you can match it with the cipher text in different positions to find a fit. In the case of Enigma the machine cannot encipher a letter as itself (due to its electrical configuration), so you can look for a place where there are no duplicates.

Given the ciphertext

1 2 3 4 5 6 7 8 9 10 1

O D P E X B A S W D Z

then the crib

E I N S X Z W O

cannot be correct at position one, as the sequence duplicates 'X' at place 5. Likewise starting at position 3 gives

E I N S X Z **W** O

which duplicates the 'W' at position 9; and starting at place 4:

E I N S X Z W O

duplicates the E at position 4. But position 2 might be a place to try.

According to Erskine[22] the original breaks by Tiltman were in 1940 and the work was then taken by Hut 8, where the wiring of the machine was solved, and then by Hut 6 from 1941 (after some months gap in its use), where the Russian front meant a great increase in traffic. Joan Murray (Joan Clarke, one-time fiancée of Turing and later deputy Head of Hut 8) confirms this,[23] saying that (while Hut 8 awaited materials that would lead to a break into Naval Enigma) the Railway Enigma early on 'was used without security precautions… This gave a 'depth", and it was from this that Tiltman was able to discern the plaintext, which turned out to be timetables. Knowing that numbers were the content, they were able to work out the wheel wirings in Hut 8, after which 'Work on the Railway Enigma was passed to Hut 6.'

An article from the NSA *History Today* also confirms[24] Tiltman making the first break into the Railway Enigma in March 1940 by discovering a 'depth', and when it resumed transmission after a break, in 1941, one thing revealed was the movement of Panzers to the Eastern Front, which prompted Churchill to warn Stalin. Tiltman shared his discovery with Sinkov[25] during the latter's visit to BP in late winter 1941, explaining that it was used by a range of 'police' forces, but in terms of intelligence produced at that time it was little more than train schedules.

The material later helped to generate reports nicknamed[26] HOR-HUG (from repeated code-groups) by BP and in 1942 these contained short reports from camps (including Auschwitz, Dachau and Oranienburg) listing: inmates at start of previous day, new arrivals, 'departures', and number at end of day in a regular format. The formulaic structure made it easier to decrypt. It was found that the system also connected with the Enigma 'Orange' key's Stecker set-up (the arrangement of plugs and wires on the front of Enigma machines which swapped pairs of letters according to the codebook each day), helping breaks into this.

1941: Research Section and Hagelin; Italian C-38M

Machines designed by the Swedish engineer Boris Hagelin were in use before and during the war. The USA used a version, which became the M-209 and was in common use for Americans before the superior M-228 which had a different system of operation.

Another version began to be used regularly in late 1940 by the Italians, for their navy in particular. This came as a relief[27] to some in the Naval Section, as the book-based system (nicknamed 'Zog') had proved intractable. Work on this soon came to the research section at BP supervised by Tiltman, where the team included the section leader Gerry Morgan, and Bill Tutte.

Tutte was recruited early in 1941[28] and joined Research. The nature of the machine itself was not a problem, as it was used in several countries and was apparently available[29] at BP. The issue was the methodology of finding the settings quickly. The machine[30] had six wheels, each with a different number of 'pins' (26, 25, 23, 21, 19, 17). Each wheel turns one place when a key is pressed, and as these numbers have no common factors with each other they will not realign in the same relative positions before about 100 million key-taps. The pins can be set to 'active' or 'inactive', and if active they engage lugs fitted to a rotating 'cage' of bars, pushing the bar to the left to form a 'tooth' which engages another gear-type wheel – there may be no, one or several 'teeth' created. The positions of the lugs and pins must of course be set from the code-book by sender and receiver.

Each individual letter is set on a plaintext wheel and a manual handle turned, moving the six wheels and engaging the 'teeth' on the print-wheel, turning it to its encoding position. It is a kind of 'additive' process (think of the letters as numbers 1–26), adding a coding letter to each plaintext letter to produce a ciphertext letter. The ciphered letter is printed onto a strip of paper and the next letter chosen on the plaintext wheel. Thus a strip of ticker-tape is produced with the ciphertext. To decode, the machine has a second setting for 'deciphering' and the process is repeated.

The essential element of attacking the messages was to find a depth (more than one message using the same setting and starting-point). As numbers of messages were sent on any day with the same basic pin and lug settings, the starting-point of the wheels had to be chosen and sent individually – often barely disguised. Tutte now says[31] that if you think of the plaintexts as P1 and P2, producing ciphertexts C1 and C2 by adding a key layer K, you can envisage two equations: P1 + K = C1, and P2 + K = C2. By subtracting the second equation from the first you have (P1 – P2) = (C1 –C2), and you now do not have to worry about the machine but try to make guesses of words and phrases ('cribs' again) in one which, by 'subtraction' in mod 26 leaves a plausible word/phrase in the other. From this the underlying key pattern can be studied.

By analysing the technique mathematically the machine became readable, and it was taken over from the Research team by the members of the Naval Section. Professor Vincent, as an Italian specialist and Tiltman's deputy in Research, came to oversee much of the work later on.

Sylvia Godden worked on this system during this time and has left us an account of its workings:[32]

Some of the interim details are lost in my memory, but after arriving at a breakthrough, we transferred the amended text to little hand-operated Hagelin machines. These machines had a series of wheels interspersed with spokes which could be moved to the left or right according to the way the code was broken. This was done by operating a small hand-operated wheel on the right side of the machine. If one's rodding[33] *had been done correctly, the decoded Italian came out printed on the paper tape we had inserted in the machine. These paper strips were then pasted on the back of the uncoded message and hastily pushed through a hatch at the other end of the office where the Italian translators worked. Speed regarding this whole procedure was important since the messages contained information on the Italian shipping in the Mediterranean and were consequently of great importance to the Allied Forces.*

See Chapter 6 for more on the impact of this success.

The Hagelin systems were not regarded as being of the highest quality. Tordella, speaking from the American perspective (he later became a senior member of the NSA), has said[34]: 'Our usage of Hagelin in World War II was abominable, and the Germans profited greatly from it' – referring to the M-209.

1941: First break into Tunny.

The Tunny break was one of the most critical of the war.

Tunny was a branch of so-called FISH traffic, German high-grade material which used a teleprinter system with an attachment, the Lorenz SZ40/42 machine. It was the army (*Heere*) version; there were others.

In teleprinting, each letter or symbol (it can cope with numbers and punctuation) is represented by a pattern of five 'marks' or 'spaces', holes or blanks, across a strip of teleprinter paper. The code for these was of course well-known and public: the Baudot-Murray code. There are 32 possible patterns of the 5 holes/blanks (or 64 if a 'shift' upper-lower case is possible).

The basic concept[35] of a machine to encipher a message in Murray code was earlier crystallized by Gilbert Vernam, an American engineer with AT&T. His idea was to 'add' to each mark or space an apparently random mark or space from a 'key'. The result generates an entirely different, generally meaningless, series of letters and symbols.

Here is an example of how this works. It uses '1' and '0' for mark and space, or cross and dot, to be clearer; the addition is like binary but 'non-carry' (or Fibonacci).

Example of Murray code enciphering

C	A	T	Plaintext
0 1 1 1 0	1 1 0 0 0	0 0 0 0 1	

Add the coding layer (non-carry addition) generated by machine

U	*5*	*R*	*Coding layer*
1 1 1 0 0	*1 1 0 1 1*	*0 1 0 1 0*	*added to plaintext*

The resulting output is

1 0 0 1 0	0 0 0 1 1	0 1 0 1 1	Transmitted
D	O	G	ciphertext

The receiver, with the same machine settings, adds the coding layer again to the ciphertext:

1 1 1 0 0	*1 1 0 1 1*	*0 1 0 1 0*	which reveals:
0 1 1 1 0	1 1 0 0 0	0 0 0 0 1	
C	A	T	Plaintext

The problem was how to generate a key without a visible pattern to it. Morehouse and Parker-Hitt[36] experimented in the USA with unequal loops of paper tape and rotors, with mixed success. AT&T had demonstrated the machine after the First World War, and the audience included some German observers who brought back the ideas. The results in the 1930s were the development of machines by the Siemens company and by Lorenz, which used rotors to generate the key.

The Lorenz attachment would add an apparently 'random' stream of 'marks' or 'spaces' to the plaintext (every possible pattern of five marks/spaces has a letter or symbol associated with it). This stream was generated by two sets of five wheels, each with different numbers of 'pins', which rotated for each symbol (all bar one were prime numbers, ensuring avoidance of frequent repeated coincident positions) before transmitting the resultant gibberish symbols. At the receiving end, a similar machine, its wheels set to the same starting positions, did a similar job to the ciphertext. The effect of adding the enciphering later a second time is to cancel it out, leaving the plaintext, which would then print out on a teleprinter attached.

Messages of this nature were being intercepted in late 1940; they were recognized as non-Morse signals but there was no capacity to do any analysis. After traffic resumed in June 1941 a farm in Kent at Knockholt was taken over to intercept the signals.

The messages at this stage began with a clear list of twelve German names (their equivalent of Alpha, Bravo, Charlie etc), and these were recognized as being the indicators of the wheel starting positions (the initial letters of the names). This betrayed the fact that two messages at the end of August 1941 had been sent with the same setting (depth) and therefore used the same additive coding layer (U5R in our example).

The second message of this pair was a repeat of the first (which the receiver said had been scrambled in transmission), but with changes (e.g. abbreviations) so it was similar but not identical. Now as each message in effect contained the plaintext and a coding layer, the effect of adding them together (two non-identical plaintexts and two coding layers) was to cancel out the coding layer (see above: adding it twice cancels it!), leaving in effect the 'sum' of the two plaintexts.

What did Tiltman then do? We do not know the exact detail, but the following example (a manufactured text, not an actual wartime one) shows something of his method, and the extraordinary patience and logical thinking of which he was capable. The reader must trust the author that the adding of letters using their combinations of 1/0 (mark/space) produces the given letter/symbol outcome! The teleprinter 'addition square' can be found in the appendices for those wishing to check.

Imagine that the 'addition' of the two ciphertexts has been done, to cancel the key layer, as described above, and the combined plaintext emerges as:

Position:

```
                  1                   2                   3                   4
1 2 3 4 5 6 7 8 9 0 1 2 3 4 5 6 7 8 9 0 1 2 3 4 5 6 7 8 9 0 1 2 3 4 5 6 7 8 9 0 1 2 3 4 5
```

Combined plaintext:

```
0 0 0 0 0 0 0 F O X U I E S M F Z S M X T 4 R O V 4 0 S T 4 V S H 5 V 0 C N H O W T Q 9 8
```

Observation showed at once that the messages began with identical letters (producing the string of '0's at the start) but began to change at position eight. Tiltman would then be thinking of possible 'cribs' – phrases likely to be such a message, based on experience and scraps of previous information from studying the Lorenz system. He would seize on a term such as *geheim* – secret – and begin to try subtracting this systematically from positions along the combined plaintext, to see what remained.

Starting at position eight (the first 'different' combination), subtracting *geheim* produces the outcome

```
0 0 0 0 0 0 0 F O X U I E S M F Z S M X T 4 R O V 4 0 S T 4 V S H 5 V 0 C N H O W T Q 9 8
              G E H E I M
              Q B D I 0 X
```

Clearly QBDI0X is meaningless, so this cannot be the right place.

A trial starting at position ten (Tiltman would have tried nine too) produces:

```
0 0 0 0 0 0 0 F O X U I E S M F Z S M X T 4 R O V 4 0 S T 4 V S H 5 V 0 C N H O W T Q 9 8
                  G E H E I M
                  U I L 0 A 0
```

Again there is no obvious meaningful language, though 'UIL' is not without hope. Tiltman would have moved on to position eleven:

```
0 0 0 0 0 0 0 F O X U I E S M F Z S M X T 4 R O V 4 0 S T 4 V S H 5 V 0 C N H O W T Q 9 8
                    G E H E I M
                    X U Y 9 G Z
```

Again there is only gibberish. Tiltman would have continued until position fifteen:

```
0 0 0 0 0 0 0 F O X U I E S M F Z S M X T 4 R O V 4 0 S T 4 V S H 5 V 0 C N H O W T Q 9 8
                            G E H E I M 9
                            I N S 9 G E H
```

Suddenly there is light. The 'INS' could well be the latter part of the number *eins* (one). The number 9 has been added to the crib as it was used as the word separator in the teleprinter system, and by adding it to our crib it produces an additional effect – we have in the 'remainder' not only part of *eins* but also a 9 where it should be, and three letters GEH which look like *geheim* again. Is one message repeating the other? We can try putting EIM onto the lower line after GEH and seeing what it gives us (when we take it away from the combined line) in the upper plaintext line. We can also insert 9E (word separator and first letter of *eins*) before the INS to see if its remainder makes sense. The E here ought to produce a 9 as a word separator before *geheim*.

Sure enough:

```
0 0 0 0 0 0 0 F O X U I E S M F Z S M X T 4 R O V 4 0 S T 4 V S H 5 V 0 C N H O W T Q 9 8
                        S 9 G E H E I M 9 A N 9
                        9 E I N S 9 G E H E I M
```

On the upper line of plaintext the AN means 'to' and Tiltman would then try a name or rank as a new crib. After a few trials he might attempt GENERAL9 on the line with AN9 (position 24). This gives:

```
0 0 0 0 0 0 0 F O X U I E S M F Z S M X T 4 R O V 4 0 S T 4 V S H 5 V 0 C N H O W T Q 9 8
                        S 9 G E H E I M 9 A N 9 G E N E R A L 9
                        9 E I N S 9 G E H E I M 9 A N 9 G E N E
```

This technique of trying out a 'guess' on one line to see what it produced on the other was sometimes called 'cross-ruffing', after the technique in Contract Bridge. By now Tiltman would be fairly sure that one message was repeating the other, but with some alteration in the earlier part to put them out of phase. Notice the 'null' zero above the two Ns at position 27 is correct; identical letters added or subtracted produce a 'null' outcome.

But what about the start? The presence of *eins* would suggest to him the word *nummer* – number – and perhaps *spruchnummer* – message number. *Spruchnummer* has twelve letters, exactly the number before 9EINS in our example. What happens if we try this on the lower plaintext line and subtract it from the combined line?

0 0 0 0 0 0 0 F O X U I E S M F Z S M X T 4 R O V 4 0 S T 4 V S H 5 V 0 C N H O W T Q 9 8
S P R U C H N R 9 E I N S 9 G E H E I M 9 A N 9 G E N E R A L 9
S P R U C H N U M M E R 9 E I N S 9 G E H E I M 9 A N 9 G E N E

Now we can see what happened at the start. The sender abbreviated the upper plaintext message, pulling it all 'back' against the other one.

Tiltman would then continue at position 33, adding RAL9 (end of 'general') to the lower plaintext, and seeing what the subtraction produced:

0 0 0 0 0 0 0 F O X U I E S M F Z S M X T 4 R O V 4 0 S T 4 V S H 5 V 0 C N H O W T Q 9 8
S P R U C H N R 9 E I N S 9 G E H E I M 9 A N 9 G E N E R A L 9 **V O N 9**
S P R U C H N U M M E R 9 E I N S 9 G E H E I M 9 A N 9 G E N E R A L 9

The repetition of VON9 added to the bottom plaintext is done in the same way, and it produces

0 0 0 0 0 0 0 F O X U I E S M F Z S M X T 4 R O V 4 0 S T 4 V S H 5 V 0 C N H O W T Q 9 8
S P R U C H N R 9 E I N S 9 G E H E I M 9 A N 9 G E N E R A L 9 V O N 9 **T H O M**
S P R U C H N U M M E R 9 E I N S 9 G E H E I M 9 A N 9 G E N E R A L 9 V O N 9

General von Thoma is a recognised name and would confirm the correctness of the process.

Tiltman spent ten days, reportedly, following this process on his actual combined plaintext. If some interruption occurred he would trial a crib word or phrase further along the message (the actual one having about 4,000 characters to try!), using the same subtraction technique, trying to find new break-in points, working forward and back, until the whole of both texts was found.

Bauer gives some detailed explanation of how the actual message might have been worked out,[37] but the example above is given to demonstrate Tiltman's skill and perseverance. He thus extracted both plaintexts from the combination.

How did Tiltman know what kind of machine process to look for? This is not fully clear. It is possible that some of the concepts behind the Hagelin machine helped to visualize it. Tiltman claims not to have had detailed involvement with the Americans until 1941 when the Sinkov mission arrived (see Chapter 7), but we do not know what he may have read. It is said[38] that he wrote, 'The next advance to be made was the demonstration that the cipher machine was a letter subtraction cipher and the determination of the laws of addition used. This was made possible by the occurrence of a number of depths.' This quotation is in the 'General report on Tunny', written just after the war, and Gannon attributes it to Tiltman (whom he says knew about Vernam-based machines and probably began from this basis), though the Tunny report is by others. Gannon also points to a paper written by Gerry Morgan, part of the Research team, about the topic. Tiltman refers[39] to experience with the *Hellschreiber*, a teleprinter device in use from the 1920s and known widely. He also states[40] that he had read a book by Parker-Hitt, one of the early workers on Vernam systems. The related Siemens cipher machine had been patented in the early 1930s and its workings were thus quite 'public'.

By now adding one plaintext to its original enciphered version, the 'two plaintexts' would cancel out, leaving just the coding layer of letters generated by the machine. It was this coding layer (in its teleprinter mark/space form) that Bill Tutte and Gerry Morgan then worked on (about 4,000 characters, thanks to the German carelessness) to deduce the mechanism of the Lorenz – possibly the greatest purely intellectual achievement of BP's war. See Chapter 9 for an example of the consequences of the success – the Russian success in checking the German assault at Kursk in 1943. The binary nature of the material was to lend itself to digital manipulation – ultimately by Colossus, first of the computers.

1942: JMA additive code (assists in break)

At the end of 1941 Tiltman, his Japanese resources thin and overstretched, had given intercepts of military attaché coded material to a group of French cryptographers headed by Baudoin, as there was nothing for the French to do after their defeat in 1940. They had made no progress, as Tiltman observed:

> *You could hardly read any of the intercepts. They were all scrawled over with red letters and so on. I had to go back to the beginning again.*[41]

Tiltman was able to show (following discussion with Sinkov's group) that 'literal additives' – patterns of letters added to what were coding digraphs (2-letter groups each meaning a set term such as directions, units, key phrases etc) entered by means of a grid – were being used. He was also able to identify a series of long messages where the sender, trying to spread his use of the additives as widely as possible, had started each one with the next additive on from the point where he finished the previous message, eventually sending enough to cover the whole additive book in sequence five times. This enabled depth to be created – the codebreaker's delight.

1942–3: German-Spanish Kryha code

The Kryha code machine worked on a similar conceptual basis to the Caesar wheel but with much more complex movement of the parts. There were two concentric discs; the plaintext letters would be found on the outer ring and the letter opposite on the inner ring was used to encipher it. The complexity was introduced by a ring which caused the inner ring to move irregularly by a certain number of steps when levers were pressed.

The machine was small and portable, and provided some security, being used by Germans in the first half of the war. However, it was weak against high-grade cryptanalysis, and a team led by Friedman apparently broke a practice message of 1,100 or so characters in less than three hours.

In a document[42] from the Friedman collection, held by the NSA, and dated to 1943, we are told that 'one of the most fruitful lines of commercial traffic exploited by Denniston's group is traffic enciphered on Kryha machine… not many messages are procured and sent to Special Branch. Such as does reach Special Branch is so… full of cover names that we have never been able to do much with it… cipher was broken by

Tiltman in June nineteen forty two and British have intercepted and read about ninety-five per cent of all messages since May One nineteen forty one.' The date discrepancy here is not explained, though David Kenyon suggests the commercial codebreakers perhaps went back to read earlier messages once the break was made in 1942.

A number of these messages were coming from Madrid under a financial institution cover. As the messages often referred to German purchases and transportation of materials – from neutral Spain – the information provided an insight into the Reich's supply and logistical situation. The Americans were very interested in this (as the British continued to be). Arrangements were to be made to forward the information, Friedman stating, 'The British are right on top of this and there appears to be little need for us to duplicate.'

1943: Japanese Army Air code 3366

Tiltman[43] says:

> *We first of all broke into an air cipher which was named '3366'. It was very badly used; the first page* [of additives] *was very much overused and there were other places, and we were able to read depth.*

The 3366 was to prove a useful army air force general purpose code system once it was broken into again. Tiltman's first breaks into it were in the 1930s, but the system was changed after Japan entered the war and had to be recovered. The code system became a British priority following the conference in early 1944 where areas of focus were agreed between the UK and the USA.

The version used during the war itself had adopted the additive procedure familiar from JN-25. Each key word, phrase or syllable (where something needed spelling out – such as CHI-YA-A-CHI-RU – which is 'Churchill') is assigned a 4-digit number, and this is in turn re-enciphered with some form of additive.[44] In the 3366 this was from a book of supposedly random 4-figure numbers where a page, line and starting-point are chosen by the sender and indicated in the message.

Decoding involved finding groups of messages with the same or very near indicator numbers, and then lining them up in 'depth' (the process is also described by Stripp[45]). Bob Biggs, who worked at Bletchley from

June 1942 until the end, firstly in Elmers school and later in Block F with the JAAF codes 3366 and 6633, explained that these codes used number groups for each item in the message, including Japanese alphabetic 'Romaji' letters, brackets and figures. After examining messages from a similar source, a depth of several messages would be lined up. By making guesses about certain things (e.g. where an 'open bracket' might be) and subtracting its (known) code-group, the additive number would be revealed. That number could then be subtracted from others in the same column (as aligned in the 'depth'), to reveal other known code groups, which then give clues about other possible contents. For example, brackets were used to enclose figures in the message, so finding a bracket gives you ten possible guesses for a following figure.[46]

So by working out a number common to each column in the depth which gave realistic known code groups after subtracting it, the residual code numbers are revealed, and then if they are known from your reconstructed code book they are translated, and if not known then from the context a fair guess can be made, which can be added to the code book as a provisional value. The process involves much guesswork about positions and numbers, and painstaking, lengthy trial and error was needed. Bob Biggs and his group, removing or stripping the additives from the ciphertext, were known as 'strippers', naturally.

The sheets on which the writing-out of depth was done were sometimes known as 'Tiltman sheets'. Further comment on his influence seems unnecessary.

An example of the value of this kind of material is pointed out by Michael Smith,[47] who refers to the manoeuvre by Slim to surround Mandalay in early 1945. His IV Corps and XXXIII Corps were moving south, with Mandalay to the south-east. Faced[48] with superior Japanese numbers, a wily general Kimura who had prepared defences, and a river (the Irrawaddy) with sandbanks and gorges, Slim sent IV Corps some 300 miles south, swinging behind XXXIII Corps and down towards a crossing near Pakokku and from there east to Meiktila, before turning north towards Mandalay. The passage was accompanied by improvised rafts capable of carrying ten tons apiece, as well as some prefabricated boats ('probably the first time that the army has constructed warships for the Royal Navy'!). A fake Corps HQ was set up north of Mandalay with wireless signals generated from it; the spearhead of IV Corps was a brigade previously attached to XXXIII Corps, to mislead any observers. The whole plan was assisted by knowledge of the enemy, enhanced by the intercept units and Intelligence Corps wireless sections embedded with each main force, and having supporting bases in the rear. One of these was Imphal, where Richard Warren served in the summer of 1944 before entering Burma with the expeditionary forces. He describes his experience:[49]

> *Three months later we crossed into Burma via the Chin Hills then turned south and began our two year Burma expedition. Using two wireless vans each containing six receiver sets we began intercepting Japanese signals and using the information they contained. I remember one such message saying that a Japanese commander would be taking off next morning at a certain time so we said thanks very much. He was duly shot down shortly after takeoff.*

It would seem Admiral Yamamoto's dramatic and fatal experience in 1943 was not unique.

By this time there were nearly 250 people[50] in the BP Japanese section working on army air force messages, a measure of the importance of this field which Tiltman's efforts had opened up.

* * *

Tiltman was also increasingly involved in the creation of code and cipher systems, sometimes with unusual results. In 1933 he created a coding cylinder,[51] a complex version of a 'grid', which he later described as 'too far ahead of its time'. He describes it thus:

> *It was based on a cylinder inscribed with 48 lines of random digits. Over this cylinder a moveable sleeve was fitted. The sleeve carried 24 lines of 4-figure windows, 5 windows to a line arranged at random, the lines corresponding to alternate lines of the basic cylinder. It could be clamped to any one message against the cylinder in 5 consecutive lateral and 48 vertical positions, i.e., 120 in all, and encryption by addition could start at any of the 24 lines and proceed for a limit of 120 groups.*

The device would have combined the grille concept with additive techniques. Perhaps the balance between ease of use and code security was inadequate to pursue it.

In 1941[52] he produced a system called 'Cysquare' for the army in North Africa, which proved to be very secure but was felt to be too cumbersome to use regularly and was gradually abandoned – but the Germans apparently paid him the compliment, when examples were captured, of refining it and using a version of it themselves in 1944! He describes this[53] in a (heavily redacted) NSA paper:

Sometime later in 1941 I produced the 'Cysquare' which was accepted by the War Office as a low-echelon cipher to replace the 'Stencil' cipher and issued to the Eighth Army in North Africa… The grille has 676 (26 x 26) squares. Each column and each line contains ten white (permitted) squares, with the exception of 3 'plus' lines containing 20 white squares each and 3 'minus' lines which contain no white squares at all. The key for the day consists of 26 letters of the alphabet in random order with the numbers from 1 to 26 written under them also in random order. For each message the operator selects a 4-letter indicator from a random list of such groups provided him for use in turn. The grille could be used with any of its sides at the top… The numerical key for the day is written from left to right at the top of the grille and from the bottom upwards on the left hand side. The plain text is written into the grille starting at the next white square after the square described by the line coordinate… and the column coordinate… using the elements of the key to define the corresponding lines and columns.

He says of his work in this field:[54]

I have also, at frequent intervals between 1924 and 1948, been forced to produce practical ciphers of varying degrees of security for British use. This is a field in which sloppy thinking finds one out more than in any other and I believe it to be a considerable factor in training the imagination for diagnosis of complicated problems. It is obvious that the livelihood of a cryptanalyst depends almost entirely on the over-ingenuity of the designers of foreign ciphers.

He also created a 'stencil subtractor' system for service use to make navy codes in particular more secure. This had been the problem at the heart of the merchant fleet and naval losses in 1942 – the German B-Dienst (a very efficient section of their naval cryptographers) were tracking convoys through code breaks. Tiltman's solution was the Stencil Subtractor Frame, which was in wide use by the end of 1943. According to Clabby[55], the SSF *consisted of a plastic grille which contained 100 four-digit-wide windows randomly spaced. This was superimposed over an additive sheet that had forty-eight lines of sixty-eight digits each. Setting squares for the placement of the grille provided 100 possible settings, and a conversion table appeared on each sheet with mixed sequences of digits from 00 to 99 for indicating purposes. Each sheet was used for one day only. The placement of the grille was determined through a substitution pattern sent to each user.*

In his role as consultant and later as chief cryptographer Tiltman had extensive connections with the British code makers, who for the duration were based in Oxford at Mansfield College, most of which was requisitioned in 1939. Initially about twenty people went there from GC&CS in London, mainly because they were close to the University Press, which did much of the printing. The place was supported by a Hollerith outstation at Drayton Parslow from 1941, and this assisted cipher construction.

In 1943 Tiltman was called into SOE to examine the types of code they were using there. Leo Marks had had growing suspicions that a number of SOE agents were compromised, in part from examining their coding activity and techniques. He felt the poem-based codes were not secure enough and proposed changes; Tiltman was the 'assessor'. See Chapter 8 for Marks' impressions of Tiltman.

And in 1944:[56]

Sometime in 1944 the War Office put up to me for security assessment a field cipher they had produced for use within divisions. I believe what the designer had in mind was an improvement on the old American 'Strip' system. I didn't like their idea much and redesigned it. My design was called 'Linex', and it was issued in the form I laid down and extensively used in the field. I was rather surprised at its acceptance as I thought it extremely cumbersome.

I was in the position – certainly from, I think I would say, from the beginning of the war – that I was the leading cryptanalyst diagnostician, if you like to put it so, in GCHQ. And from early in 1941, I was called chief cryptographer [Tiltman took this role officially more than a year later] *and I was actually personally responsible for the attack on anything we weren't reading or anything that was undiagnosed. This was, of course, a quite impossible responsibility to carry, but we did our best. I had a very small research section of about twelve.*

The description of Tiltman by Christopher Andrew[57] as a 'brilliant mathematician' might well have amused (or puzzled) him. Tiltman's own assessment of himself was simple: he said he had 'no knowledge of higher mathematics'! The estimation of colleagues was very different, and perhaps a comment by Henry Dryden[58] is telling. The 'phoney war' saw the dispatch of a group to support the French cryptographers at La Ferté-sous-Jouarre. Dryden comments that intercepts were few in number, and this period saw, according to Dryden, the 'only recorded case of failure by John Tiltman... to break a system he had attacked'. This is an affectionate comment on the awe with which Tiltman's skills were viewed by his colleagues, from a man with much to thank him for (see Chapter 8).

Tiltman was a pragmatic thinker about cryptography. He outlined his key concerns in a 1973 article[59] where the priorities as he saw them were stated. For example:

A. *A cipher system has to be a compromise between security and practicability. It should be designed specifically for the task it has to perform. Anyone can produce a secure cipher, e.g., one-time pads, but OTP becomes impractical when the system has to be used for frequent intercommunication among a number or holders.*
B. *The responsibility for the security of a system has to be taken completely out of the hands of the cipher operator, who should virtually be told how to encrypt each message. Further, a system has to be proof as far as possible against attempts by holders to circumvent the instructions through laziness, i.e., the instructions should take account of this possibility.*
C. *A system is as strong as its weakest link. Cryptanalysts make their living out of the sloppy thinking and enthusiastic over-ingenuity of designers of cipher systems. When the security of a system is assessed in advance, the possible damage due to compromise of part of the cryptographic materials, e.g., the codebook, has to be taken into account.*
D. *All transposition systems are dangerous. If they are overcomplicated, they breed mistakes.*

Within words like these he shows how his experience counted. Idea C was at the heart of breaking the Japanese codes, when they changed the codebook but not the additives, or *vice versa*; idea B was manifest when operator errors often gave the clue to breaking Enigma systems (the early Russian codes were transpositions).

The instinct for finding clues is well illustrated in a story from Jean Nissan,[60] who worked initially in Hut 4 at BP but spent the major part of her time in the diplomatic section in London. She recounts:

> *The messages went to one of the military sections, I think, who worked hard on them and reached a point where they felt they were one stage from converting them into a plain language. They tried French, German and Italian and various languages they all knew, but they could not read the messages. So they took them to Colonel Tiltman who wondered if the language might be Hebrew transliterated, because the letters 'im' kept coming up together, as in cherubim and seraphim. These messages were in letters, not figures. He first asked a Captain in the ATS to translate it and she confirmed that the language was Hebrew, but said she wouldn't translate it, obviously a Zionist.*

Chapter 5

The Diplomat – Part One

Tiltman's value as negotiator, representative and diplomat from the late 1920s onwards is seldom appreciated. His travels were considerable. The benefits gained by British cryptography were great. His own personality and character played an important role in the success of these adventures. In this section we review some of his early involvement.

After his return from India at the end of 1929 (when he was appointed head of the GC&CS Military Section), he visited Berlin three times, between 1931 and 1934. In 1932 he visited France and met with Bertrand to discuss French progress on Russian cyphers (though he was not supposed to tell the French what he already knew of Russian codes). He and Bertrand were able to be mutually open, and this led to great trust and respect. Clabby[1] describes the occasion thus:

> *Bertrand immediately indicated that he knew where British sensitivities lay. He handed Tiltman a paper that contained exactly what the French knew, setting aside any qualms Tiltman's instructions may have caused. Tiltman responded to this openness in kind, and a relationship was established that served the British well throughout the decade… The cooperation established in this exchange led to frank exchanges in dealing with the German Enigma machine.*

Tiltman recognized the integrity of Bertrand and the French, and was prepared to respond. It enabled the 1938 enquiries about Enigma details to proceed without hindrance. He describes his own later meetings in 1940, when he went to France during the 'Phoney War', and when the attack came:[2]

> *When we sent the British Expeditionary Force to fight in France… we also provided them with a liaison officer named Macfarlan, 'Pinky' Macfarlan, who worked in their most secret office;… a typical interview with Bertrand, who as I said didn't know English, would be in Bill*

> *Dunderdale's office. Bill Dunderdale is half English/half Russian… our representative in Paris of our secret service… I would be talking, Bertrand would be sitting on the edge of his chair opposite to me, and when he saw you were about to ask a question that he couldn't answer, always he'd say 'ne pas demander'… he always knew what was going on. After the Germans attacked into France – I think it must have been about May 14 1940, I was in the French GHQ, negotiating the return of our party, and Bertrand said, 'We value your party very much; we'd like to keep them, but you'd better get them out while you can,' and they were evacuated through Bordeaux. He then said, 'And please tell your chiefs in London that none of your secrets will get into enemy hands'* [modern underlining]. *Now how he made such an impossible statement I don't know, because there must have been a hundred French officers who knew what we were doing on the Enigma and everything else. But they never did get into enemy hands.*

Engagement with Far Eastern traffic made demands on his travel time and diplomatic skills. Tiltman held that the years from 1935 to 1937 were dominated by Far Eastern codes. He says:[3]

> *My time for the three years, 1935 thru 1937, was almost entirely taken up with research on the intercepts from Hong Kong. The major part of the traffic was in a succession of military systems used for transmission of intelligence reports from China, especially detailed as to the characteristics of key personalities.*

In 1937 he went to Hong Kong to negotiate with the Far East Combined Bureau (FECB) station to take over military traffic, as the more experienced navy cryptologists in London were overloaded. FECB did not want this – they were preoccupied with navy codes. Tiltman says:[4]

> *It seemed to me that this was something that ought to be done and dealt with… it was intercepted in Hong Kong and just as the Navy did their own exploitation in Hong Kong, that we ought to have a military party dealing with military in the Far East and not with us. So I got permission; I went out by sea to Hong Kong and when I'd been there a short time I found that there was really an awful lot of work to be done… and I found a very good Japanese interpreter… on Stonecutter's island which is in the middle of the harbour in Hong Kong, where the military intercept was*

taken. I applied for Marr-Johnson to be attached to me, and the first time applied it was refused. The second time was after the Japanese had come down into China and they agreed to let me have him half-time. And then when he just got not only interested but useful, they took him away from me for a translating job in North China. I was so angry that when I got home [November]... *I made a row in the War Office and they actually flew him from Hong Kong home.*

He returned to the Far East, with his desired Japanese-skilled entourage following by sea, in 1939 having won his point.

That year he had been meant to be at the July meeting about Enigma with the Poles, but was interrupted by the need to go once more to Hong Kong. He again visited France, being appointed lieutenant colonel on 19 September (he recalls), arriving not long after.

I then was presented a temporary Lieutenant Colonel in charge of a mythical body called #4 Intelligence School, which included my own people and quite a large TA party which worked in London under Colonel Stratton.

There were in fact 'intelligence schools' within MI6, and no.4 (army) had a base at Bletchley, linked to the Military Section. It is found in Block F later in the war, having been based earlier in the Mansion.[5]

In January 1940 Tiltman visited Finland where he was able collect Russian code information. Smith says[6] that he made arrangements with the Finns to send Russian code traffic, to continue the process of building up their ability to break Russian ciphers – Tiltman may well have led the breaks into two high-grade ciphers then in use. Smith quotes from Denniston who said that Tiltman

spent a fortnight in Finland and established a close and friendly liaison with their cryptographic unit, and his persistent drive... may well seal an alliance which will prove of the greatest value to the intelligence departments of all three services.

According to Tiltman[7] (he told Sinkov during discussions about what could be shown to the mission in February 1941):

I said, 'Sometimes we have to make the decisions without authority.' For instance, I've recently been in Finland and I promised the Finns certain things that I had no authority to provide them. And when I got back I got a rocket in the war office who said I had no right to do this. I simply said, 'Well, that's what I did, and that's the way it is.'

It is unclear what precisely these promises were. It may refer to radio equipment which was paid for only after some arguments with Menzies, by then in charge of MI6 and thus director of GC&CS, and this seems to be confirmed by a report he made after his return (March 1940) to BP.[8] Certainly the Finnish connection continued to help the British monitor Russian code until 1941 when Operation Barbarossa (Hitler's invasion of Russia) changed the nature of the war and its alliances.

Something similar had been arranged in the early 1930s with Estonia.[9] Again, Russian codes were the target, and again the offer of equipment to the Estonians made the deal work. Information came through for GC&CS from as early as 1933, but then in 1940 the Russians muscled their way into the country and the flow stopped.

Tiltman was back in BP to meet the February 1941 US party headed by Sinkov (see Chapter 6), but returned to Finland in March. He was there for a fortnight, where he learned of Finnish success against the Russian systems which were using additives, but also of problems against Russian submarine codes. The latter Tiltman was able to work on, after recognising that the messages had repetitive formats.[10] By April he had returned to BP, to work again with the Sinkov mission. He was to go to the USA in March 1942 and again at the end of that year, remaining there in early 1943, and again in 1944 (see chapter 7).

Kullback has recorded[11] his impression of Tiltman and his instinct for finding clues, and his account seems to show Tiltman's 'diplomatic' discretion. Kullback had visited Britain between May and August 1942 and apparently been able to see all he wished, including work on the Lorenz codes. He was impressed by Tiltman's patience and persistence in pursuing possible key material from dictionaries, poems and other out-of-the-way sources which were used in a range of hand ciphers and codes. Kullback thinks it may have been Tiltman who called him in to see some Lorenz decodes, which happened to reveal (in a message from Egypt to Berlin) that the Germans were reading American coded messages (from an inferior machine, the M-10). Was this some gentle diplomacy on Tiltman's part to show a problem discreetly without embarrassing anyone? Certainly Kullback reported the matter, the system was changed and the decoded US material ceased to appear in the German messages.[12]

Chapter 6

Early War Years and the Japanese Work

Tiltman's achievement at GC&CS was increasingly obvious, but the added pressure of war was to magnify his importance beyond expectation. We shall examine his role and contribution as the world moved towards another global conflict. It is a story of a mix of action and responsibility – the utterly mundane administration and the most sublime cryptographic achievements.

With the clock running down on the European situation in 1939, Tiltman now achieved a vital breakthrough in the Japanese work. He recognized the nature of the new Japanese Operational Code for the Imperial Navy, which came to be known as JN-25 and was arguably the most influential system in the Pacific war to come. He identified its additive nature (with a 5-digit system), the garble-check 'divisibility by 3' rule, and the approach needed to solve messages (see Chapter 4). Hugh Denham[1] estimates that this system carried about seventy per cent of the Imperial Navy communications, so it was critical in the war. The breakthrough of course did not mean that everything was at once readable; the painstaking work of 'bookbuilding' – gathering the codebook content and the additive pages from hours of collating, comparing and trial-and-error, to enable decoding to take place – was needed time and time again when new books were issued. But Tiltman's analysis showed the codebreakers what to look for and how to use the information for decrypting. It also brought Alan Turing into the mix, and mathematical methods of approaching the analysis of additive groups began to be devised[2] which were also to bear fruit when the Tunny problem appeared.

Following the Nazi-Soviet pact of 23 August 1939 the stage was set for war. This time it was no false alarm. Anticipating matters, the GC&CS began their move to BP on 15 August. The codebreakers were summoned to their war station. Initially, numbers of new arrivals from London at BP were to sleep in the house, but of those doing so at the end of September only one of something over a dozen was apparently a codebreaker, somewhat to Denniston's annoyance.[3] The building was shared with other MI6 people, which was not so surprising, as BP was an MI6 war station, including a radio section – the tenth on the organisation list, hence 'Station X'. But it meant that codebreakers had to be billeted elsewhere with all the administrative problems this brought. Tiltman himself was billeted at the Swan Hotel in Leighton Buzzard at this time with half a dozen other codebreakers. Later he was to move to a house close to the Park – 43 Buckingham Road;[4] he is attested there in 1943 when Friedman was a guest.[5] The house was a spacious red-brick town house built in 1919 by Major Chadwick,[6] and set in a pleasant garden space on a corner. It stood within short walking distance of Bletchley Park and was undoubtedly convenient. Interestingly, there was a large and very strong bomb-shelter installed at the back of the house; it was much more substantial than the typical 'Anderson' shelter, and remains of the concrete walls (about 50 cm thick) can still be seen. Any connection between the unusual nature of this and its important wartime occupant is as yet unclear.

Initially the Military Section may have used part at least of the main dining room, but hut provision was already under construction. Part of the section may have moved into the original Hut 3, just north of Hut 2 close to the Mansion[7] and south of the tennis courts (the location has some doubt), but Hut 5, in front of the Mansion, was being prepared, and in January 1940 at least some of the Military Section moved into it, remaining there (with some people using Elmers School for a time in between) probably until the section moved to Block F in February 1943.

Rooms for Tiltman's team were also found in the main house in Rooms 1 and 3, with Tiltman having an office in room 2, all on the first floor (later in the war he was to move to rooms 33–35, and at the end of 1944 he was occupying room 11, as indicated in a distribution list from the Drama Group).[8] The rooms may have been a slight surprise to him; apparently they had been a nursery some years before the war, and it is said that the walls still had 'Peter Rabbit' wallpaper.[9] His duties, apart from the codebreaking work, were to include mundane administration for his Military Section. On 11 July Denniston had written a memorandum[10] which included reference to billeting, saying:

> *It is to be hoped that similar arrangements to those of September 1938 should obtain, namely, Departments to pay full subsistence rates and the staff, being in receipt of lodging and food, should pay over 2/3s and*

> *retain 1/3 with a maximum of 5/- per day. Mr Clarke should clear up this question for Naval officers, Captain Tiltman for Military officers, Mr Cooper for RAF officers.*

Tiltman's Military Section team at the start of life at BP held a number of personnel key to its ultimate success. In addition to Tiltman and Freddie Jacob, there were[11] Professor Frederick Norman, often called 'Bimbo', a lecturer in German from London,[12] who quickly became involved with Hut 3 intelligence and worked closely with R.V. Jones, the Air Ministry scientific Advisor, to counter the German radio guidance systems; Arthur Hatto, a Foreign Office civilian, worked on German police messages and contributed to Hut 3 before moving to the section on German agents' non-Enigma messages; the Italian section featured Elizabeth Anderson,[13] who worked in Hut 5 until 1943 when she transferred to the Air section and subsequently to the diplomatic side; Major Francis Thompson (the victim of the pay squeeze before the war?) went for a time to Beaumanor in 1942, but returned to BP in 1942 and headed the Japanese section, as well as becoming a Deputy in the Military Section; Daphne Sercombe had been with the Military Section[14] before the war as an effective codebreaker and worked in Hut 5 and later in Block F; in Japanese work, apart from Pritchard (see chapter 3), Henry Dryden was to contribute overseas and had Tiltman to thank, in several senses (see later chapters).

There was a range of ciphers to deal with already. A memo[15] of 7 November 1939 apparently for the War Office lists a range of systems being used, among them the Enigma (an optimistic assessment that 'messages can be read in considerable quantity... early in the New Year'), the '*Satzbuch E*', a code-book with reciphering element, the double-transposing *Handschluessel*, the stencil *Heftschluessel*, 3-letter German air codes (already being solved) and an unknown '*Fronsschluessel*'. The memo indicates that the Military Section was working on much of this, although a great deal was Air material.

The Nazi-Soviet Pact of August 1939 meant that Russia continued to be a target for the codebreakers. Tiltman was charged[16] with setting up a Russian section in the new surroundings. This he did, at the nearby village of Wavendon where a suitable country house, Wavendon Tower, existed. As well as housing the codebreaking section, the house was used for recording and preparing 'black propaganda' during the war. The village also saw a number of BP workers billeted there, and a local hall served as a focus for social gatherings and activities of music and drama groups.

Tiltman is named in a memo[17] of 24 November 1939 from Denniston to the War Office, replying to a query about sharing information with the French:

> *We now have a very close liaison with the Deuxième Bureau of the* [French] *Army and the Navy and we interchange everything with them. By this means also Tiltman and the Military Section will be in touch with a similar organisation at the French GHQ.*

It was desired[18] that Bertrand visit Britain to discuss exchange of material in more detail, but a letter[19] of 19 December 1939 indicated lack of time and workload would prevent any visits before the end of the year – Tiltman was referred to in this. He had had contact and another letter was to follow. The French were reluctant to allow the Polish codebreakers (who had taken refuge there after escaping from Poland) to come to England, but they kept in touch by sending reports on their findings, as a detailed one which survives from the end of February shows.[20]

In March 1940 Tiltman was appointed chief recruiting officer[21] for Services' SIGINT requirements. Perhaps his teaching background contributed to this, and certainly his pre-war role in recruiting, interviewing and training fitted him for the task. As the war progressed however, government control over this increased, and BP was to work through the national system under the Ministry of Labour headed by the scientist and author C.P. Snow.

Tiltman found himself going to France several times up to May 1940, when the French guaranteed that they would never betray Enigma (a promise kept – see above, Chapter 5). On some of these visits at least he was accompanied[22] by Sergeant John Manson. There are two 'J. Manson' names on the BP Roll of Honour. One (perhaps more probable) is Quarter-Master Sergeant J.D. Manson, who worked in Hut 5 (Military Section) from 1940. The other is John B. Manson, listed as in the Intelligence Corps and part of the Military Section and SIXTA; no rank is given or date of joining.

For part of the time a British support group worked at Ferté-sous-Jouarre with French codebreakers. 'Mission Richard' remained in place until May when the real shooting began. Dryden's account of his escape[23] is worth reading.

Freddie Jacob was set to make a visit to Bertrand in May 1940 as BP representative, and his visit was to lead to some French intelligence officers going to some British sites.[24] The War Office suggested some visits to 'Y' sites, and Denniston agreed though with concerns about whether the French would duplicate British work (they might better try for signals not received in Britain instead). Events were of course to overtake France very quickly, but a visit by the French was made.

Tiltman had visited France in the first half of May 1940. In response the French wrote back[25] to Denniston:

> *Tiltman, who is on his way back, has brought me lots of information about you and your activities. Permit me on my part to send you these various pointers on matters which have emerged...* [a range of cryptographic items are covered, including the capture intact in Norway of an Enigma] *Tiltman tells me that you do not yet have machines in sufficient numbers to decode material currently. I hope that you are now receiving our decodes. We are somewhat behind with our daybooks of decoded telegrams but you will have these as soon as possible.... Tiltman has given me to understand that you have demonstrated a certain awkwardness at having Macfarlan with you, he being ignorant of Enigma matters. Could he not be brought up to date on developments if he is sworn to secrecy about how it is used?*

The French material may have contributed to the break into *Barbarameldung* material (see Chapter 4), but the swiftness of the campaign made this a short-term gain only.

Tiltman was brought into another discussion in mid-May 1940, this time about GC&CS organisation. Commander Saunders, then in charge of Hut 3, suggested[26] in May that a 'Central Intelligence' section with a sorting officer should receive all incoming intercept material on a 24/7 basis (he excludes 'FJ' – i.e. Enigma-derived in Hut 3 – material, already working round the clock) and an intelligence room for rapid dissemination – to include all services. Saunders was apparently showing concern about possible service parochialism, a problem that intensified in 1941. Frank Birch, from the navy side, was opposed to the idea as it stood, and Denniston suggested that there should be instead a copy of every outgoing piece from each service to a central inter-services intelligence centre. Tiltman[27] writes:

I agree with Commander Denniston's note. There should be an inter-service intelligence office which functions day and night and receives copies of all information passed. It must not act as a bottleneck to delay information for the ministries. I do not understand Saunders' reference to 'cribs' [Saunders was suggesting that his version of the system could help identify possible cribs from one area to another] *as they are frequently only recognisable by cryptographers.*

Freddie Jacob concurred. Following this, in June, a Standing Advisory Committee was formed,[28] with Denniston as president, including Saunders as a member, and co-opting others including Tiltman. It first met on 13 June and examined the dissemination of Hut 3 material, its methods and security, as well as considering the work of Hut 6 and potential expansion.

After the fall of France, Tiltman worked with some French cryptanalysts,[29] led by Baudoin. He gave them some work to do on the Japanese military attaché code system, but they were unable to make progress and he took it over himself, more successfully. More urgent was the realisation that British codes had probably been compromised following the Dunkirk evacuation. Tiltman was to join Travis, Josh Cooper (Air section) and Foss[30] on an advisory committee for the services with a view to changing codes. Amid all this, the plaintive, short and increasingly desperate flimsies of messages from Bertrand in June 1940, to be found in the National Archives, make chilling reading of the position on the continent. Remarkably, Bertrand was to survive, sending further material back to Tiltman and BP, and living through the war.

Later, in November 1940, Tiltman's position as an expert and his leadership of the Military Section meant that he was brought in to advise on codes which were to be used by the Free French under General de Gaulle.[31] Churchill had agreed to support the General's call for active French resistance, and ciphers would be needed to enable the organisation's communications. Tiltman was to evaluate the new ciphers delivered by Lieutenant Norman.

In similar vein around the same time he was involved[32] with the free Polish forces:

In I suppose late in 1940, I was called in to examine the ciphers being used by the free Poles, who had a headquarters in London, and they were using sheets of 4-figure additives and I suggested that they should put masks on these with windows [i.e. grilles – see Chapter 4] *and so on.*

As Bletchley Park grew the organisation and management needed to change. Demands on Tiltman especially were increasing, and not helped by his dual role as Head of the Military Section at BP and as part of the War Office under MI8. Denniston recognized this at the end of 1940 in his report[33] to Menzies, when he said,

Were it not for the loyalty of Colonel Tiltman (Head of the Military Section) and Mr Cooper (Head of the Air section) I hardly know how this large interservice office could have been run. Tiltman and Cooper both owe loyalty to their service chiefs. But they have never failed to back our main duty, attack on enemy ciphers.

In early 1941 a new administration group was set up: the Joint Committee of Control.[34] Valentine Vivian (deputy to Menzies) chaired, with Tiltman, Travis, Bradshaw (retired captain and a senior administrator at BP) and other senior people as members. Tiltman and the others had to deal with matters such as the use of Elmers School, and (in April 1941) the decision to build the new BP dining hall, which took shape just on the edge of the Park (as it stands at the time of this writing), as well as the continuing work on e.g. Playfair ciphers and (for the diplomatic section) Floradora. There is no doubt that Tiltman's position was a difficult one with this range of responsibilities. That he seems to have retained the respect and approval of all is tribute to his character.

This was also the time when Tiltman was involved off and on for two months with the Sinkov mission, assisting the American visitors with their tours and discussions.

Before the arrival of the 1941 Sinkov mission, in August 1940, Americans led by General Strong, senior officer in US Army G-2 (Intelligence) were visitors to Britain.[35] Naval and army personnel were involved. US army codebreaker William Friedman had helped to draft proposals for full exchange in cryptanalytic work, but at this stage the navy (then headed by Lieutenant Laurence Safford) would only consider exchange of traffic. The situation was crystallized by an urgent message from Strong on September 5; would the USA 'exchange full information on German, Italian and Japanese code and cryptographic information therewith? Are you prepared to agree to a continuous exchange of important intercepts in connection with the above?' The British were apparently surprised (as was the US navy!), but pleased. Strong's initiative went to General Marshall and ultimately the President, gaining acceptance in early October. While this was taking place, the American break into the Japanese 'Purple' cipher was achieved.

Efforts to get the US navy as well as army to agree to full technical exchanges of information (as well as more general information on codes and intelligence) were slow to succeed – the US navy was strongly opposed.[36] But Roosevelt agreed near the end of October 1940.

So two army personnel – Abraham Sinkov and Leo Rosen – and two navy experts – Prescott Currier and Robert Weeks – appeared at BP in February 1941. According to Tiltman,[37] Friedman was due to have been one of the two army personnel, but he became ill (one of several breakdowns from which he suffered) and Sinkov was his replacement. It was Tiltman who arranged for the transport and met them in London[38] after their voyage from the USA to Scapa Flow and then down the North Sea, bringing with them boxes of materials, including a copy of their 'Purple' machine analogue (one of only four), which they were to present to BP. They were then met at BP by Denniston, with Tiltman again present. Currier describes[39] that first encounter:

> *There were blackout curtains up everywhere, everything was absolutely black, went through a doorway with two blackout curtains, one ahead of the other, walked through into a rather brightly lit office and there was John Tiltman… the first time I saw him, standing there in his regimentals with his hands behind his back, he and Travis and Denniston, Denniston was in charge. And that was coming out of the dark into the light and seeing the three of them sort of standing there in a row and John went over to one side like this and so we all went around and shook hands.*

Barbara Abernethy, as Denniston's personal assistant, provided the sherry, and was sworn to secrecy, as the meeting could have been construed as in breach of various neutrality acts which limited Roosevelt's freedom of action.

Tiltman certainly gave much time and attention to the visiting party. Sherman[40] says that he 'perhaps had become closest to them', and he accompanied a number of their visits, joining them occasionally for their pub lunches (though specific details are not recorded). But arguably his most important role was in February 1941 when he raised the question of allowing access to the Americans for information on Enigma successes, as a response to the generosity with the 'Purple' machine. Denniston was unwilling to agree to this, but allowed Tiltman to speak to Menzies, who was persuaded (perhaps with prime-ministerial approval) to allow this access. See Chapter 7 for more discussion of the significance of this.

For the latter part of the visit (after his return from Finland) he was, in his own words, 'more or less in charge of them'. This being 'in charge' may well have included making arrangements for the visits by Currier and Weeks to some of the direction-finding centres (including Scarborough, as well as Dover and Flowerdown) to see the HF-DF system and the use of signals information for military use. The whole group visited London twice, and saw something of the effects of the Blitz; a club that they visited on one evening received a direct hit from a bomb the next day (the following week, as some remembered it). Tiltman accompanied the group as they prepared to leave on 18 March, driving north with them to Greenock to board their ship for the return.[41]

Some research sections were, as mentioned, also housed in the main house, as well as those breaking some hand-ciphers. It was in mid-April 1941 that a formal 'Research Group' was organized[42] at BP to look at 'unknown' systems of cryptography, as well as examine BP techniques to improve them, and it was to report to Tiltman. Major Gerry Morgan was to lead this team (he arrived in May) and his previous work on both Hagelin and Vernam-related codes (see Chapter 4) was to be invaluable. Other team members[43] included Bill Tutte, a Cambridge chemist turned mathematician, Gerry Morgan's brother Stanley, and Norman Sainsbury from the British Museum's books and manuscripts section. Tiltman oversaw much of this work. Their brief ran widely, including diplomatic codes from France, Ireland, Poland, Czechoslovakia, the Vatican and even America (not yet an official ally), as well as Vichy, Japanese and Comintern material. When they had mastered new systems so as to define a good working procedure they would hand these over to other groups to handle the regular breaking. Thus for example the Hagelin work (with Morgan and Tutte prominent) was regarded as secure by the end of June 1941 and handed on (e.g. to the Italian naval section, which worked on Italian convoy supplies to Africa – with important results. See below).

This was also the time when Tiltman's work on the Railway Enigma bore more fruit (see Chapter 4). The ability to read some traffic revealed Panzer movement to the east in the late spring of 1941 – an indicator of Hitler's preparations for the attack on Russia. The powers that be were slow to believe the indications, however, and it was only in early June that there was conviction of the reality of his intentions.

According to Noel Currer-Briggs,[44] the other German hand ciphers attacked included Double Playfair in 1941, a team led by Tiltman in rooms 1–3. The account indicates that Tiltman was not 'above' the others but worked alongside at the coalface. Gerry Roberts, who initially worked on Playfair until his section was moved to the new Tunny material, describes[45] his own recruitment in 1941 to the organisation: he recalled Tiltman appearing in his full uniform 'complete with red tabs', looking extremely daunting for a new member coming face-to-face with a full colonel. He was, however, to get to know that Tiltman had 'a very positive and friendly attitude'. Major Tester, later to be important in the Tunny operation, was also involved in this group with Roberts.

Training for cryptanalysts was not always consistent. We have seen that for the new pre-war recruits there was a series of courses in which Tiltman took part. But for numbers of people reporting to BP during the war their experience of training was, as one put it, 'sitting by Nellie' (i.e. watching an experienced worker and learning from them). Tiltman, with his teaching experience, set up[46] a cryptanalytical school in 1941 in Bedford, one of the lead teachers there being Major Masters (see also Chapter 8).

Later in 1941 Tiltman was involved in liaison with Norwegian experts.[47] At this time part of the Military Section at least was based in Elmers school (just west of the main BP site), and questions were being asked about the Hagelin machine. Tiltman's Research section (including Bill Tutte for a time) had been working on the system, and the Norwegians were keen to find out what the British knew. On November 15 Tiltman received a copy of a report[48] on the working of the Hagelin device, which was being used by the Norwegians in exile in London; Major Roscher Lund was the main informant. Denniston's covering note shows that Captain Morgan contributed greatly to the technique of breaking the Hagelin system.

From late in 1941 the work emanating from Tiltman's Research Group's success with the Hagelin C-38m became increasingly important. Stephen Freer describes his experience:[49]

> *In my first job at Bletchley Park, I was working under Gerry Morgan, head of the Research Section. What I remember most about this time was working on some of the Italian Navy ciphers, which used a Swedish machine called Hagelin. We had to decipher messages and write them out in various ways, trying to find any repeats or other significant features, usually the answer was no. The Italian Navy had a base at Naples and outstations in Rhodes and Libya, and took supplies to the German army in North Africa. Every now and then, after we had deciphered a message about a convoy from Naples, a few days later we would read in the paper that a convoy had been bombed on its way to North Africa, and we thought we had achieved something there.*

Much information was sent on the C-38m in 1941–2 regarding Italian transport from Europe to North Africa. Hinsley has said[50] that thanks to the reading of the C-38m, GC&CS was able from the middle of 1941 to warn the services in advance of most of the convoys and other shipping in the Mediterranean, especially those carrying troops or supplies, including identification of the ships and forces involved. In particular, the targeting of Rommel's supply convoys in 1942[51] 'probably turned the scale against Rommel in 1942'.

The autumn of 1941 saw Tiltman execute one of his finest pieces of analysis. The teleprinter code material, generated by the Lorenz machine, was being gathered at Denmark Hill under Harold Kenworthy, but with little insight into its workings (at this stage the system was still experimental and was not to go fully 'live' until next year; it was desirable to analyse its functions before its use spread). It had been theorized that the signals were teleprinter form, and it was recognized that, as with many codes, a 'depth' was needed to assist in breaking. Messages being sent from June 1941 were being examined, and a preamble in clear showed that starting settings for theorized rotors were being selected by operators – a list of names not unlike the phonetic alphabet, where the first letters of each were perhaps some rotor start-points, for example (as Enigma had). Tiltman was amused[52] to find the word KAEFERBOECKS as one such setting; the word means some kind of bug and may have been an insult in some way! One can compare the use of 'dirty German words', as Mavis Lever found herself expert in, for Enigma settings.

It was also found in July and August 1941 that several messages contained similar short letter-patterns at the start of the preamble, suggesting stereotyped openings, and when one such pattern – ++xxx88 – was used as a 'plaintext guess' for one of a pair of depth messages and subtracted from the combined ciphertext (see Chapter 4 for how the Lorenz addition and subtraction worked), the start of the word *spruchnummer* ('message number') appeared.[53] These early attempts at depth however failed to produce any great length of additive material from the machine.

It was at the end of August 1941 that two long messages were sent, using the same twelve-letter setting, HQIBPEXEZMUG. Tiltman, who had been involved in the earlier work, followed the process of adding the two messages together to eliminate the additive layer and produce a stream of letters representing the combined plaintexts. See Chapter 4 for a full description of how it is believed he then dealt with this. Tiltman revealed nearly 4,000 coding layer characters that had been added by the machine to encode these messages.

Gerry Morgan may have assisted, and certainly was involved with the subsequent work of Bill Tutte, who took over the analysis of the coding layer and from it analysed certain repeats at different intervals, which were thought to be rotors of some kind, and thus deduced the structure of the machine.

What Tiltman, Morgan and Tutte had exposed was nothing less than the functioning of the system being prepared for use by German High Command. It was for use even by Hitler and his top coterie for communication with his generals. While the Enigma or Hagelin systems were for the battlefield and short-term material, the Lorenz material was strategic and of long-term value.

The overall name 'Fish' was given to teleprinter traffic, with 'Tunny' given to the Lorenz-generated army traffic. As the war developed, individual connections were also christened with 'fishy' names (Bream, Jellyfish, Squid etc.).

The resultant ability to decode Tunny material revealed some of the most important enemy information of the war (see for example Chapter 9). It is hard to overstate the significance of this achievement by the Research team; Tiltman's success in his part was vital.

In September 1941 Tiltman was receiving reports from 'the Polish expert working under BERTIE in France'. 'Bertie' was Bertrand's nickname and the Pole is probably Rejewski, Zygalski or Rozycki (or their team), who had arrived in France and were now under cover in 'Unit 300' (based in Vichy France at Chateau des Fouzes, not far from Avignon). Tiltman's work earlier on maintaining good relations with Bertrand was continuing to be felt. Among other materials was a long exposition of how the Double Playfair system functioned; it is unclear whether it provided fresh information to the BP workers on the subject, but it shows that it was understood there as well. Further reports[54] contain revealing notes concerning the Eastern Front. Referring to the 1 SS Brigade and its halting-place at Berdyczów, Tiltman read:

> *26.8* [26 August]... *46 prisoners, capture of 2 guns, shooting of 82 Jews... The Pol. Reg. Sued. shot on 26.8 – 849 Jews, and on the next day they recaptured 22 German prisoners, and shot 914 Jews... The 320 battalion, after having cleared up the region of Kamieniec Podolski,... have shot 4,200 Jews.*

Regarding the Reiterbrigade that August, he saw that 'Up to 3.8.41 the Kavbrigade liquidated 3,274 partisans and Jews.' This material corroborated Tiltman's work on the police codes which had begun to reveal similar killings.

The working of Hut 3 and improvements in its efficiency were to be scrutinized by Tiltman[55] and others in November 1941. Denniston's memo of 6 November, in encouraging greater depth in research and the development of individual specialist knowledge, asked Tiltman to investigate better training of military officers in the watch teams at Matlock, focussing on German army matters. However, the issues of Hut 3 here were trifling compared with what was emerging.

The most difficult problems at BP in 1941–2 were linked to its relations with the three Services and the production of intelligence of use to them. It had been a struggle for BP's work to be recognized as of value. The navy, for example, as the 'senior service' felt it did not require the contributions of unproven outsiders. A case in point was the sinking of HMS *Glorious*: Harry Hinsley from Hut 4 had tried several times to warn of the danger to the aircraft carrier from the *Scharnhorst* and the *Gneisenau* but his messages were discounted by the Admiralty; *Glorious* was sunk soon after.

Once the credibility of BP information was recognized, attitudes changed, but not always for the better. The events in Hut 3, in which air and military advisors tried to manipulate their position to their own section's advantage (see below), led to their departure as well as the transfer of Commander Saunders who was in charge of the Hut, and showed that Denniston may have been lacking urgency in such matters of management. Tiltman's wisdom was brought into the issue of Hut 3, which came to a head in the winter of 1941/2, by which time it had become clear that the products of Hut 3 intelligence were worth having.

Hut 3 at BP was the intelligence analysis centre, particularly for army and air force Enigma decodes, which were performed in Hut 6 next door. Decoded messages were passed across for emending (solving gaps, garbles etc), translating, and analysis of intelligence. The Services, through some of their representatives in Hut 3, began to seek control for themselves. At the time, the Hut was directed by Commander Saunders, a naval man chosen in the early days for his competence in German, in spite of the Hut being focussed initially on army and air force Enigma and related material (naval work emerged when the Mediterranean campaigns began in earnest).

The senior advisors (one for each main service) were the key people apart from Saunders. Group Captain Humphreys was the air force leader, and appears to have wanted control of the output to be in his hands. One witness of the situation was F.L. (Peter) Lucas, who said that Humphreys was very well qualified for his work both with the German language and with the resultant intelligence, but became determined to take control for himself and his service – he therefore tried to run a semi-independent group linking directly with the Air Ministry instead of following the established channels. The army counterpart, similarly minded, has been described as a 'charmingly naïve plagiarist' in some accounts (e.g. R.V. Jones), less politely (Smith says) by others; Tiltman names him as Captain Curtis. The result of the intrigues, in Ralph Bennett's words, was that 'something like chaos sometimes reigned' for some months from late 1941 into the New Year, with 'a regime of divided control'.[56]

Tiltman says:[57]

I was shown a report which Curtis had made to one of the Deputy Directors of intelligence in the War Office that the reporting would never be satisfactory until the whole of the Enigma operation was put under the services. So I took this report to the Director of Military Intelligence, Davidson, who was a friend of mine, and I said, 'Isn't this a bit out of order?' and he said, 'Certainly it is, you're my representative at Bletchley Park; Curtis mustn't take any action except through you. And he will be told so.' Well, he did it again, so I reported it. I reported this to the Director of Military Intelligence and they [this must mean the managers at BP] *had a board meeting on what they should do about their representatives... They all agreed, of course, Curtis got to go anyway; we can't leave a man like that in the outfit – told how he must do things and doing the same things again. And then they got to Humphreys. They talked about him for a bit and the Director of Air Intelligence turned to me and said, 'Tiltman, you've been very silent all afternoon – what do you think of Humphreys?' So I told him. I told him he was a very clever man, but he was creating all kinds of difficulties for us. So he said, 'Well, Humphreys will have to go too, and if so, then the Navy must give up their man too.' Quite innocent, Commander Saunders, who had been with us before the war and who was a friend of all of us, was then turned adrift and they started again and after two or three tries, they put Eric Jones in, who was an Air Force officer.*

Brigadier van Cutsem was sent by Menzies to enquire and report, and in February 1942 Menzies responded with a plan[58] to reorganize that affected Tiltman. The work of GC&CS was to be divided between Services and civil/diplomatic sections with Denniston leading only the latter in London:

The Deputy Director (S) (Commander Travis) with headquarters at BP will control the Services section... Colonel Tiltman, in addition to his duties as Commandant No. 4 IS, will act as Chief Cryptographer and will take charge of the Research Section... Colonel Tiltman will be responsible for liaison with the FECB and the USA Bureaux.

Late in 1942, Professor Vincent was appointed Co-ordinator of Cryptography under Tiltman to assist him.[59] Vincent, a Cambridge professor, had specialist Italian skills and had been involved with BP for some time but apparently was contemplating the possibility of leaving; he decided to remain.

Wing Commander Eric Jones was brought in as a result of the report to analyse the situation, and on the basis of his response was put in charge of the Hut. Jones's management skills, including the establishment of Duty Officers who had final say on all outgoing material from the Hut, restored order and confidence in the section and set the pattern for the rest of the war. He was to make a major contribution at BP and with GCHQ for the next twenty years, and ultimately become a director.

Commander Edward Travis thus took over as supremo at BP from Denniston in 1942. A naval man who had served with Jellicoe in the First World War, he moved into cryptography, it is said,[60] when he showed that Jellicoe's codes were vulnerable by breaking them himself. Decorated by France and Italy at the end of the war, he moved into GC&CS and became a deputy to Denniston by 1925. He was therefore experienced in codes and in organisational matters for GC&CS by the time the Second World War broke out. It was Travis who approved the plans of Gordon Welchman to develop the organisation which tackled the Enigma problem and cajoled the authorities into action.

Under Travis, Tiltman (he says) became chief cryptographer. In practice he had been the lead for much of the previous year because of Dilly Knox's illness, and Denniston had often used him as an advisor before the war. Now, as Tiltman puts it:[61]

> *I became officially Chief Cryptographer. This was only a name, but it meant that I was not only responsible for ciphers that were not being read, but I was also technically responsible for the security of all British ciphers… I was the last word on security. I attended a meeting in the Admiralty once a week on Wednesdays… I was brought in, in every case where there was a technical point involved, and I was asked to try and cope with this bad situation in the British Navy.*

It was this that led him in due course to create the Stencil Subtractor Frame (SSF) which went into use in 1943 and greatly improved navy security (see chapter 4).

A document survives[62] which indicates something of the organisational set-up from about this time. Though undated, it details known wartime elements, such as Commander Hok's oversight of the codemaking section at Mansfield College, Oxford, and the now-dated insistence that 'Cryptographic work [is] done only by commissioned officers, warrant officers and sergeants.' Tiltman is named as Cryptanalytical Advisor to the ISCSC (Inter-Service Cypher Security Committee), which included a representative from each service, and Edward Travis, and met fortnightly at the Admiralty – more or less as Tiltman described above. The navy representative, Commander Wilson, appears later (Chapter 9).

As a result of the reorganisation centred on Hut 3, Tiltman was confirmed in charge of all army personnel[63] at BP. This affirmation seems to link with the issue (see above) of previous military officers disregarding the protocols at BP in favour of the War Office, and underlines the control of BP in what was happening to its material.

With all these organisational matters going on, the background work on codebreaking continued relentlessly. The success of Tiltman in breaking an example of the Lorenz system, and the analysis by Bill Tutte of the machine structure, had led to mathematical techniques evolved by Tutte, Turing, Jack Good and others which assisted hand-breaking of the 'Tunny' traffic. The appearance of the 'Robinson' machines for speeding up the maths process also helped. An example of the outcome of this was the information on German manoeuvres leading to what became the Battle of Kursk in July 1943. But in early 1942 war on another front threw up additional problems for BP.

Tiltman explained his earlier work in the 1930s on Japanese codes as follows:

> *I think either at the end of '35 or the beginning of '36, I was getting military intercepts back from Hong Kong which were not being worked on by anybody else and this was before they used additives. They had various systems, more or… greater or less complication which I kept in touch with until September,* [or] *December 1938 when they began to use the kind of additives that they used all through the war and which I broke into during the Munich crisis.*

This bland outline hides the tremendous effort made by Tiltman and the Japanese section, in which Hugh Foss also played an important role, in the run-up to the war. The outbreak of the European war meant that German materials took priority in terms of personnel and resources, and when the Japanese threat became imminent (and actual on the fall of Singapore and the sinking of the battleships *Prince of Wales* and *Repulse* early in 1942) it was clear that more would be needed to boost the capacity of the Japanese section.

It was in the middle of the crucial American liaison work that he took his other well-known initiative – the setting up in early 1942 of a Japanese teaching course under Captain Tuck – to train codebreakers in Japanese within six months, something the School of Oriental and African Studies [SOAS] were maintaining needed five years (or two for absolute basics).

It was at SOAS that the few trainee Japanese codebreakers were being instructed at first.[64] The eruption of action at the end of 1941 had suddenly heightened the need for Japanese expertise, but the section at BP consisted of only thirteen people. It including Hugh Foss, who had had some early success in 1934 against the Naval Attaché Type A machine and was continuing to attack other cyphers,[65] but the chronic problem of too few people and too little material (there were few places listening and any progress came far too late to be of practical use) remained an issue.

Perhaps it was Tiltman's sense of tact that persuaded him to call his proposed new course 'experimental'. In early 1942 he approached Captain Oswald Tuck, RN, retired, who had learned Japanese on his own initiative. Tuck had his reservations but agreed. The venue was to be Ardour House Gas Board showrooms in Bedford. Later larger rooms were used in St Andrews Road.

Hugh Denham describes his experience as he began the course:[66] he described Captain Tuck as 'an impressive figure, with an impressive white beard'. The lesson began with a little introduction: 'When I come into the room… you are to stand up. I shall then say SHOKUN OHAYO, which means "all you princes are honourably early".' The students were then to reply OHAYO GOZAIMASU, which meant 'honourably early it honourably is'. The captain then left the room, returned and the words were exchanged – the lesson had begun.

The early trainees were generally Oxford and Cambridge classics students (the departments were delighted at having demand for their students for once). They worked for three hours each weekday morning and afternoon, and on Saturday mornings. The initial course began on 2 February 1942 and ended in late June, after which the recruits were drafted to various jobs – a few to diplomatic work in London, others to BP or towards overseas postings. Denham describes the use during the course of plain-text telegrams and Japanese newspaper items, and the long wait for dictionaries. Michael Loewe comments[67] on the excitement at the realisation that their work was connected to codebreaking, and on Tiltman's personal interest in the students and willingness to speak to them. One candidate, Lance Corporal Eric Ceadel, became the assistant for Tuck on future courses.

The courses were very much focussed on practical Japanese related to the war and military matters; there was no room and no time for niceties of poetry or other literature.

As matters progressed, interest in what was being achieved began to grow. Tiltman[68] tells this story about the reception when visitors came:

> *I took two bright boys of mine from the school in Japanese. We were met by the director of the School of Oriental Studies and a very formidable lady… and a Japanese named Yoshitake and, to my horror, General Piggott… General Piggott, who was a very famous Japanese scholar and had been our military attaché in Japan before the war and had written the standard textbook on handwritten Japanese. And they walked side by side down the main passage of the school… I explained we didn't have time to teach spoken Japanese like we wanted, so we had very special selected students who were all fascinating scholars.*
>
> *We gave them a feel of the written language as it's taught. Then we'd been talking about this and General Piggott said to me, 'I want to hear one of your boys read some Japanese.' I said, 'Have a heart General, I told you we don't have anything to do with the spoken.' He said, 'I just want to hear the sort of noises they make.' To my horror, Yoshitake produced out of his pocket, a piece of green paper… One of my boys took this in his hand, and he not only managed – they'd only been working four months – managed with very little problem to get on, only leaving off the few things he didn't know. Then that went full swing.*

In March 1942 Tiltman visited the USA for a month. In his report on his visit[69] submitted in May, Tiltman, who was instructed to visit only army and navy and to avoid other organisations such as the FBI, explained that he handed over his materials gifted from GS&CS on 27 March. There was much that was new to the US, including information on European and Far Eastern ciphers. Tiltman recognized that US army and navy cryptography would not be unified, and did not press the issue. As both US army and navy sections were 'suffering' reorganisation, Tiltman observed that the navy (under Redman and Joseph Wenger) seemed to have a good set-up at the top but the army, with new personnel (apart from Friedman – 'by far the soundest and most experienced expert in either service'), still had progress to make. Tiltman admitted that he had not judged the best arrangement for handling Japanese army traffic the previous September. The Americans' capacity for use of Hollerith machines in helping analysis was smaller than anticipated, but was to improve rapidly, and Tiltman arranged for a shared approach to attack on the systems for the time being. In his view US capacity to handle German codes was low and they did not have structures for analysis and interpretation akin to BP's Hut 3. Tiltman was hopeful of future success in US development of electronic counting machines, but found that Agnes Driscoll,[70] much deferred to as a veteran in US codes and currently in naval research, was 'making no original contribution at all.' He says he was 'obliged to point [this] out,' which if he did so directly (as he implies) might have been a reason for repercussions later in the year. There was much discussion of training for Japanese work, and interest in Tiltman's Bedford-based Japanese course, as the US was also short of Japanese-speaking workers.

The long process of involvement of the USA and Bletchley (including the handling of the Japanese material) has been described by a number of writers. Some suggest that it was rather the Americans who created the major difficulties, over Japanese codes and Enigma matters. In *The Codebreakers of Bletchley Park* a positive view of the liaison approaches and British contributions is given by Alvares (specifically citing the diplomatic codes section managed by Denniston from 1942), but (on the military side) this is not the impression given by Budiansky in the same publication, who sees British reluctance to be open about its military work as at least equally problematic. The problems revolved around sharing of technical expertise, sharing the results of intelligence gained, and the security of the information (a particular and not completely unjustified British concern). See Chapter 7 for more detail.

Tiltman was still head of the BP Military section at this time, thus the buck stopped with him even when seemingly mundane matters arose. A selection of his activities in the autumn of 1942 gives an idea of the range of his responsibility.

He was involved in discussions with Freddie Jacob in October 1942[71] regarding the appointment of SIGINT officers to postings in the Middle East. Jacob had been sent to lead the Combined Bureau (CBME), but Tiltman was also in discussion regarding his return from Palestine and reassignment with MI6. He was involved in discussions with Nigel de Grey at the start of October[72] regarding prospective pay levels and inequalities between civilians and enlisted people (the latter with allowances not subject to income tax and therefore gaining against civilians). Also on his plate was a Romanian[73] cipher message picked up in the Middle East, with a request for decoding, and various missives from Edward Crankshaw concerning 'Y'-service material gathered from Russia.[74] Crankshaw had been GC&CS liaison with the Russians for a while, trying to maintain open exchanges of code information in the face of increasing Russian evasion. One message listed a series of questions Crankshaw's Russian contacts raised – referring to an analysis of naval traffic that Tiltman had been doing (apparently on Black Sea and Aegean areas) – and arousing suspicion that the Russians were 'fishing' for information (they were providing little of their own).

Tiltman was consulted (because it affected military personnel and their functions) over an organisational change in November[75] regarding the operational control of the Fusion Room and log readers linked to No. 6 Intelligence School and Hut 6, to be under the direction of Gordon Welchman as head of Hut 6. The aim was to improve efficiency in production; at this point, Welchman and Captain Lewis (log reader officer) argued,[76] their work largely concerned Enigma material and it made sense to link with the Enigma hut.

Other examples of the 'mundane' can be found in November and December 1942 (just as USA issues were demanding attention). One[77] involved the redeployment of a sergeant (characterized as a 'dud'). The suggestion was that he be posted, but the view expressed is to keep him and give him work he can do. In another[78] he had to write to MI8 (the section dealing with radio) about shortages of military transport drivers. The reply of December 15 indicated sympathy and says that there were 'a certain number of MTC drivers, insufficient however to run all the vehicles... It is therefore submitted that the army contribution of 6 drivers IC (may be ATS) is thoroughly justified and should be accorded permanent WEC approval.'

But it was in liaison with the USA that Tiltman's tact and wisdom would find their stiffest test.

Chapter 7

The Diplomat – Part Two

T is for Tiltman, just one of the boys
Red tabs he won't wear with brown corduroys
When billets were scarce, Dame Rumour doth say,
He lived in the States and flew in each day.

This extract from the 'Bletchley alphabet' (an affectionate poem written and performed late in the war about a number of 'characters' at BP) is indicative of the times when Tiltman was away, elsewhere in Britain or in the United States, on a range of missions, generally connected with US-UK liaison, helping to build what became the 'special relationship'.

This writer's impression from reading some of the letters and memos, as well as the NSA materials of the time, is that Tiltman's role as 'ambassador' and liaison officer during and after the war was more critical than has sometimes been recognized. He seems to have felt the British were too guarded; he had to combat mutual distrust through his own personal integrity, and he was successful in establishing personal trust and sincerity with most of his US counterparts. In particular the contact with William Friedman, chief cryptologist on the US army side, was vital, and the correspondence between them gives us an impression of his standing.

William Friedman was born in 1891. His father had a Romanian background, his mother a Russian. After school in Pittsburgh and a short spell in agricultural college he went to Cornell University, New York, in 1911, graduating in science in 1914. A spell at Riverbank laboratories, Illinois, introduced him to Elizebeth [sic] Smith, later his wife, and through her to codebreaking (like Tiltman, almost casually). He was in the army in June 1918 (after training), commissioned as lieutenant, and joined the American Expeditionary Force doing code work. He was honourably discharged in April 1919, and after eighteen months at

Riverbank, a private research facility under Colonel George Fabyan, went to the US War Department and the Department of Defense, for whom he worked until his retirement in 1955 (by which time he had transferred to the NSA). In late 1940 he suffered a nervous breakdown and was hospitalized for a few months, and the effect of this remained with him thereafter. As a civilian in a military context, he was to be presented[1] with the army's highest civilian award, the Exceptional Service award, in 1944, and the nation's highest civilian award, the Medal of Merit, in 1946.

The USA was recovering its confidence in codebreaking following the closure of the 'Black Chamber' operation a decade before (and Secretary Stimson's notorious comment that 'gentlemen do not read each other's mails'), and both army and navy had evolved increasingly brilliant (though numerically small) organisations and teams. OP-20-G was the navy group, led by Lieutenant Safford in the Navy Dept, Washington. The army Signal Intelligence Service (SIS – not to be confused with the British 'SIS', an abbreviation for the organisation better known as MI6) was set up in 1930 and led by Friedman with new recruits Frank Rowlett, Abraham Sinkov and Solomon Kullback, all of whom had pivotal roles during the Second World War.

The Sinkov mission (named for its ranking officer) in February 1941 is key to understanding the development of USA-UK relations from 1941 onwards. The practicalities of it have been outlined already (see Chapter 6), but its political significance, both in its context and in its effects, and Tiltman's role in it, also need examination.

The arrival of the mission should be seen in the context of other discussions and exchanges – in particular the Tizard mission of August-September 1940.[2] This mission was led by Sir Henry Tizard, who headed the Committee for Aeronautical Research in Britain, and agreed to, after some reluctance about revealing British secret inventions, by Churchill. The mission sought to develop contacts with US industrial resources and to exchange technology and development. The British brought information and details about radar (most notably an example of the new cavity magnetron which for the first time made possible much more accurate centimetric radar), some background about jet engine development (in which the UK was ahead of the US), as well as details of gyroscopic devices and plastic explosives. The magnetron was described in

America as 'the most valuable cargo to reach our shores'. In return Britain hoped for information about the US Norden bombsight, and cooperation in manufacturing. The US response was limited by various Neutrality Acts, and both sides showed the wariness that the codebreakers were to demonstrate later, but there was much interest.

An important element in the Sinkov visit was the American delivery of a 'Purple' machine. Frank Rowlett had been at the heart of the efforts to break the system, one used for Japanese diplomatic messages and created by a machine known as 'Type B', which had replaced 'Type A' (readable at the start of the war) and was a lesser priority than military codes for the British at the time. It was Rowlett who recognized the 'six and twenty' letter-structure used, and Genevieve Grotjan who spotted depth in a number of messages in September 1940, which led to the successful analysis of the machine's workings, whereupon Leo Rosen, a young engineer, began work on an analogue device. It was a copy of this that came to BP.

Tiltman refers to the Sinkov mission initiative in his interview[3] in 1978:

> *And one of the first things they did when they came across was this magnificent gesture that before really having any information from us, they set up the Purple machine analogue in our office and I had nothing at all to do with it. I never worked on the Purple machine. So I haven't very much to tell you there, except that it was, as I say, presented to us before… I gave them everything I could. Eventually we had to argue out about the Enigma, but I gave them everything I could… They made the first gesture and I think perhaps it's safe to say the Navy was just about level with us if not a little in advance on Japanese Navy. They presented to us a most beautifully bound book with all the keys… and all the recoveries and so on, which was something we couldn't do for them. We didn't do it on quite the same scale.*

He clearly regarded the Americans' generosity with the Purple machine (before America entered the war officially) as very important. However, it soon became clear that, despite the hopeful initiatives of the Sinkov mission, there were mutual concerns about intent and motivation. The British delayed telling the Americans about the extent of their penetration of Enigma, and provided a paper version of how the machine worked.

Tiltman later explained[4] the diplomatic awkwardness (as he saw it) posed by the British position (which dated from the time of the Sinkov mission and continued to be held by many) in an interview:

> *I handed over everything I could. The Enigma wasn't my job. It had an entirely separate staff and so on. But I tried to get the Director to give way on this, but he wouldn't do it. By Director, I mean Denniston. So I got permission, and went up to see General Menzies, who by that time had succeeded Admiral Sinclair… I said to him, 'Unless you give way over this and show the American Party, allow them to see all our work on the Enigma, I don't see how we are going to have any kind of successful collaboration. Apart from anything else, they can't help seeing something like a quarter of the office to which they're barred.' General Menzies agreed with me that this was something that had to be taken into account. He said, 'All right, but if you disclose it to them, they must sign a document which lists all the people to which they'll make the disclosure when they get back to Washington and any fresh spreading information must also be reported back to us, otherwise we won't do it.' They* [the Sinkov team] *were junior officers, they didn't like having to make this sort of decision without being able to refer back. Eventually, after I'd left them alone for about an hour and a half, I went into see them and I said, 'You know, this is something you can't go away without, or the whole thing will break down.'*

The Americans seem to have signed in early March, not without some concerns about the view of their superiors.[5]

As the above shows, Tiltman was uncertain about how even-handed the exchange of information was. For Safford, as head of the navy side of codebreaking, this (and other factors) made it a terrible imbalance of generosity; the USA had been 'double-crossed' in his view. This was not the view of Prescott Currier, who says:[6]

> *All of us were permitted to come and go freely and to talk with anyone in the area that interested us… we watched the entire operation and had all the techniques explained in great detail. We were thoroughly briefed on the latest techniques applied to the solution of the Enigma and in the operation of the Bombes.*

The Sinkov mission should therefore be seen as another stage in the pattern of Anglo-American cooperation, and the generosity of the British in the Tizard mission could be said to be matched by the delivery of the Purple machine in 1941 (just six months later), this in turn being matched on Tiltman's arrival with diplomatic ciphers (see below, in March 1942).

Denniston's visit to the USA in the summer of 1941 followed up the Sinkov visit and continued the process. But the question of 'balance' in the cryptological exchanges was an issue, and argument remains about this. The withholding of aspects of Enigma irritated some in the USA, but Smith considers[7] that what the British gave the USA in other cipher areas, including the Japanese, was very useful and greatly helped the 'balance'. Currier seems to indicate that the Americans did take back a great deal of material, not just from BP but also some radio equipment collected on the way to their returning ship.[8] This included Marconi 'Huff-Duff' receivers and their masts and antennae – valuable technology. Currier goes on to explain[9] that the materials went missing in transit:

> *So Bob Weeks and I walked… or drove up and down the Clyde side, checking every warehouse until we eventually found it… This was about two tons' worth of gear… But when we got it to the* [ship] 'Revenge', *they didn't want to take it because it took up too much room. They didn't… They weren't told that there was going to be anything like this. But eventually we saw the captain and got it squared away; and we eventually got all our gear on the 'Revenge'.*

Two tons doesn't sound like a small return – the Americans had brought nearer one ton with them!

Was the Sinkov mission ultimately a success for US-UK relations? In spite of Tiltman's reservations, it probably was. Sherman's view is a positive one, and includes the opportunities the Americans had to visit other British installations,[10] notably the sites where Huff-Duff (HF-DF, high frequency direction-finding) technology was based, in which the US navy had special interest. Though enough questions remained to cause friction later, Tiltman's actions facilitated this and he must be seen as a prime force, particularly in overcoming the reluctance to divulge the Enigma situation. Sherman's view is that, Tiltman having been persuasive,

> *it saved both sides from having to overcome the ill will which likely would have been created if the exchange during the Sinkov mission had been judged to have been more or less one-way. Bletchley Park and its American*

partners would experience enough lingering suspicion of one another during 1942 and early 1943 as it was. Had the Sinkov mission failed, these doubts might have continued to late in the latter year or even into early 1944.

Denniston visited the USA in August 1941, after the Sinkov mission departed, and communications with Friedman in September suggest reasonable hopes. In a letter of 10 September he says:[11]

After a week's wait in Montreal I made a safe passage home and am just beginning now to describe my visit to my colleagues who are all extremely interested... I am extremely sorry that the arrival of Stevens from Singapore has been delayed so long but I feel it may give your staff an opportunity of close study of the material they already have and I am sanguine of your success when the extra material and background reaches you... I hope soon to hear of further progress made by Dr Kullback's party.

Geoffrey Stevens was to be liaison officer with the army in the USA later on, from July 1942 with G-2. Herein perhaps lies another of Tiltman's many problems: Stevens made a doubtful impression on his hosts. According to Budiansky[12] he

arrived in July 1942 and immediately ruffled feathers with what the Americans took to be his pompous manner, accentuated by his habitual costume of Sam Browne belt, polished black riding boots, and swagger stick.

His letters back to England were at times flippant and full of complaints, including 'the "regimental gossip" of American women at a dinner party to our fat friend Kully' – Solomon Kullback, no less, whom Stevens accused of being obstructive and over-organized. If this is the impression Stevens created, Tiltman would have his work cut out.

It is possible that Edward Hastings too, when he took up liaison on the naval side, sometimes left the wrong impression with his US hosts. Elizebeth Friedman tells a story:[13]

On the afternoon of 7 Dec 1941, soon after the attack on Pearl Harbor was announced, Captain Hastings came to the Friedmans' house in Washington. He sat down and proceeded to "laugh and laugh" about the Pearl Harbor attack. Mrs Friedman was shocked and offended and never understood his behaviour on this occasion. Apparently Hastings found the surprise element of the attack amusing.

Another letter,[14] undated but likely to be from a similar time to the September missive, shows Denniston sending Friedman three reports on various ciphers and promising others, as well as requesting information from Kullback. Here at least there were signs of understanding and cooperation.

It should also be remembered that, at this stage (the summer of 1941), the Americans were not yet involved in the European war. Consequently their need for European code information, especially that of Germany, would have seemed to be much less justified. The security of material extracted from Enigma codebreaking might well have been weighed as being of greater importance along with reservations about US security. The distinction between the capacity to decipher the codes and the exploitation of it to derive intelligence, which required the experience and cataloguing to be found at BP alone, must also be considered. The exploitation of intelligence was to become an issue later.

With the entry of America into the world war following Hitler's declaration on 11 December, the barriers to cooperation and collaboration with the USA were ostensibly lifted. It was not to prove so simple.

Discussions opened on arrangements for liaison and this coincided with the problems of management at BP which were coming to a head. On 5 February 1942, 'C' (Menzies) had decided that Tiltman was to be the liaison man. Denniston questioned this decision, and it seems[15] that Menzies recognized Denniston's case.[16] But changes were coming at BP, and a week later the decision was made to move Denniston to head the diplomatic section, leaving Travis in charge of Services matters at BP. Tiltman was thus assigned to go to the USA. Edward Hastings, navy liaison in the US, wrote to Tiltman[17] on 7 February 1942 extolling the start Stevens had made in liaison and hoping that Tiltman, with his technical competence, would not be long in coming.

Tiltman was accompanied[18] by Captain Sandwith (navy) and Harold Kenworthy, as well as RAF representation. Sandwith was to play a major part in the April conference on Radio Communications, with US, UK and Canadian representatives present. Tiltman brought letters from Denniston to several people including Friedman, Denniston recommending Tiltman to Friedman as someone 'you will enjoy meeting… not only on technical grounds but on personal grounds'. He was to carry papers for Oliver Strachey (then in Canada on BP liaison work) and for

Prescott Currier, as well as some RAF materials to be shared with the Americans. Tiltman also carried important cypher material: the codes of the Spanish and the Vichy French, and[19] material on the German diplomatic Floradora system (books and microfilm). 'Given the arrival of American forces in the Mediterranean, this was valuable material' is the assessment of Aldrich,[20] who points out that subsequently more and more material went to the USA from diplomatic codes of the Middle East (Iraq, Iran) and Eastern Europe (Greece, Hungary). If Aldrich is correct in this assessment, then, together with the Italian ciphers already shared, this would certainly constitute 'reciprocation' of the Purple machine. It might also perhaps not have been appreciated in navy circles for what it was, because European diplomatic material was generally handled in the USA by the army at Arlington. As a naval man, Safford, complaining of a lack of balance, might not have realized its significance. Messages exchanged in April 1942[21] make it clear that there was sharing of Japanese military cipher and Japanese weather codes, as well as German and Vichy diplomatic cipher material.

Yet before Tiltman's arrival there was hesitation from Britain about providing even training materials on various aspects of codebreaking. A British memorandum[22] of March 1942 states

> *Your A.25. Colonel Tiltman will bring with him descriptions of German and Italian methods. To copy all of the tables reconstructed and now in use would involve nearly 1000 photostats and before doing this we should like confirmation that they are all required.*

Tiltman went to the USA in late March 1942. He met with navy personnel and, according to Budiansky,[23] 'assessed the situation with a clear eye'. The British position, helped previously by information being passed to the USA about naval matters, was weakened because of the current lack of submarine Enigma decodes. The 'Shark blackout' caused by the introduction of a fourth rotor on the U-boat Enigma system, with the consequent inability to locate U-boats – and a reluctance to admit it – at a time when U-boats were turning their attention to the US East coast, caused bitterness and complaint that there was no information forthcoming. Perhaps this growing concern lies at the bottom of the increasing divisions across the 'pond'. There were also issues with the quality of some of the materials sent: Tiltman sent a memo[24] to Travis on

1 April outlining some things not received or desired, including Vichy books, information on French diplomatic traffic, and the basic material from the vital Lorenz break (August 1941).

It is therefore perhaps not so surprising that the USA was also coy about sharing some of their systems, in particular their own cryptographic machinery. Among other issues was the practicality that the USA was using the ECM/SIGABA machine as their standard, while the British used Typex (a rotor-based encoding machine, with similar principles to Enigma but using five rotors and able to print out; it was not apparently broken by the Axis during the war). The two were not compatible.

The ECM 888/889 was the name the navy had (Electric Cipher machine) for the army SIGABA, which was in both cases the same machine, ECM Mark II.[25] It had its origins in the work of Friedman and Rowlett in the mid-30s, looking for improvements in earlier Hebern machinery. They shared information about this with Wenger, who with his experience in machinery improved it on the technical side and persuaded Safford, then in charge of navy codes, of its value. The result was that by August 1941 the machine had become standard across army and navy in the USA. It was, so far as is known, not to be broken at all by Axis powers.

A letter of April 1942[26] shows how, while the advantages of mutually-compatible machinery were obvious, American security concerns predominated. Tiltman had shown the Americans some British field cipher systems, which the US army felt too cumbersome and possibly lacking enough security, proposing instead adoption of US devices (including the M-209, a Hagelin-based product which ironically was to prove insecure). The letter continues:

It is proposed, if possible, to work out with Colonel Tiltman the basis for joint cryptographic systems using the Y-138-A and M-209 devices so as to permit of expeditious intercommunication between American and British units working together. However, these systems would be in addition to cryptographic systems (using these same devices) which would be restricted in distribution to American units, and which would therefore not be readable by the British. The discussions would specifically be restricted to these systems and devices and would exclude any discussion of our electrical converters.

Both sides were hesitant about going too far.

It was clearly also an expectation on Tiltman that he would negotiate to dissuade the Americans from 'taking over' the Enigma work by using its industrial muscle and manufacturing capacity. On 25 April 1942, Tiltman was allowed (by agreement with army and navy) to observe the ECM/SIGABA machine[27] which was the heart of the US machine ciphers. In return he conducted a demonstration of the British Typex machine – which was considered good but not adequate by the Americans, who preferred their own.

Tiltman described what happened:

I came over on an American troop ship, with a naval captain by the name of Sandwith. The cipher officer on board the ship, with great pride, introduced Sandwith and me to the ECM, which actually he had no right to do. It didn't actually make a difference, but he had no right to do it. But after I'd been here for a bit, Wenger and Friedman had got permission to show me the ECM machine... Joe Wenger had his permission on paper... and Friedman didn't, and Friedman was in very serious trouble with General Strong who heard about this and hadn't been consulted. That was the cause of one of Friedman's breakdowns.

They had sought authority to show me, as part of the complete exchange, the ECM, which would have had to have happened very shortly, because you'll remember there was a machine, the CCM, which would convert ECM to TYPEX.

Tiltman presented his visit report[28] on his return at the end of April, with results and recommendations for the future of US-UK cooperation. While optimistic about future development, he was critical of a number of aspects both of US competence and of organisation. But he had continued to make a good impression on William Friedman at Arlington. Tiltman received the following friendly message[29] from Friedman when he returned to Britain (late April 1942):

I was very glad to learn of your safe arrival, notice of which was communicated to me by Miss Chaplin. I cannot begin to tell you how much I enjoyed your visit and how beneficial it was. Please give my very best regards to Cmdr. Denniston and tell him that I still have some letters of his crying for answers.

The letter also refers to gifts of books on ancient 'codes' which were of interest to Tiltman (a generous gesture indicative of warmth), and to the imminent arrive of Captain Kullback who was to figure in liaison in the future and would become interested in the Fish material. Tiltman's return flight, incidentally, in a Liberator, ended in a crash-landing at Prestwick[30] and he was fortunate not to have sustained injury.

Tiltman's reply[31] confirmed arrangements including the initiation of Kullback into the details:

Dear Friedman,

1. *In the first place, very many thanks for all your kindness to me during my stay in Washington, both in the office and at your home. Please tell Mrs. Friedman how much I appreciated her kindness during my long stay with you, which must have caused her a very considerable amount of extra trouble. I hope you and your family all keep well.*
2. *Kullback has been here for several days now. He is being shown everything he wishes to see, is working very hard and seems perfectly happy. He was apparently quite favourably impressed with the work of the party in London which deals with FLORADORA* [German diplomatic code broken probably in 1942].
3. *Stevens goes back to Washington shortly with our blessing. I propose to write him a letter every month, and have asked him to do the same by me…*
4. *Considerable progress has been made here both in my absence and since I arrived back, in the investigation of the Japanese Military Attaché cipher. Details will be forwarded to you as soon as a definite stage has been reached. In the meantime it will all be shown to Kullback.*

This is a reply which is positive and open, and sets a tone for future work with Friedman – and a desire to do so with the navy, as Wenger is included. It might however have been part of the background to problems with the US navy in OP-20-G, since they and the army were not colleagues but rivals in the area of codes.

In June 1942 another version of the US machines, the HCM, was examined in London by Dudley-Smith. His report[32] on it shows concerns and refers to Tiltman's awareness of the ECM, a model of which was apparently on its way to Britain at the time. The concerns were with possible compatibility of the HCM with Typex, and some potential weaknesses in repetitions of rotor positions.

Friedman replied to Tiltman's message quoted above in a letter of 21 July. He says[33] that Stevens has arrived, and that there are plans to exchange letters each month. Over receiving information on the '*Geheimschreiber*' he says:

> *There seems to be some delay of a nature that I do not understand in connection with the establishment of the local 'Y' Committee, and I imagine that somebody high up has become confused. I shall get busy on this and see if we cannot prod the necessary people.*

Friedman (according to this letter) had by now sent Tiltman material for him to read on American techniques; Tiltman himself had sent various texts[34] the other way at the end of May, and apart from the training manuals the enclosure contained an archaeological report – which seems to be a personal copy for Friedman, knowing his interest in ancient writings, and is also indicative of a warm and positive relationship.

July was the time when US navy personnel Robert Ely and Joe Eachus arrived at BP and were shown the details of construction of the Bombes. According to Johnson[35] in his account of early SIGINT liaison, it was Tiltman who was persuasive in setting up this visit, having made it clear that failure to give the US navy information about the Enigma developments would be detrimental to the accords. Tiltman intervened again in June to ensure that the visit took place. Navy Bombe development was to be key for the future. Small groups of other Americans now began to appear at BP. Tiltman's work on his first US visit, according to Clabby, had ensured that these groups, when involved on the ground, would be under British control (something Travis, by now in charge at BP, was prepared to give away).

At the same time Denniston was writing (from his by now Diplomatic section point of view) to Friedman,[36] saying:

> *Speaking for the Diplomatic Sections only, he* [Kullback, about to return to the USA] *now knows what all of us are doing and has seen weak points in the liaison in the case of the French and South American, and will, I hope, take steps on his return to clear up any misunderstandings. I consider that in Japanese, German and Italian we are now walking in step, and I hope soon to see the other subjects equally efficient.*

It seemed like cooperation was working.

However, the reference by Friedman to 'some delay' might indicate awareness of what was to happen next; Denniston's optimism was premature, partly based on the greater success of the diplomatic cipher cooperation of which he was now in charge, back in London, and where connections were less troubled than in the Services sections represented at BP. There were barriers in the US army regarding exchange of information, in spite of Strong's apparent early interest in 1940. It was as a result of this that on 9 July Roosevelt asked Marshall[37] to develop similar links for the army to those which the navy already seemed to have with the British cryptographers over information exchange. General Strong, replying on the same day to Marshall's query, stated,

> *Intimate exchanges of technical cryptographic information have been in progress for over a year and the discrepancy with Navy practice was solely due to the Navy ones having been in place for longer.*

This very generalized reply, passed back to Roosevelt on 11 July, did not show the true situation.

Meanwhile Jeffrey Stevens had been sent to the USA to liaise and report with a view to further developing cooperation. At the end of July he sent Tiltman back a description[38] of the current state of USA work, their organisation, and progress on various topics. His time had included a number of visits to William Friedman (who sent Tiltman good wishes), and he had also met Joseph Wenger.

A series of events and situations now began to disturb the US-UK liaisons.

Perhaps annoyed by the fact that the ECM machine had been shown to Tiltman and the British without written authority, General Strong[39] now placed an embargo on sharing new army developments with both British commanders and the US navy. The ban also extended to some social and informal connections. Friedman maintained that the veto was lifted in the autumn of 1942 by Colonel Bullock, but this was contested. If such restrictions were in place it might explain why there was delay, e.g. in producing documents requested by Tiltman,[40] promised in July but which had not arrived in November. (Strong finally made it clear in May 1943 that he had never meant at that stage to lift the restriction but was prepared to accept whatever had happened as a *fait accompli* without further impugning Friedman's position.)

In August 1942 the US navy cryptologists of OP-20-G, led now by Joseph Wenger, who had considerable experience in using automation to analyse problems and was impatient about the lack of British U-boat information,[41] prepared a plan to build hundreds of Bombes and do the job themselves. Hastings as navy liaison officer was told of this[42] early in September.

Travis and Frank Birch visited the USA and finalized the 'Holden agreement' in response, which conceded American dominance over Japanese codes (in the face of Tiltman's pioneer work) and provided US participation in naval Enigma work and output. Travis kept Tiltman informed[43] of this. Stevens also referred to it in his letter[44] to Tiltman of 4 October – the US navy had taken to Frank Birch, but the army 'appears to be working up to something'. The one-sided nature of the Holden paper probably had an influence on future British negotiations; it would be hard to concede such territory again. Tiltman also had continuing reservations about US security, which he detailed in a memo[45] of mid-November 1942.

The Holden agreement (2 October 1942) was very much to the advantage of the USA in most respects. Apart from the concessions to sharing Naval Enigma material, it provided among other things for[46] the US to take control of FRUMEL (Melbourne intercept and cryptological base), which was then shared between British and US personnel displaced by the Japanese advances. British cryptological efforts at Kilindini (where cryptologists from the Far East were now based) would wind down, and instead they would work on materials sent by other units. The Americans would pass to GC&CS or the Admiralty relevant Japanese traffic, radio intelligence and Japanese cipher recoveries.

All this placed the British in the hands of the Americans regarding SIGINT in the Pacific sector of the war. However, it became impossible to hold fully to it in places, when the US end failed to share or pass things on and the British were driven to do some things themselves (not without success). It was nevertheless a striking agreement, sharing, even though primarily in naval circles only, the most sensitive of secrets with another nation.

In spite of 'Holden', the US navy was unhappy, and Admiral John Redman, head of OP-20-G Intelligence, seems to have been a leading player.[47] In his earlier visit to the USA, Tiltman had previously met with Safford who was then at the top of OP-20-G, the US navy code organisation, but Safford was soon to be ousted from this position, with Redman and Wenger put in charge, Tiltman commenting later,[48]

> *Wenger wasn't the sort of person for any sort of underhand action, or anything like that, and Redman would ride roughshod over anybody.*

Speaking of his later 1942 meeting with Admiral Joseph Redman, Tiltman described something of it in interview:

> *Goodman:* *You, of course, talked to Redman?*
> *Tiltman:* *Did I – Yes. when I could get a word in edgewise…*
> *Goodman:* *Or rather he talked to you. What were your impressions of Redman? Was he knowledgeable of the business, or was he out for himself?*
> *Tiltman:* *I don't know the answer to that. He was rough with me, particularly because of the restrictions we'd laid down over the Enigma, which I claimed to have cleared by sending a telegram home saying that the situation was ridiculous. He was pretty rough with me then saying German submarines were operating on the east coast of the United States, and we were withholding life and death information.*

This meeting with Redman had been towards the end of the time (February to December 1942) of the 'Shark blackout' – the inability to read U-Boat Enigma messages on the new 4-rotor machine Enigma – which was leading the US (the navy especially) to move towards creating their own Bombe machines, effectively usurping the British effort. Feelings were therefore running high, and the British had been reluctant to admit the full extent of the problem for a while. Tiltman was 'ambushed' during his later 1942 visit[49] when veteran US codebreaker Mrs Agnes Driscoll[50] arranged an apparently innocent meeting. Tiltman says:

> *I was to see Mrs. Driscoll. I was not aware that there would be a formal amphitheatre with everybody that could possibly be interested sitting around – Sinkov, Kullback, Rowlett; Mr Friedman, and the heads of both services were there and so on; and I didn't know my stuff. I've told this story before. Mrs. Driscoll had decided that she had a better method of breaking the Enigma than we had, but there was one bit of information which we had which we had not disclosed, so that in all her methods she*

always allowed one piece of information, what I call a bisque. I was not in the position to argue with her because I really didn't know my stuff. I always thought this was a very unfair way of dealing with me.

Tiltman suggested that this meeting might have been Redman's idea.[51]

Tiltman arrived as a liaison officer at a similar time to Turing's arrival in America with the specific task of liaising and advising over the building of Bombes and discussing voice encoding equipment. But there were great difficulties, due in part to the mix-up earlier over the main high-grade US ECM cipher machine and US caution about other such revelations. Tiltman explains:

For some odd reason we sent Turing, who was by no means an expert... we regarded him as a genius in our office. While he was on the high seas, General Strong heard about it and said he couldn't see it. And I had a telegram from England, I should think in December of '42, telling me not to come back until General Strong changed his mind, decisively.

The story of the Turing incident[52] and its repercussions, alongside negotiations with the army over 'Special Intelligence', created serious friction between the USA and Britain over the next two months or so and had echoes beyond that time. It brought Tiltman into a difficult situation vis-à-vis General Strong and other senior War Department officers in the US. The account in detail is necessary to understand fully what Tiltman had to overcome in his work at this time. Some of this dates back several months; a long report dated 8 June 1942 by Lieutenant Commander Kroner, USN, shows his distrust of the ways in which the British seemed to work, suspicion over the role of Captain Hastings, whom Travis had arranged to be GC&CS liaison in May 1942, and concern over apparent involvement of both the FBI and the State Department more widely.

Distrust of other organisations (even on your own side) was a recurrent theme then and later; both US army and navy were against the inclusion of other agencies in their secret work, such as Hastings had already done by his liaisons with the FBI and others. Tiltman experienced this late in 1942 when he was invited to meet with William Stephenson, the British secret service coordinator in New York. At the meeting, Stephenson indicated that he would like Tiltman to meet General Donovan, chief of the US Office of Strategic Services (OSS), who was in the building. However, Tiltman had been warned by Admiral Redman, 'As long as you deal with the United States Army and Navy, we're your friends, but we will not have you getting mixed up with any other organization.' A 'diplomatic' absence was needed and Stephenson undertook to say that Tiltman had 'missed his connection'.

So the background to the feelings shown in the Kroner report (which is a lengthy and unfriendly review of past liaison), Strong's suspicions, and the awkwardness of the ECM secrecy being 'breached', was there when Turing arrived at the end of November 1942. He was to offer some help with Bombe development but was also now working on voice encoding projects such as 'Delilah' in the UK. Tiltman was now to help resolve this situation.

On 2 December, Field Marshal Sir John Dill, senior army representative in Washington for the British, wrote to Marshall[53] expressing surprise that Turing had been denied access to the Bell laboratories, and asking for this to be reversed. A draft reply dated the same day, but not apparently used, says that Turing arrived unannounced, without accreditation, and without contacting the Signals Corps, Security or the Army G-2 section, asking to see most secret materials. He would be welcome, the reply was to say, with proper authorisation.

Two days later, Carter Clarke, a senior member of Strong's staff, wrote to Strong. Clarke had spoken with Colonel Crawford in Signals; Turing had come

> *posing as a cryptographer and cryptanalyst, but that in his opinion [Turing's] real mission is to obtain information relative to the scrambling device… This is just one more 'back door' attempt to gain information.*

Strong sent a memo the next day to General McNarney (Deputy Chief of Staff in the US Army) setting out his view: that Turing came as

> *a representative of the British Post Office, supposedly as a cryptographer and cryptanalyst. He did not contact this office and, as far as I know, is not vouched for by the British Staff mission. However, Captain Hastings, who is accredited as a liaison officer between the British Admiralty and the Navy dept., and who has no standing whatever with the War dept., did approach an officer in the Signals corps… in connection with the highly secret telephone scrambling device… This incident constitutes just one more pain in the neck resulting from the consistent practice of British representatives to this country using back-door methods to gain information.*

Marshall meanwhile wrote back to McNarney on 8 December indicating that Dill had explained Turing's position to him and asking for the ban to be lifted. He clearly received a negative reply because of the status of the machine, for on 9 December he wrote to Dill explaining in his turn that the voice encoder was on their 'ultra-secret' list and therefore not covered in the exchanges. The mix-up apparently came from Turing conferring with lower-ranked officers instead of getting the proper level of authorisation.

On 15 December Dill wrote again to Marshall, expressing concern that full exchange of ultra-secret developments was not happening and promising action. Some of what was in doubt might be seen from Carter Clarke's memo to Colonel Bratton dated 17 December, where he mentions 'about eight thousand words per day of German clandestine traffic' not being made available – with concern as now the Americans were beginning to be involved in Europe and such material could well be important.

By now Tiltman was becoming directly involved in the liaison role. Carter Clarke wrote to Strong on 17 December outlining waspishly visits with Hastings (on 12 December) and with him and Tiltman (on 14 December), where Tiltman was keen to offer expertise in identifying weaknesses in devices – in reality, Clarke says, just a ruse to get information. After liaising with Crawford, Clarke was satisfied that the US disclosed everything bar the voice encoder and their cipher machines' technology, but the British were not disclosing German clandestine material (meaning espionage intelligence, such as the *Abwehr* messages), German field traffic, Slavic material (probably here meaning Russian) or details of their 'high-speed analyser' (meaning the Bombe).

It must be remembered that this last point was written from an army viewpoint; Joe Eachus and others from the navy had been to BP to see the full detail of the Bombe, but the US War Department was a separate case.

Marshall wrote to Dill on 23 December explaining what the perceived shortcomings were in British openness, as stated by Clarke. Dill's reply on 26 December stated that these materials were indeed made available in the UK, to accredited representatives. But issues had arisen due to procedural misunderstandings.

> *The duly authorized British organisation which controls these matters is named the* [GCCS] *under the direction of Brigadier Stewart Menzies under the Foreign Office. This body has a representative in Washington,*

Portrait of John Hessel Tiltman. (*Courtesy of the family of Tempe Denzer. Shows him in the 1920s*)

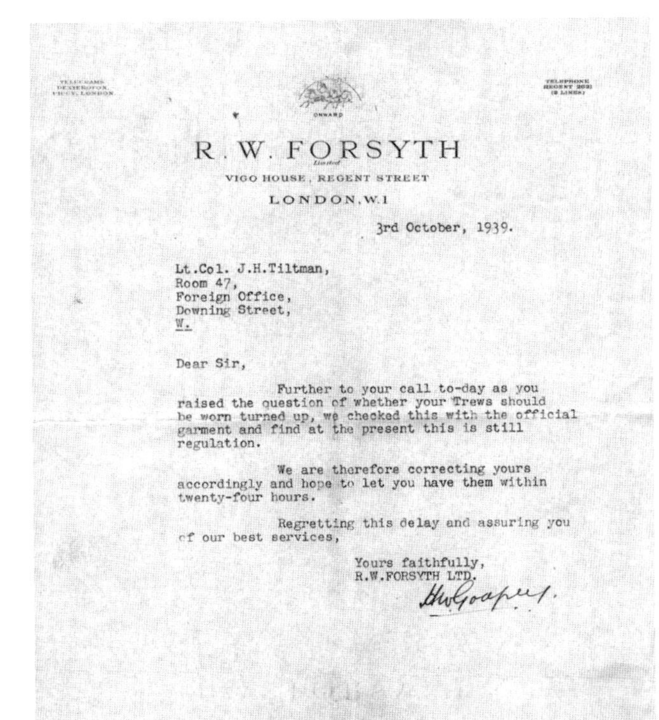

ONWARD

R. W. FORSYTH
Limited
VIGO HOUSE, REGENT STREET
LONDON, W.1

3rd October, 1939.

Lt.Col. J.H.Tiltman,
Room 47,
Foreign Office,
Downing Street,
W.

Dear Sir,

Further to your call to-day as you raised the question of whether your Trews should be worn turned up, we checked this with the official garment and find at the present this is still regulation.

We are therefore correcting yours accordingly and hope to let you have them within twenty-four hours.

Regretting this delay and assuring you of our best services,

Yours faithfully,
R.W.FORSYTH LTD.
[signature]

RENFIELD STREET, GLASGOW & PRINCES STREET, EDINBURGH

Letter from R.W. Forsyth, tailors, apologising for incorrect 'trews', 1939. (*Copyright BP archive*)

Tiltman with William Friedman in the 1950s. (*Courtesy of National Cryptological Museum, NSA*)

Tiltman with Friedman and Josh Cooper, 1960s. (*Courtesy of National Cryptological Museum, NSA*)

Conference March 1949. In front row, Tiltman front left, Travis next but one, Friedman right. Also present Corderman, Wenger, Sinkov and Kullback. (*Arlington Hall photo collection HIST-200-001. Courtesy of National Cryptological Museum, NSA*)

28 March 1953, meeting of Canada-US-UK conference, Tiltman second from right in front. Bill Bonsall (glasses & moustache) and 'Bill' Millward are in the back row. (*Arlington Hall Photo collection HIST-136-001. Courtesy of National Cryptological Museum, NSA, cch@nsa.gov*)

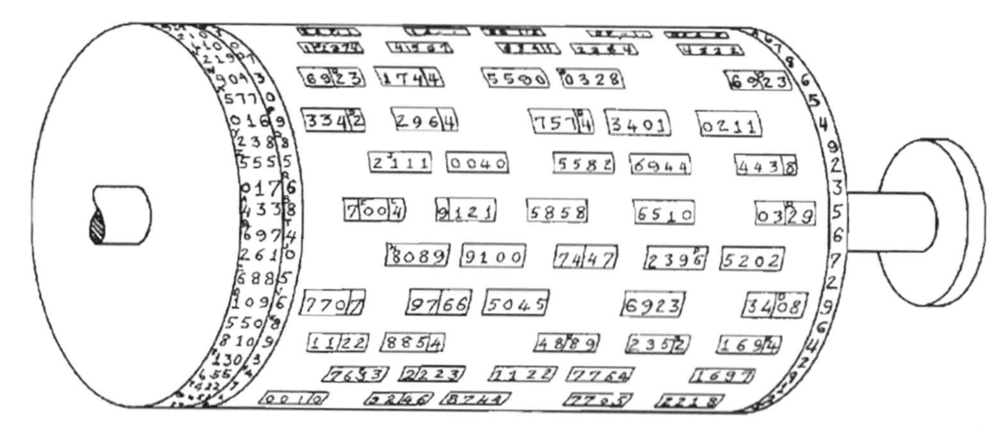

Cylinder cipher device, created by Tiltman in 1933. (*Courtesy of National Cryptological Museum, NSA*)

An ECM/SIGABA Mark II code machine from WW2. (© *Mark Pellegrini, Creative Commons CC-BY-SA-2.5*)

Joseph Wenger, USN. (*Courtesy of National Cryptological Museum, NSA*)

Robert Weeks (left) and Abraham Sinkov (both post-war), two of the 'Sinkov mission' in 1941. (*Courtesy of National Cryptological Museum, NSA*)

28 March 1950, presentation to AFSA director Rear Admiral Stone of antique maps, from Travis. Tiltman was the intermediary. Seen second from front inspecting example. HIST-139-003. (*Courtesy of National Cryptological Museum, NSA*)

Tiltman with Professor Vincent and Alastair Denniston in London early in the war. (*Courtesy of National Cryptological Museum, NSA*)

The Lorenz teleprinter cipher attachment, for enciphering teleprinter messages, used by German army High Command – the so-called 'Fish' traffic (Tunny section). (*Courtesy of Bletchley Park and by kind permission of GCHQ*)

The reconstruction of 'Colossus', built by Tony Sale and team, now at the National Museum of Computing, near Bletchley Park. (*Author's photo and courtesy of the National Museum of Computing*)

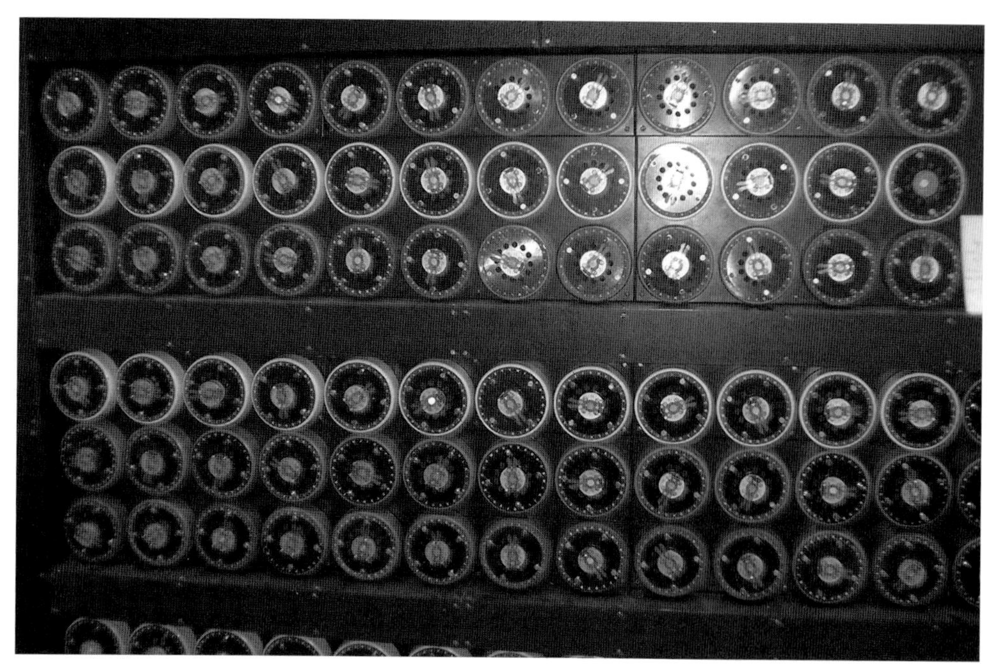

Model of the Bombe machine, showing the three blocks of twelve 'Letchworth Enigmas' which could be tested at once for finding the settings to decipher a particular crib. (*Courtesy of Bletchley Park and by kind permission of GCHQ*)

An Enigma machine, 3-rotor version with lid open showing rotors and lights, plugboard and spare rotors. (*Courtesy of Bletchley Park and by kind permission of GCHQ*)

TOP SECRET

GEHEIMSCHREIBER (GERMAN SECRET TELEPRINTER MACHINE)

DIAGRAMMATIC PRESENTATION OF THE ENCIPHERING ACTION OF THE MACHINE

A. CLEAR TEXT

EXTENDED PSI

C. DE-CHI

D CHI

E CIPHER

TOP SECRET

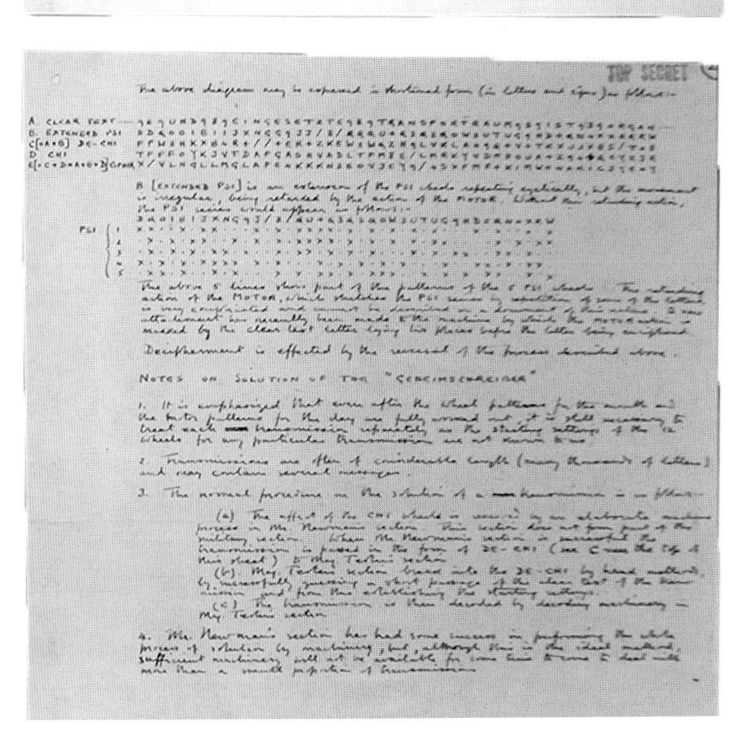

TOP SECRET

Decipherment is effected by the reversal of the process described above.

NOTES ON SOLUTION OF THE "GEHEIMSCHREIBER"

Handwritten analysis of Lorenz material, showing the Murray code and the process of addition to encode and decode, believed to be the work of John Tiltman, 1941–2. (*Courtesy of Bletchley Park and by kind permission of GCHQ*)

Bletchley Park – view of the front of the Mansion, the 'ugly monstrosity' for some, and centre of the code-breaking of GC&CS 1938–1946. (*Author's photo*)

Ardour House, Bedford, where the Tiltman Japanese course took place in 1942. (*Modern view, courtesy of Nick Cooke*)

Views towards and from one of Tiltman's probable rooms in the earlier days of the war (nos. 1 and 3) in Bletchley Park. (*Author's photo, courtesy of Bletchley Park*)

One of Tiltman's probable working rooms (33) at Bletchley Park, during the later years of the war. (*Author's photo, courtesy of Bletchley Park*)

The Swan Hotel, Leighton Buzzard, former billet of Brigadier (then Colonel) Tiltman at the start of the Second World War. (*Author's photo*)

Number 43, Buckingham Road, Bletchley, where Tiltman lived during the war. (*Author's photograph, with kind permission of owner Geoff Banbury*)

A German Kryha coding machine. (*Courtesy of National Cryptological Museum, NSA*)

Nos. 27–30 Torrington Square, Bloomsbury – nineteenth century housing in the area of Tiltman's birth. No. 70 has been demolished. (*By kind permission of Sally Williams and London Gardens Trust*)

TILTMAN – BRIGADIER J.H. C.B.E. M.C. PERSONNEL

D.D.4.

Page 2.

Date 1945	To	No:	Ref	
8-3	O'CONNOR	AZ/2610	–	To be Chief Cryptographer to Civil & Commercial Sections – 8/5.
24-4	[illegible]	[illegible] 350	–	Accom: booked for DD4 & party, 26, 27 & 28/4 in Paris.
14-4	SCOTT	PROC/3721	–	To take party to France re French security. DUDLEY-SMITH, BULL & EDWARDS
19-4	W.O.	FWD/19472	–	Party to go to SHAEF main 28/4 re French signal & cypher security.
20-4	C.S.S.	AZ/2726	–	Draft sig to STRONG re meeting, Subjects for discussion.
20-4	G-5	PROC/3942	–	Party hope to arrive Le Bourget 26/4 – for discussion with STRONG, SCOTT-BICHER (Cypher)
21-4	STRONG	PROC/3980	–	Discussing French cooperation in F.E. & probable Anglo-French post war.
25-4	SHR	PROC/4105	350	Thanks. Party due Le Bourget 26/4.
25-4	SCOTT	PROC/4104	–	Party arriving Paris 26/4, Staying at Raphael Hotel.
5-10	C.S.S.	WO/47	–	Future. SRS. be demobilized and posted as civilian to GCCS.
10-10	D.D.4.	DDR/36	47	Agree to suggestions – go ahead. (Enc. draft reply to W.O.)
12-11	GCCS	BSC/49	–	Expects to be home 18/11.
9-12	OP-20 T069	GCCS/17277	–	Informal BOURBON meeting held 9/12. Another to be held on 18/12. Shortage of linguists.

Tiltman's personnel record card of 1945 from GCHQ. (*Courtesy of Bletchley Park and by kind permission of GCHQ*)

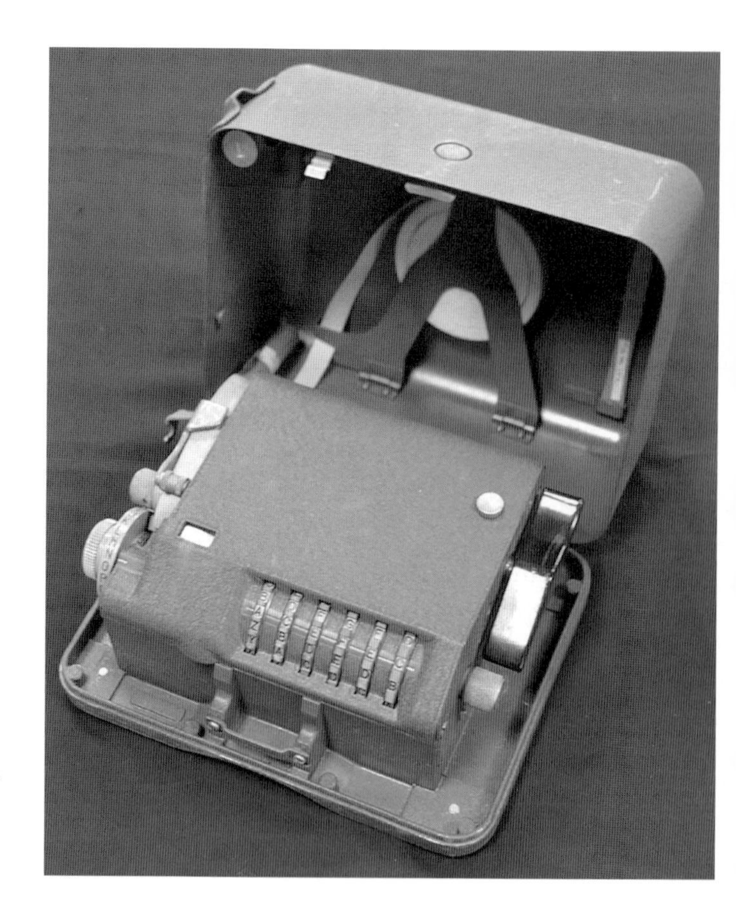

A Hagelin machine (version M-209, as used by Americans). (*Courtesy of Bletchley Park and by kind permission of GCHQ*)

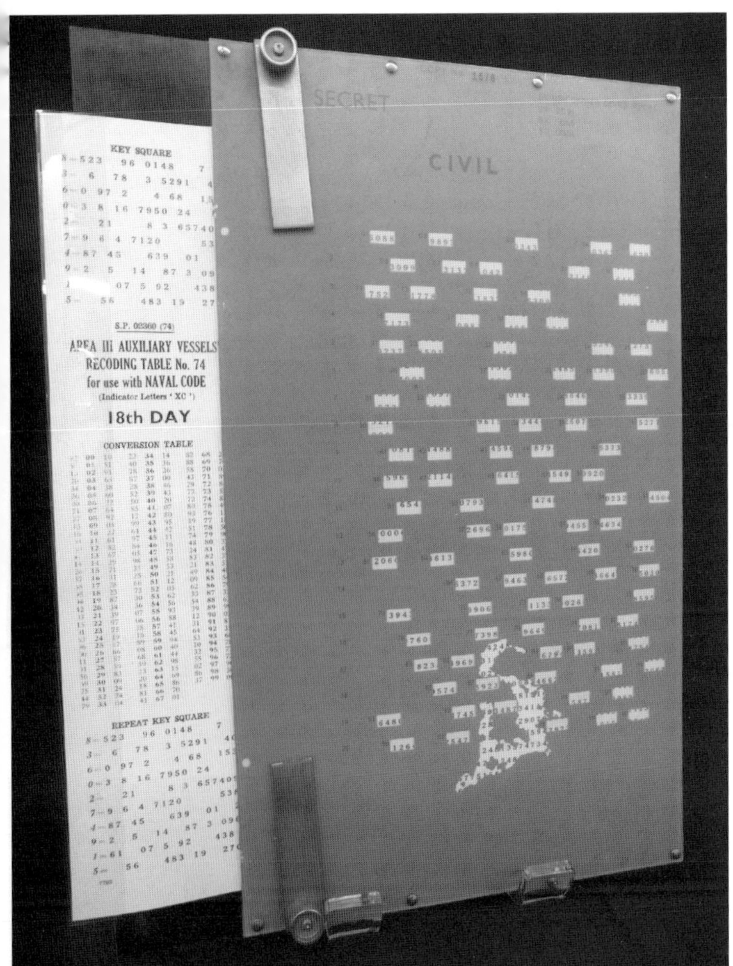

A stencil subtractor (SSF), believed to have been created by Tiltman. (*Courtesy of Bletchley Park and by kind permission of GCHQ*)

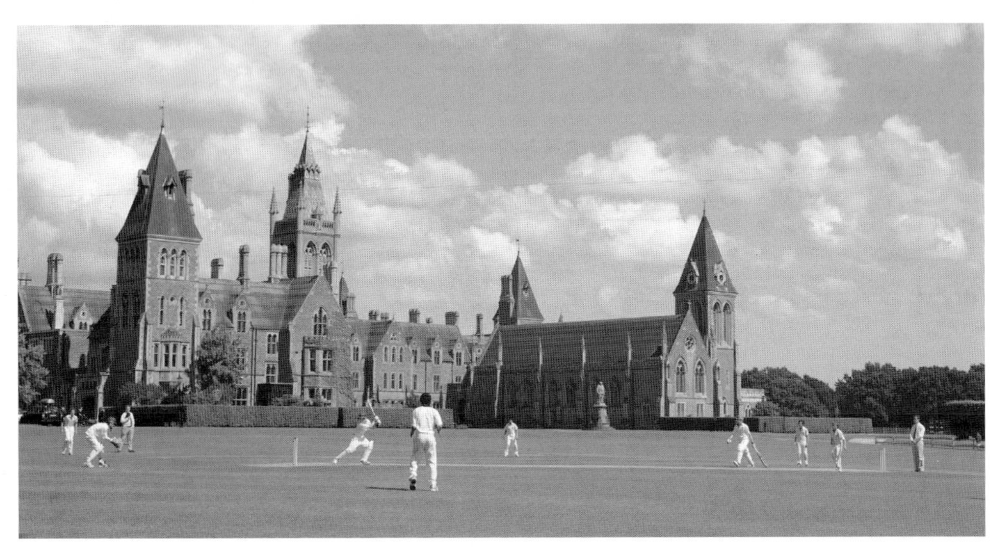

Charterhouse, Godalming, Tiltman's senior school until 1911. (*Copyright Charterhouse School, courtesy of the archivist*)

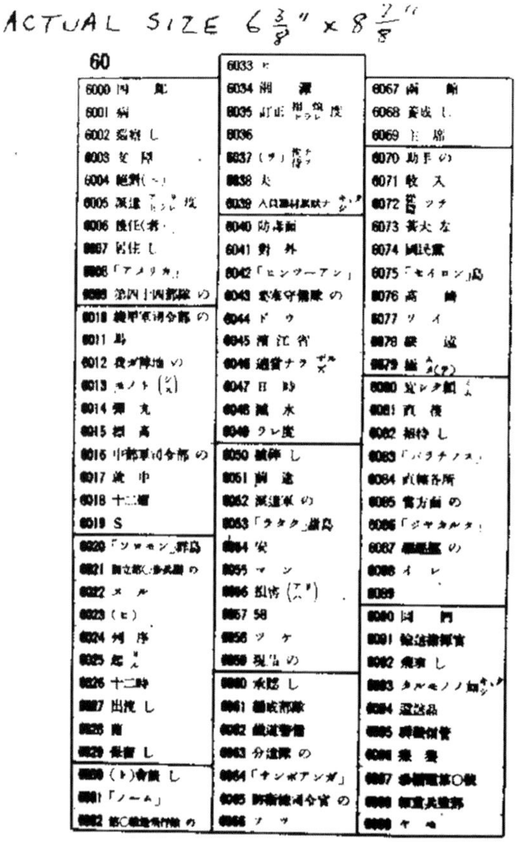

ACTUAL SIZE 6 3/8" × 8 7/8"

60

6000	[illegible]	6033	[illegible]	6067	[illegible]
6001	[illegible]	6034	[illegible]	6068	[illegible] し
6002	[illegible] し	6035	訂正 [illegible]	6069	上 席
6003	[illegible]	6036		6070	助手 の
6004	[illegible]	6037	(ツ) [illegible]	6071	收 入
6005	派遣 [illegible]	6038	[illegible]	6072	[illegible] ツチ
6006	[illegible]	6039	[illegible]	6073	[illegible] な
6007	[illegible] し	6040	防毒面	6074	[illegible]
6008	「アメリカ」	6041	對 外	6075	「セイロン」島
6009	第四十四部隊 の	6042	「ヒン[illegible]ーアン」	6076	高 [illegible]
6010	[illegible]司令部 の	6043	[illegible]守備隊 の	6077	ツ イ
6011	[illegible]	6044	ド ウ	6078	[illegible]
6012	我ガ陣地 の	6045	[illegible] 江 省	6079	[illegible]
6013	[illegible]	6046	[illegible]ナラ [illegible]	6080	[illegible]
6014	[illegible] 丸	6047	日 時	6081	[illegible]
6015	[illegible] 高	6048	[illegible] 水	6082	[illegible] し
6016	中部軍司令部 の	6049	クレ度	6083	[illegible]
6017	[illegible] 中	6050	[illegible] し	6084	[illegible]各所
6018	十二[illegible]	6051	[illegible] 途	6085	[illegible]方面 の
6019	S	6052	派遣軍 の	6086	「ジャカルタ」
6020	「ソロモン」群島	6053	「ラタク」諸島	6087	[illegible] の
6021	[illegible] の	6054	[illegible]	6088	イ レ
6022	メ ル	6055	マ ン	6089	
6023	(ヒ)	6056	[illegible]	6090	[illegible] 門
6024	[illegible] 序	6057	58	6091	[illegible]
6025	[illegible]	6058	ツ ケ	6092	[illegible] し
6026	十二時	6059	[illegible] の	6093	[illegible]
6027	[illegible] し	6060	承認 し	6094	[illegible]
6028	[illegible]	6061	[illegible]部隊	6095	[illegible]
6029	[illegible] し	6062	[illegible]	6096	[illegible]
6030	(ト)[illegible] し	6063	分遣隊 の	6097	[illegible]
6031	「ノーム」	6064	「サンボアンガ」	6098	[illegible]
6032	[illegible] の	6065	[illegible]司令官 の	6099	[illegible]
		6066	ナ ツ		

Japanese naval code-book, sample page showing 4-figure code numbers and their meanings. NSA document 41709969074927. (*Courtesy of National Cryptological Museum, NSA*)

ACTUAL SIZE 4 7/8" × 7 1/8"

80

⌐	6	0	5	7	8	3	9	1	4	2
8	1113	7312	0627	4138	8194	3635	9490	6915	4125	4313
0	2817	6119	7238	8976	9830	2893	9922	4527	8685	8594
3	6470	0244	3449	7797	2714	4003	4171	4784	6250	5430
4	5786	4507	7893	2116	8365	5756	2121	5145	5897	3257
5	6034	0921	6149	0994	2288	8416	3558	0874	9473	8709
9	2153	4421	4608	1970	7133	7343	3208	1245	8242	0386
2	5820	5131	7100	2795	9519	0841	2642	1444	5539	7705
6	1002	9315	9563	9537	4236	1292	5905	0379	8627	7821
7	2388	1769	7778	9549	3819	0661	5352	3559	1264	3982
1	0683	1360	8247	2097	7317	8701	8683	9011	3506	7543

Japanese naval code-book additive page, showing 4-figure numbers to be added to coded figures (non-carry addition). (*NSA document 41709969074927. Courtesy of NSA Cryptological Museum*)

Captain EG Hastings, RN, and the senior officials make occasional visits on liaison work. One of these, Colonel JH TILTMAN is at present in this country [USA] *and I am directing Captain Hastings and Colonel TILTMAN to clear up any misunderstandings which still obtain.*

This is plausible; the US War Department and Navy Department were strictly military with their intelligence sections, and would be trying to liaise with their counterparts, the directors of Military and Naval Intelligence in the UK, not with a branch of MI6, the GC&CS. Stevens was sent as liaison with the War Department and G-2; Hastings was the OP-20-G liaison; and both were, from GC&CS's point of view, valid personnel from one organisation. But to the USA, Hastings' arrival at G-2 where he was not accredited would be a mistake, accentuated by his not getting on well with Strong (and perhaps with the legacy of Stevens' earlier attitude). This impression of Hastings is confirmed by Telford Taylor in his oral history, where (speaking of the end of 1942) he says:[54]

And then [Carter Clarke] *told me that, 'You know these bloody English --we don't get anything they're getting out of the German traffic and that Naval guy they have over here, Captain Eddie Hastings is ****' - his profanity was extreme. But he said, 'They've got all this stuff and we ought to have it.'*

The navy (as Kroner indicated) was unhappy too at Hastings' previous contacts with the FBI and the State Department; the former in particular were receiving information from him which was pertinent to navy matters and which was 'filtered' or delayed by this. But this position was symptomatic of the contrast between the separation of US organisations and the comparative unity at GC&CS. Benson in his account of the situation[55] agrees that this is at the heart of the confusions which emerged.

It is worth considering at this point the situation as it stood as 1942 ended. The US army were concerned that they were not getting the information they needed and felt entitled to know they were engaged with Europe. They were also preventing cooperation with Turing's visit. The US navy (see above for the attitude of Admiral Redman) were accusing the British of withholding vital submarine information which was costing American lives, and were about to proceed with a Bombe-building project which threatened to undermine and sideline the British effort. The liaison officers, Stevens and Hastings, had managed to annoy both US army and navy sections with their attitude earlier in the year. The report by General Kroner was suspicious of British motives and critical of their manoeuvres. The Holden agreement, while making concessions to the USA in the naval area, had not removed many of the concerns. In response the British, led by Travis, were considering counter-measures. The possibility of a serious rupture in Anglo-American cooperation and relationships was a 'clear and present danger'. In the vortex of this situation was John Tiltman.

His responses showed firm but reasoned common sense to both sides. He managed to convince the US army of his fundamental integrity, and persuade the British that there were sensible ways to cooperate.

By 1 January 1943 Tiltman had had a crucial and lengthy meeting with General Strong. The latter informed Marshall[56] of this in a 1 January memo, also explaining that both army and navy concurred in denying Turing access to the scrambler. That same day Edward Travis wired Tiltman urging him to make another effort to get Turing cleared to see the Bell laboratory. Feelings were running high on both sides now, as Travis intimates that he was considering blocking Johnson, who was representing Arlington's army codebreakers in England, and interested in technical items. Tiltman's reply on 2 January explains what had happened at the meeting:

> *He* [Strong] *accepted my word that nothing was deliberately withheld by us. His interest is chiefly on long term intelligence grounds and I suggested that he would get best satisfaction if he applies for access to all decodes and intelligence evaluations at BP for a permanent competent representative of G-2. He is sending Lieutenant Colonel McCORMACK on short visit and will direct him to report on the best method of implementing my suggestion.*

The Turing question was being taken 'to the highest level'.

What had been said in the crucial meeting with Strong? A memo exists in the NSA papers[57] which looks like notes from Tiltman explaining the issues of the four areas listed as 'withheld'. The 'high-speed analyser' (Bombe) was fully outlined in 1941, shown to Colonel Bicher and Toner, and fully studied by Kullback on his visit. The special German submarine machine (surely the 4-rotor system?) had been revealed to the navy, whom it concerned. US staff now in England were seeing the

German field traffic. The 'clandestine traffic', the writer says, was less clear and may indeed have been delayed in passing over (it may well refer to the monitoring of Abwehr and similar material by BP) but 'I believe this has been cleared up.' The Slavic material appeared to have been Russian SIGINT, which had been officially discontinued after the German invasion of June 1941. The writer of these notes mentions that the US army Bombe was 'not known to me till 5/1/43' – which is what Tiltman's position was. These notes, if passed on to Strong and others in January, as it appears they were, certainly answer the points of concern voiced by Carter Clarke and Marshall in December. They read like notes of Tiltman's words.

It was now time also to take a stand with the British upper echelons. On 4 January Travis told Tiltman[58] to refer McCormack to the Director of Military Intelligence, and that 'Director' – presumably Menzies – 'does not (repeat not) approve [of a GC&CS-based US representative].' Tiltman's reply on the 5th shows his preparedness to stand up to senior people where he felt it necessary. It also reflects the US army's slowness to accept Arlington's advice:

> *Does he* [Menzies] *understand that G-2 under Strong has complete control of Y policy? Recent serious misunderstanding in matter of Turing and suspicion of our sincerity arise largely from G-2's reluctance to take advice on policy from Arlington experts with whom all our contact has been hitherto. I am convinced there is a danger of further misunderstandings unless G-2 is placed firmly in picture at BP… Situation is becoming involved and I feel it is necessary to adopt a realistic attitude.*

Another memo dated the same day, apparently by Tiltman himself though not signed, and referring to Menzies as Director, GC&CS, underlines the importance of General Strong's role linking the army and SIGINT, and underlines his trustworthiness. McCormack should be received by GC&CS and not diverted to DMI (Military Intelligence).

On the same day (5 January) Dill wrote[59] to Marshall. Tiltman had reported back on his crucial meeting, and that mutual trust was established. Strong had told Tiltman that the Turing matter was now out of his hands. Marshall wrote back the following day, and while it was disappointing that the Turing matter was not resolved (it was 'beyond the War Department' in its ramifications), Strong was persuaded by

Marshall that there was risk in sending British ULTRA material directly to the USA and this should not be pressed too far.

On 4 January, Tiltman and Turing had also been finally brought up to speed on the new design of the army bombe, which was to be a very different design from the navy ones.

This was the so-called 'Madame X' device. It was not to be fully ready before July 1943, but consisted of a number of 'frames' about 8 feet high and 6 feet long which used telephone selector switches instead of rotating wheels (as the British and navy bombes did). A 'crib' of about sixteen letters could be tried.

> *An electric impulse was sent through successive frames. The reciprocal board, representing possible* steckers, *furnished a series of return paths through which the current flooded back to other levels of the ENIGMA chain and eventually back to the test relays. At wrong settings, all twenty-six paths would usually have current indicating no true single reciprocal circuit existed. Accordingly the machine stepped to the next setting, continuing through the cycle or* 26^3 *or 17,576 settings, testing all possible* stecker *assumptions at every setting. When one or more of the test relays failed to get current the machine stopped and a recording device printed a record.*[60]

The device could take ten minutes to do a 'run', somewhat faster than a conventional Bombe, but only half a second to change the equivalent of the rotor order – very time-consuming on the British machine where up to 100 or so wheels had to be changed and their rear brushes carefully checked.

Tiltman's reaction[61] was that 'the Army and GC&CS had better get together'. The army promptly sent requests to BP asking for intercepts and cribs to be sent. Tiltman had to explain (somewhat disingenuously, as Budiansky sees it) the concerns the British had over security and interference with further exploitation of material if it were sent overseas – though navy material was already now being sent. It was more convincing to suggest, as was quietly done, that because of long-standing British expertise and experience with German Enigma (the indexes of Hut 3, for example, had been built up over the course of the war and could not be duplicated) this field should be left to them to explore, while the Americans took the lead in other areas, especially the Far East. But the barriers to full disclosure here were to extend to these other areas of 'co-operation'. Speaking of sharing success with Japanese code breaks, Tiltman says:[62]

> *The cryptanalysts had difficulty in getting permission to hand this bit of information on to us. This was a particularly foolish incident, because it was broken into in Australia and India. Everybody who handled the thing got on to this there and we had a liaison officer, my very good friend, Geoffrey Stevens, who wrote a very amusing paper headed, 'Odd Behavior At A Hall', obviously trying not, trying to obey their instructions not to pass this information on, but to let them know it was done personally.*

On 7 January Dill wrote[63] again to Marshall. For once his letter was harder in tone and he was concerned about frankness between the parties. It was easier in Britain, he said, because the dealings were with just one organisation (GC&CS), while the US had several sections. Marshall's recent letter, he felt, deviated from true reciprocity: the British would show the Americans everything but reserve the right to refuse to allow 'exploitation' in the USA of ultra-secret information unless convinced of the need. The position, Dill indicated, could affect the navy where exchange is vital – a clear threat to withhold ULTRA derived from Shark and the like.

Moves seem now to have been made on both sides. Tiltman received a message, probably from Menzies' office (and perhaps responding to Tiltman's clear advice to be more realistic), to be forwarded to Strong, expressing regret about misunderstandings involving Travis's rather threatening message of 4 January and confirming that Eisenhower, as relevant commander, was receiving all relevant RSS material. The same day McNarney messaged the British staff mission that G-2 had been instructed to permit Turing to visit the Bell laboratories to see (but not 'exploit') the devices.

In the course of these exchanges it appears that Travis had the 'bright idea' of sending a huge contingent of British cryptanalysts to the USA to work alongside their US counterparts,[64] and Tiltman had to use all his powers of persuasion (and a preparedness to go to higher authority if his concerns were not reported) to get his reservations expressed on the practicability of this move – which the Americans in any event rejected.

It was clear from these developments that clearer policy on army cryptology exchange, limitations and exploitation on both sides of the Atlantic would be needed. Friedman wrote a report in February[65] stressing the value of having material to exploit on the new army Bombe – in the course of which he noted that Tiltman 'felt bad' because of lack of consultation over the development. Strong wrote on 17 February to Marshall outlining the advantages of having such material, and Marshall referred him to Hastings, who took this to Menzies, GC&CS and the British Chief of Staff on 26 February.

All this led to agreement signed in draft by General Strong[66] dated 1 March 1943 and finally confirmed in June. General Strong had clearly removed his earlier veto on sharing information. Tiltman had had, on the one hand, to convince the Americans of the sincerity of British motives and, on the other hand, to persuade the British of the reasonableness of the American requests. That he had succeeded to a great extent is a tribute to his character.

The text,[67] the basis of what is often known as the BRUSA (BRitain-USA) agreement, defined spheres of leadership for each party and how materials were to be shared. Key clauses included:

(2) The U.S. will assume as a main responsibility the reading of Japanese Military and Air codes and ciphers…

(3) The British will assume as a main responsibility the reading of German and Italian Military and Air codes and ciphers…

(6) British or U.S. Commanders-in-Chief, Military or Air, will receive all Special Intelligence necessary to them for the conduct of their operations from either British or U.S. centers as may be mutually agreed. Liaison officers will be appointed as desired for facilitating this. They will be given full access to all decodes…

(11) All intelligence available from decodes shall be made available to Liaison officers, and if they deem necessary it will be exchanged between London and Washington. These Liaison officers will be specially appointed and given full facilities for this purpose.

The agreement made fundamental statements about the relationship. Each side was to give full access to the others' liaison officers. Sharing both of technical code information and derived intelligence was to be full. For the British this meant concessions from GC&CS, hitherto extremely guarded about allowing information out. Appendix 'A' made it clear that US personnel would come, work and participate at BP. For GC&CS this was very much a change of ethos. It was a remarkable agreement, to share such intimate matters with another nation, one whose codes the British had been secretly breaking only a few years before. It set a course for future history and policy for decades.

It is hard to see anyone other than Tiltman with the expertise and 'qualifications' (technical and personal), as well as possessing the respect and integrity, to handle these discussions. Tiltman's role was particularly valuable in handling the relationship between Hastings and Stevens and their US counterparts. Dill's contribution too was vital: he was willing to 'get tough' at the right time, after striving for agreement with Marshall. The US held most of the cards regarding industrial and economic resources, so arguing the British case was difficult. Without Tiltman and Dill in the places they were, there might have been complete breakdown, with profound consequences for future agreements and relationships. He 'could be said to have contributed personally to the ultimate creation of the most secret special relationship' (Bradley Smith).

Amid all this had been a conference, held in January 1943, between Britain, the USA and Canada, regarding diplomatic and commercial traffic.[68] Tiltman, along with Kenneth Maidment (a GC&CS member who was linked to the British Security Co-ordination team in the USA), and Major Drake from Canadian Military Intelligence, met their counterparts (including Friedman, Rowlett and Telford Taylor, then a major in US military Special Branch) to agree on responsibilities in this area.[69] Denniston had achieved considerable success in his revised role, as William Friedman was to find in the spring. Agreement was reached on exchanges of information on intelligence and what was being monitored; the USA was anxious to have more of a role in this. Maidment and Major Brown for the US took on the work of establishing the exchanges. The formal meeting took two hours and in its diplomatic area was a contrast to the military negotiations.

It was in late April of 1943 that Tiltman felt able to convene a conference[70] at BP to discuss further army developments, progress in breaking Japanese army codes, including new success with the Japanese Army Air code 3366 (see Chapter 5), organisation of areas of responsibility for interception and liaison arrangements. His team had made inroads by April 1943, and this followed further success against army codes by March of that year. A new Army Air section was formed in the Japanese section at BP following the work done to break in during the spring.

But continuing difficulties with American liaison (or rather, lack of it) in the navy areas of the Far East made life difficult. The BRUSA agreement was between the US army and Britain, and did not encompass navy matters, the two forces being distinct (and rivals) in America. The US navy team in Melbourne, Australia, which had come from the Philippines after evacuation, was led by Lieutenant Rudi Fabian, who was apparently antagonistic to sharing material with non-US-led people.[71] In this he was backed by Admiral Redman, whose responsibilities included directorship of Naval Communications in this area. Tiltman was therefore having to ensure that there would be agreements on future cooperation, with sharing out of priorities and avoiding duplication, against a background of suspicion.

But he had been able to continue liaising with the US army, and in particular with Friedman at the army code centre, Arlington Hall. Once the interruption of full communication with the army codebreakers seemed to have been ended early in 1943, Friedman was able to pay a visit to Britain. He arrived at BP in April with Telford Taylor who was to lead on the intelligence-gathering side – thus fulfilling the essentials of what Tiltman had insisted was important three months earlier.

Tiltman's role in this visit was as facilitator and negotiator. Friedman states:[72]

> *On Monday, May 3, we made our first visit to Bletchley Park, arriving there on the noon train. We were met at the station by Colonel Tiltman, who took us to Commander Travis' office. There we had a few minutes discussion relative to their organization, sources of raw material, methods of getting the latter to BP, and its routing thereafter. We were informed at this preliminary conference that we were to be permitted to see everything at BP except Naval material. This latter decision, we were informed, had been made at the request of our own Navy, for reasons best known to them… The afternoon was spent by me in discussions with Colonel Tiltman and some of his assistants, at the end of which Colonel Tiltman took the three of us on a quick external survey of the buildings at BP.*

Friedman's diary[73] also shows that on this day Tiltman found the time to discuss the SSF device, and variant gadgets.

The conference itself began three days later, on 7 May. Friedman writes:

> *Commander Travis, who was about to depart for Washington, then asked me to act as chairman, an honour which I declined in favour of Colonel Tiltman, in accordance with the requirements of protocol. After lunch the conference reconvened and began its work. My next few days were taken up with this work and a copy of the minutes of the several meetings held have already been received.*

Protocol it might have been, but it also indicates the recognition of authority in Tiltman's role between the various parties.

Friedman's diary[74] now demonstrates Tiltman's continued involvement with his visitors and the conference. The next day (Saturday, 8 May) saw them in conference again (over Japanese matters), and that evening Friedman was Tiltman's guest at his home, which at that time was close to the Park (he had moved by now from his hotel billet). 'Then Mrs. T and daughter joined us for dinner (prepd. by Mrs. T), very pleasant, substantial food (hot soup, cold meat, hot sausage roll, vegetables, choc pudding)' – Friedman's account is full of culinary details! During the day Travis informed Friedman that he would after all see 'their new E [Enigma] machine', the US navy having raised objections previously (ironic given their previous complaints about non-communication; Friedman found their attitude frustrating).

On Sunday, 9 May 1943, Friedman met Tiltman again, in his research section, along with Major [Gerry] Morgan, and learned of some of their work. They met less formally the following evening after a session with Welchman about Enigma.

Friedman spent some time in London, looking into the diplomatic section, but was in touch with Tiltman on the morning of Sunday, 16 May, to sort out some confusions over information requests (which had apparently been duplicated by Captain Nenk). The next day, scheduled as the last of the main conference, involved all the principals, and ended with a cocktail party at the Tiltmans' house. However, there was more for Tiltman to do for the American guests. He had been in touch with the USA, and on Tuesday, 18 May, he reported, 'Pretty good news about what is going on in [Washington] on the controversial discussions. We shall probably do things on E both over there under George and back at

AH [Arlington Hall].' The pair met on Saturday, 22 May, and again on the 24th, when Tiltman assisted in the preparation of a schedule for the rest of Friedman's time in England. It was at this point that Friedman heard that the US navy was raising objections to his seeing more about the British Enigma equipment. De Grey appears to have conveyed the news; it is tempting to speculate how unhappy he might have been, given his intervention later in the year (see below) to reduce the amount of sharing taking place. Friedman was livid with the navy.

It was Tiltman who rescued another situation on Tuesday, May 25, when Friedman was to visit Beaumanor, only to discover that Colonel Lycett (on paper Tiltman's boss in MI8) knew nothing of this and objected. Tiltman explained the position and Lycett gave the go-ahead. Two days later Friedman was again a guest for dinner at Tiltman's house ('pleasant chat'). There were further sessions where Tiltman met the US party over the next fortnight, before Friedman returned to the States. Friday, 4 June, saw an afternoon session looking at the 17 May agreement in detail. A week later Tiltman was at a meeting in London with Menzies where farewells were said.

While it could be said that much of the wining and dining only represented the necessary wheel-oiling for such guests as Friedman, Taylor *et al*, the general impression of this continual interaction is nevertheless one of detailed business discussion together with the cementing of a positive working relationship of mutual respect and trust. In Budiansky's view, the three (Tiltman, Taylor and Friedman) were the architects of ultimate success in US-UK cooperation.

Agreements with the army on 17 May and confirmed in June – the BRUSA agreement, the landmark of future Anglo-American intelligence cooperation – led to the increasing despatch of intelligence of ULTRA to the US army at Arlington, with Telford Taylor playing a vital role in selecting the key materials to be sent to the USA. The agreement had confirmed US predominance in the Far East and the British in German/European areas, as well as full access to information. Though far from being the last word, the BRUSA agreement was fundamental to US-UK cryptological relations for the rest of the war, and pointed the way to the 'special relationship' to come.

The willing cooperation is reflected in an incident in London while Friedman was visiting the War Office on his way to Beaumanor.[75] He heard about the development of a new version of the Typex machine:

It was described to me and was stated to have an operating speed of 90 characters per minute. When I expressed a desire to see a model, arrangements were at once made with Wing Commander Johnston or the Air Ministry to see one.

Such an immediate and positive response would have been improbable six months earlier.

A letter of 17 June 1943 from Friedman shows the positive tone which Tiltman had created, following the former's visit to BP where he had been given access in depth:

I cannot at the moment undertake to mention by name specifically each of the many persons who gave me so much of their time, but I must not fail to ask you to convey my sincere thanks, especially to Travis, DeGrey, Vincent, Welchman, and Jones. Just as soon as opportunity affords, I hope to write them each a brief note of thanks together with several others whose names will develop as soon as my notes arrive. Please be sure to thank Lycett [Deputy to Director of Military Intelligence in London] *especially and tell him that I expect to write to him very soon.*

There were still hiccups. Nigel de Grey, deputy director at BP, was not happy about sending material so freely to the USA. In the summer of 1943 he negotiated with General Strong to modify the agreement, so that only selected materials were sent back to the USA. Telford Taylor records:[76]

I gather he [Strong] *was a very good man in his day and I know Clarke* [US general] *thought well of him. But Strong certainly did not impress me very much at his performance when he came over at that time… I had sensed before this that Nigel DeGray* [sic - Nigel de Grey, deputy at Bletchley Park] *did not like what was going on with us at all. That he wanted to cut it down to a minimum. And Strong was persuaded by Nigel DeGray, apparently with the toleration of Travis, that they really didn't need much back there. The order of battle was being handled by the American Headquarters and was being set up in England by then, and that, therefore, I should stop sending stuff back. And Strong agreed to that.*

When this was recognized, there were reactions. Taylor goes on:

Well, I wired this, of course, posthaste on my little private channel back to Clarke. Of course he saw red when he saw this happening… I heard from

> *Travis, though not from DeGray, that that was just a bad mistake on our part. We should have known you needed it and so go ahead again.*

This account reveals how much Tiltman was still having to work against in his liaison and negotiation with the Americans. His reply to Friedman's letter (dated 25 July) shows the pressure he and others were under:[77]

> *I see that you managed to get a letter off to me over a month ago and I haven't yet written. But I am afraid my efforts as a correspondent are far below average. I find I have been getting more and more tired and I am going off for a fortnight's holiday with my family. I have taken the precaution of persuading the doctor to give me a medical certificate, not because there is anything much wrong with me, but so that any attempt to drag me back from leave early might be frustrated.*
>
> *Travis also appears very tired. I am afraid these policy trips abroad are no holiday… I imagine you must have felt this too, especially after covering such an enormous amount of ground and in such detail.*

Nevertheless there was now finally agreement about sharing army information in place, and with the arrival of teams of Americans from the end of August 1943 to begin working alongside the British, the fruits of the work began to be garnered. William Bundy's group was the first of several to appear, soon dispersed to Hut 6 and Hut 3 to work at the heart of the organisation. Eventually numbers of US personnel linked to SIGINT came to well over 400.[78] About 80 of them were billeted in Little Brickhill, in the old Manor House.

A year later, and Friedman was writing[79] again, in the same warm tones of previous letters:

> *My sincere congratulations on your advancement to Brigadier. I learned of this well-deserved promotion only recently… I learned that Lieutenant Colonel Jacob has been promoted to Colonel and has taken over much of the administrative duties of the Military wing, thus relieving you of a considerable burden of non-technical activities. If that is the case, I am sure you will probably be much happier and better able to do the sort of work for which you are so eminently qualified.*

Tiltman's reply,[80] a rapidly-scrawled letter, is equally relaxed, confirming his new position as a deputy director (and brigadier) and outlining other changes.

Tiltman had in fact been back to the USA in early 1944, with Travis and others, to discuss further work on Japanese ciphers. Sinkov joined them ('more Australian than the Australians', commented Tiltman),[81] flying in from the Far East; Corderman and General Mark Clark were also there. The outcome of these and further discussions was another agreement later in the year on the sharing of work.

Tiltman sometimes had to overcome residual issues left by others in the field of negotiation and liaison. When meeting with General Strong in 1942–3 he found out that Captain Hastings, British representative in the USA and liaison in SIGINT matters (and later a deputy at BP), was without doubt the General's *bête noire*. Consequently he needed the utmost patience and tact when speaking with the general. He says:[82]

> *We used to have long conversations with General Strong in which he would talk about everything under the sun except Turing. Eventually Brigadier Dykes, who was Staff Officer to our Field Marshal, Sir John Dill, he told me, 'You know, your trouble is that you'll never get anything out of Strong if you take Hastings along with you because he doesn't like Hastings'.*

It was Tiltman also who had to tell Lieutenant Burnett, the British Far East codebreaker who had been involved with JN-25, and was keen to act as liaison officer with Wenger and the US effort in the Pacific, that he would not be considered for this task[83] as he was regarded as 'intolerant' and clashed with or demeaned colleagues.

The interference by de Grey in the matter of what information might be going to America has been described, and would not have helped matters. Throughout this time Tiltman had needed to strike a balance between respect for his superiors and the need to oppose what were in his views mistaken or foolish policies.

The letters to and from Friedman, and the details of the negotiations and disputes underlying the exchange of information, also begin to reveal more of the 'human being' behind the master cryptographer, and to this we must now turn.

Chapter 8

The Human Being

What sort of a man was Tiltman? What were his qualities? In this section we shall try to answer these questions.

Stephen Budiansky has described[1] Tiltman as 'the accidental cryptanalyst par excellence'. For him Tiltman was a man who could see and sense patterns, and would not give up when trying to find something but explore every avenue, every permutation, which was, Budiansky says, 'the hallmark of great codebreakers'. In modern parlance, we might see him as a visual and kinesthetic thinker and learner, and this is borne out by the story Dryden tells of his solution to the German police code (see Chapter 4) by creating a matrix from cork board and card (subsequently remodelled in more permanent materials). Tiltman preferred to write out lots of his own depths; it gave him ideas, he said, as he did it.

His attitude to others around him – one frequently of warmth, helpfulness, generosity and tact – will now be examined.

Gordon Welchman in the early days was indebted to Tiltman for providing him with material support. Welchman[2] had begun work in the Cottages at BP, but his relations with Dilly Knox there were less than rosy (though there is disagreement about the exact nature of this), and according to Welchman's own account he had to remove himself to the newly-acquired Elmers School nearby. Here he was somewhat adrift of information and materials, working only with Tony Kendrick, and even this for a short time only. Welchman[3] wrote that no-one else took much notice in their work 'except Josh Cooper and Colonel Tiltman. Cooper and Tiltman were not only heads of expanding sections, they were both distinguished cryptanalysts.' It was Tiltman who arranged for one of his sergeants to bring Welchman quantities of material from the Chatham intercept station, on which he worked, and from which he became enlightened about the nature of the traffic. It was also Tiltman who helped Welchman to get a visit to Chatham in September 1939, where Welchman met Commander Ellingworth, who showed him how things worked and gave him a clear insight into issues about traffic. This led to the creation of the 'Huts' organisation so vital for the success of BP during the war. Welchman names Tiltman one of the select seniors who 'gave their full support to the plan'.

There were times when Tiltman seemed to embody the impression at Bletchley that rigid formality did not matter much. John Clabby[4] states:

He surprised many with his lack of concern for the mundane protocols of military life, this in spite of the fact that he remained, throughout his life, most military in bearing himself. Upon being recalled to active service in 1939, he readily admitted that he could no longer remember whether his insignia of rank should be mounted above or below the crown on his uniform. He repeatedly drove his adjutant at Bletchley Park, a major consumed with enforcing proper military bearing and decorum, to distraction with his informal practices such as granting weekend passes to subordinates who merely knocked on his door and asked, bypassing the adjutant completely.

Instances of this can be found in the accounts of Bletchley people. Several quote the example of Private William Filby[5] approaching Tiltman, coming to attention with a stamp of the feet and saluting, only for the officer to turn and say, 'I say old boy, must you wear those damned boots?' Filby thus gained the distinction of being authorized to wear battledress with white running-shoes!

'Old boy' seems to have been his term for informal address. Filby experienced it; Henry Dryden experienced it when he was 'asked' to go to the Mediterranean 'for a month, six weeks at the outside, old boy' (the assignment took two years).

Clabby offers[6] the following story to illustrate Tiltman's preference for looking at the human element rather than just the rule-book:

Tiltman, as a senior officer, had to deal with his own chauffeur who had 'borrowed' Tiltman's official vehicle for a tryst with his girlfriend, and then had the misfortune of crashing the vehicle. Tiltman's inclination to deal with the matter quietly and personally had to give way to military propriety, and he was forced to convene and preside over a court-martial, his first. Again, he frustrated his adjutant, and provided mirth for everyone else involved, by constantly asking the major what he was

> *supposed to do next during the proceedings, and by asking the accused if what was happening met with his approval.*

Tiltman's preparedness to be casual with protocol could extend to uniform. He was partial to wearing the KOSB 'trews' with their tartan pattern. But one day[7] he was spotted by two Free French officers at BP as he walked wearing the trews and a completely unrelated ordinary jacket. Their reaction: 'Ce pantalon-là, c'est de rigeur ou de fantasie?'

However, when it came to his formal presentation, Tiltman could sometimes be pernickety, especially where the trews were concerned. There is a letter in the Bletchley archives[8] from the company which provided them:

> *In response to your call today as you raised the question of whether your trews should be worn turned up; we checked this with the official garment and find at the present this is still regulation. We are therefore correcting yours accordingly and hope to let you have them within 24 hours. Regretting this delay.*

Clearly this lapse in protocol was a bridge too far for a man proud of his Scottish regimental background!

Another example of boundary-pushing is apparently found[9] in the recruitment of Dennis Babbage, a Cambridge mathematician known to Welchman who was to prove his worth throughout the war. He was brought into the pre-war training sessions in cryptology but was not immediately contacted when war broke out. There was some concern about limitations on numbers who could be enrolled. But Babbage took the initiative in making contact, and it was Tiltman who 'eventually… "smuggled" him in as a soldier of sorts,' and he joined Hut 6.

Tiltman's kindness has been noted, and Henry Dryden speaks of it being shown to him.[10] Dryden was in France with the liaison group 'Mission Richard', working on such messages as they could (the phoney war at first being his experience). But on 10 May real shooting began and the commander ordered him to 'burn that bloody suit of yours, my boy, and get into a battledress' – necessary to avoid recognition as a specialized civilian if captured – and informed him that he was receiving an emergency commission in the field. He had no idea what the War Office would say.

He was right. The War Office did not start paying him when he returned home, and neither would the Foreign Office now he was enlisted. It was Tiltman whom Dryden approached, and Tiltman arranged for help. A cheque arrived soon after and his pay was sorted in due course (though Dryden says the back-pay was not received until 1941).

Tiltman's concern about the pay and conditions of some other civilian members of his Military Section (compared with those in the services) has already been noted (Chapter 3). Major Thompson was also a victim of pay restrictions and Tiltman tried to intervene on his behalf. The response generally from the upper echelons was that civilians who were recruited as such should continue to serve as civilians (thereby being paid less in effect) – an understandable economic view at the time, but disheartening for some.

Much later, William Lutwiniak[11] recalls another incident which illustrates Tiltman's kindness:

> *The Brig was a shy man, but warm and generous in his friendship. He couldn't do enough for friends. I recall a conversation about nonwork hobbies, and mentioned lapidary; he mentioned weaving, and I asked some questions. Next day there appeared on my desk a book on weaving and operating a hand loom.*

Tiltman's relationship with Dilly Knox has been referred to already (Chapter 3). Knox was clearly someone with whom it could be difficult to sustain a good rapport – Welchman, for example, found himself apparently not liked, though the reasons for this impression are mixed and may result from misunderstanding. In the case of Tiltman there seems to have been sustained good professional mutual respect. Years after the work on 'Mask', Mavis Batey quotes Knox[12] as writing (concerning his work in the section ISK – Illicit Services Knox) in praise of his 'capable' section, and his own determination not to have interference with their approach: 'The Brigadier [Tiltman] was on the whole very cordial' and appreciative of what Knox's team were achieving. Knox noted also Tiltman's preparedness to assist if any difficulties should arise.

Clabby[13] refers to another incidence of Tiltman's thoughtfulness to others, in the 'Lady Macbeth' matter. A German map showing the Luftwaffe North Sea grid system had been captured from an aircraft shot down near Edinburgh and was put on display in Josh Cooper's office. It bore the bloodstains of one of the airmen. Tiltman felt that this could upset the ladies who worked with Cooper, and consulted a colleague with a pathologist's training. As a result, the stains were cleaned without wrecking the map. Cooper thereupon quoted from 'Macbeth':

> *Will all great Neptune's ocean wash this blood*
> *Clean from my hand? No; this my hand will rather*
> *The multitudinous seas incarnadine,*
> *Making the green one red.*

Hence the nickname for the document. In 1940 Tiltman presented the map to Bertrand at one of their meetings, a gesture in response to Bertrand's frankness over their understanding of Enigma at the time.

The same kind of thoughtfulness is attested by Elizabeth Langstaff (later Reid), a senior member of Hut 3 (secretary to Eric Jones) and talented in music and drama. She explained that

> *Colonel John Tiltman rescued me once when I missed the train. I was always missing trains. He was there with his staff car and driver and popped me in the car to get back to the Park.*

Leo Marks[14] tells of his meeting with Tiltman in 1943. Tiltman had been brought in to assess proposed developments in SOE codes, of which Marks was in charge: 'A very decent chap, by all accounts' was the description given by Marks's boss. Marks' own reaction was of 'a large teddy bear of a colonel with amused eyes'.

Tiltman had done his homework and was ready with technical questions. Marks commented flippantly that he had not been a good host, as Tiltman had not done any codebreaking that day and 'might be suffering from withdrawal symptoms', and so embarked with Tiltman on an unbroken message to demonstrate the working of the process under discussion. He marvelled at Tiltman working through the standard processes (four 'movements' as he puts it) but at the equivalent speed of 'a one-minute mile'; Tiltman would then look briefly at the tables they had laid out, and '*calculate in his head which letters would appear in the first line of the message* – an awesome achievement even for a cryptographic supremo' (Marks's emphasis).

Tiltman was clearly committed to the whole process of recruiting and training people for the work. Some aspects of this were less than developed pre-war. Tiltman[15] says:

When I first came to the office, nobody would tell you anything; you had to find out for yourself. Early in the war; fairly early in the war, I devised a training program for the entire department. I don't know why, I think it was really a rather successful idea. We had a course at Bedford for all kinds of people, with all kinds of information, because normally it was a 3-month course. It was supposed to assess what the best use of a particular man was.

Perhaps there is something to be seen of the ex-teacher in this aspect of his character and for years he had regarded the WO approach to induction as flawed (see Chapter 3). He helped to prepare some of the teaching material for the cryptography training. Arthur Maddocks, who ended up in the Testery (Block F) at BP, where work was done on the Tunny messages, says:[16]

There was a good deal of competition between the three of us in working our way through the text book which had been prepared by John Tiltman. This was a brilliant technique, I think, for instructing people in the basics of cryptography. He would set out on one page an idea or a new technique, and he would follow it with exercises. And the exercises were very cleverly worked out so that they didn't all depend on what you had read on that page. Many of them referred to previous pages, that even tempted you to jump ahead and guess what was coming on the next page. So it was a very cleverly constructed work, and it really did take a lot of working through.

Tiltman himself interviewed a number of people who became key to GC&CS. Harry Hinsley was interviewed by him at St John's College, Cambridge, in 1939. Arthur 'Bill' Bonsall, later important in Hut 3 and later still chief of GCHQ, was interviewed[17] on the same visit. In 1940 William Filby remembers being interviewed by him. In an article of 2003, Anne Garside writes:[18]

As Bill had studied German at Cambridge, he found himself being interviewed by a Lt-Colonel John Tiltman who asked him for references. Bill gave the name of Professor F J H Stratton of Cambridge University, which caused Tiltman to shout 'Tubby!' and in walked Lieutenant Colonel Stratton. Stratton commented on my dirty uniform, then turned to Tiltman and exclaimed, 'You want him, John?' John did want him, and Bill spent the next six years working in Intelligence.

Tiltman's role as leader in recruitment was formalized in 1940. In 1942 it was Hugh Denham – 'How is your health?' Tiltman asked, and 'Do you have any religious scruples about reading other people's correspondence?' Bill Sibley[19] was interviewed in September that year as a Balliol student, 'a five-minute one-to-one interview'. In 1943 Julius Gould (also Balliol and later a professor of sociology) was the candidate. He says:[20]

> *I was interviewed by a very remarkable and gifted man named Brigadier John Hessell Tiltman; I was a mere civilian of 19 years old. He was sitting in the wooden hut and he introduced me to the man next to him, a kind of secretary called Captain Kaye. They got me talking by asking me questions about what my interests were, things like crossword puzzles and so on. This took about half an hour while they assessed me, after which they said I would be hearing from them in due course.*

Sometimes Tiltman worked through college tutors. Jon Cohen[21] thinks it was prodding by Tiltman that brought his name to BP's attention, and this may have been Maurice Wiles' experience too, along with Mervyn Jones and Roland Oliver. In 1943 Hugh Melinsky[22] was similarly recruited in Cambridge before going on the Japanese course and thence to the Far East.

American visitors to BP offer comment from a different cultural perspective, but seem to appreciate equally Tiltman's qualities. Kullback was to offer the following comment:[23]

> *and, of course, Tiltman was a real gem and his capabilities. The things he could do all by himself and what he had done finding the books which some of the agents were using... He spent quite a number of hours in some of the libraries in Europe hunting for these key books and finding them.*

This account of his methodical persistence, so well summed up by Budiansky (see above), can be seen in Tiltman's own account[24] of searching for keys used in the Russian codes of the 1920s, and finding them in obscure English poets from a volume in the British Museum (where the British Library was housed at the time – see Chapter 2).

Commander Howard Campaigne, USN, served at BP from late 1944 until the end of the war. He was part of Block F, the Newmanry, and became involved with the TICOM mission material (see Chapter 9) at the war's end. He met Tiltman and was impressed with his work, including the break into the Fish material. He says:[25]

He also had administrative duties, which he apparently carried off pretty well, there at Bletchley Park. And of course, he was a human being who was very pleasant to deal with. He was very nice... Tiltman was a real gentleman. I was proud to have known him.

US codebreaker Juanita Moody points out[26] his willingness to do things 'out on a limb' at times. Speaking of a wartime analysis of a particularly intractable system, she explained that neither the US nor the British were ready to document the issue:

You will never have an admiral or anybody at GCHQ... one person did write this up, and you showed me that was Brigadier Tiltman. That was just the time when I was caught up in other things and didn't get around to it. But his is strictly a technical journal treatment of it, but I take my hat off to him. He was a very... he was the one person that would have done it.

And Wilma Davis (formerly Berryman) worked with the US army codebreakers at Arlington and met Tiltman a few times in the USA. She says[27] in connection with him:

As a matter of fact, Mr Black Chamber [Herbert Yardley, who ran the US 'Black Chamber' codebreakers in the 1920s until they were closed down, and later wrote a book on the subject] *was running a restaurant up on K street. I went there with the Brig, when the Brig (John Tiltman) used to come over. I was single and widowed and he was so sweet. He used to take me out to dinner. One night he said, let's see if we can go find... Herbert Yardley, Herbert O. So we went and found Herbert O. and his wife was at the cash register. We had dinner.*

This reflects an unusual aspect of Tiltman's life in the USA – the social side – which apart from his time with Friedman is not well documented. Mrs Tiltman's reaction to this is not recorded. Wilma subsequently married John Manson in 1949 and they moved to Canada.

Of his relationship and work with William Friedman much has already been said. Budiansky's view[28] was that the emergence of the 'special relationship' was a 'remarkable story, which reflects greatly to the credit of three men in particular, William Friedman, Telford Taylor and John Tiltman'. In May 1942 when Tiltman sent Friedman[29] a batch of cryptanalytical technical papers and methods, he also enclosed a book about the archaeology of India, knowing Friedman to be interested in antiquities of various kinds. In 1943 Friedman was a guest of the Tiltmans on a number of occasions while he was visiting England, and his gift in July to Tiltman's wife in token of thanks was much appreciated.[30] These simple gestures are more than formality; they are indicative of warmth and friendship beyond the professional association. The closeness of purpose comes out in one matter arising from Friedman's diary[31] of his visit in May 1943: it was Tiltman that he turned to when an issue regarding Turing came up. An awkward message to Washington was going to be needed, and the pair of them worked out the draft text, before getting approval from other seniors and having it encoded and sent. 'Now comes the deluge… I hope not', commented Friedman. The letter sent by Friedman to Tiltman[32] in August 1944 also reflects the warmth of the relationship, as well as the generosity of Tiltman:

> *We were all so very much charmed by the print you sent us and which will be framed in due course. I dare say you are getting a great deal of fun out of your mezzotint work. I wish I could do something like that but instead I have been practicing* [sic] *a bit with our newly organized symphony orchestra. If I didn't feel so rusty on the violin I probably would get more fun out of it and in the hot weather it is difficult to find the energy to practice at home to wear away the rust.*

Against the comments described here it is possible to raise some questions about Tiltman's 'first impressions'. A reading of his 1942 report on the codebreaking operations in the USA[33] suggests a man who did not suffer fools gladly – he is blunt in assessing lack of skills and capacity at G-2 and OP-20-G; he was not impressed by French codebreakers. If he spoke to Agnes Driscoll (given her distinguished career) as directly as he implies, there is little doubt she would have bridled, at the least. Lewin has described him as 'abrasive', and codebreakers such as Gerry Roberts were overawed by him on first meeting. We have seen examples of his 'straight talking', including to his superiors where he was convinced that he was right. He could at times feel aggrieved, and we shall see an example of the discord with Admiral Redman continuing after the war's end (and his fury, much later, at Winterbotham's revelations). The evidence from accounts of him by others seems to suggest that such times were very much a minority.

The NSA website contains a few sound recordings of Tiltman's voice, talking about various aspects of his work.[34] Hearing these, one gets the impression of a well-spoken, educated man of reasonable class. He does not sound forceful or bombastic at all, but genteel and calm. He sounds closer to Marks' 'teddy bear' than a brigadier, though of course some of the recordings date from his last years.

Who disliked him? Admiral Redman, perhaps, is the only person to sustain serious disagreement with him. Agnes Driscoll also seems not to have liked him, though their acquaintance was brief and intermittent. It is hard to find anyone else. Even if there were initial differences, Tiltman generally won over others to a position, if not of affection, then at least to one of admiration and respect.

There is one area of the work with GC&CS during the war in which Tiltman's judgement has been called into question, and that is his attitude to the application of machinery to cryptology.

It has been suggested that Tiltman opposed the introduction of sorting equipment and Hollerith machines. At Bletchley Park, Freddie Freeborn's Hollerith section was initially in Hut 7, and later transferred to Block C (1943) where it became a vital centre for the rest of the war. The Hollerith machines, which worked with punched cards, produced and processed the datasets so increasingly vital for BP analysis. The system, importantly, could collate patterns of letters emerging from enciphered material of various kinds, so that searches could later be made when similar material came to the codebreakers, who could save time by rapid machine sorting. Edward Simpson describes[35] their importance in the routine attack on JN-25, where the Hollerith system could record and analyse 'good groups', probable values of the additive book which had appeared before, and their relationship with other groups. This allowed indices of groups to be compiled and searched, speeding up the decryption. The machines could be used similarly for recording and analysing outputs from Enigma, so that searches for previous patterns could be made to find rotor settings; there was a plan[36] to use the machines for finding repeat of Steckerboard settings more rapidly in 1944. Tiltman was a man who liked to do things for himself; he preferred to write out all his own depths, because for him it produced fresh ideas and insights; and he had the patience to persist for days or weeks. In 1978[37] he said:

> *I had nothing to do with the introduction of scanning machinery, Hollerith machinery. To my shame, I have to admit that back in about 1934–1935, a man named Guy Liddell* [who became prominent in the late- and

> post-war work of MI5 and MI6 and rose to be director] *in the SIS, took me down and gave me a demonstration in Hollerith and I didn't understand at the time its application to our work. I had so little – well, by then Sir Edward Travis introduced a rival form of the scanning machine into the office… and I did a test and I found that I could beat* [the operator] *in time in an analysis job. This was a completely unfair test, of course, because the development of machinery is not dependent on one person pounding one machine which is what happened to her… When we did take on Hollerith, it was done on Sir Edward Travis' responsibility and we approached it in a slightly different way.*

In his interview[38] where he shared a platform with Prescott Currier, he dates the Hollerith encounter earlier – 1932–3 – and simply says, 'I didn't think it would help us.' This is a little different from actively blocking the use, though his opinion would certainly have influenced movement on the possibility of machine methods.

Other factors, such as availability, may well have been more important. Michael Loewe,[39] Japanese codebreaker at BP, says:

> *At the outset we had very little opportunity to use Hollerith machinery, as that was reserved for German and Italian problems. After the Italians left the war there was a little leeway and we found that long lists of code groups and meanings, which we would have compiled by hand, could be transferred onto Hollerith cards. In addition, the messages we received could be put onto Hollerith, which made it possible to do certain things rather more quickly than otherwise.*

So shortages might have been the heart of the matter, at least earlier; Hollerith machines were leased rather than purchased and were dependent on suppliers.

Ferris points out[40] that in 1939 Tiltman began using some kind of 'sorter' to help in the work on revised Japanese codes. In 1944 Tiltman was called in[41] to the JN-25 team, where simultaneous changes in the codebook and additive book, and the introduction of a stencil super-encipherment process, had shut out the codebreakers. He recommended a full-scale indexing of code groups by the 'Freebornery' to assist searches (the effort was in vain). Clearly by this time he was supportive of such processes. Around this time he also assisted Welchman in assessing the American M-228 machine for its security (see Chapter 9). He has also said:[42]

> *But we did a lot of work on GEE* [a German one-time-pad system used later in the war]. *In those days, we had Hollerith machinery, but the Hollerith man, Freeborn, used to come in at night and work with me on it. It was very late in the war. How much it affected the outcome of the war, I'm afraid I don't know.*

After the war he was involved in US-UK negotiations about a range of machinery (including the future US-UK machines for the 'special relationship') and clearly was not only comfortable with but also knowledgeable about what machines could do.

Currier[43] has said,

> *There were certain things that he could not do, and admits that he cannot do, just the way I do. High-level mathematics is absolutely out of his camp. He does have no use for computers, and while he's certainly willing to use their product, he would much rather sit down with a pencil and paper, and he has solved some extremely difficult problems, some that many others have failed at, and he's been doing it for a very long time, and he has a sense (an inborn sense, I think) that gives him a true feel of the problem by the time that he is gotten into it far enough to start forming conclusions which is something that many people never acquire; I mean, they can on working for the rest of their lives and punch buttons in the computer, and still not really get a feel for the problem and know precisely what lay in the minds of the people who produced it in the first place. As a result, he has, for instance, he did, certainly during the war and before the war, he was, for instance, their chief cryptographer, and this means that he was not only a cryptanalyst, but he did, in fact, produce quite a few systems for their use… not machine systems, mind you, but hand systems which were beautifully devised, and he has a great, great ability in this regard.*

It may be arguable (given for example the account of his experience in the 1930s' demonstration above) that Tiltman was sceptical of the value of automation in the earlier stages, perhaps because it might undermine the importance of acquiring essential fundamental skills, knowledge and concepts in cryptology. But it is clear that by the later stages of the war this attitude was no longer the case.

Chapter 9

Towards Victory, and Post-war

In between the vicissitudes of the US-UK liaison work, the growth and development of BP and its work meant changes in organisation and structure. The 'debs and dons', if such a reductive view of the nature of BP was ever applicable, was certainly a distant echo. A highly-organized intelligence factory was evolving by the end of 1943, in which codebreaking was no longer the only essential task. This could have an impact on groups and individuals. We shall examine how Tiltman needed to adjust to the changes.

Tiltman's own position within the organization remained to an extent 'special'. In June 1943 Friedman reported back to the USA on his visit to Britain. He mentions:[1]

> *Another interesting thing to note is that although the military wing which comprises No. IV and No. VI Intelligence Schools of GC&CS belonged to MI-8A, Colonel Tiltman, the commander of the military wing reports directly to Colonel Lycett and not to the Chief of MI8, Colonel Vernham.*

Lycett in turn reported to the Director of Military Intelligence (at the time Major General Davidson), which indirectly reflects the importance of Tiltman's position. Friedman also refers to Tiltman's role as general 'troubleshooter' for cryptological problems:

> *When a problem requiring cryptanalytic techniques does arise it is referred to Colonel Tiltman in his capacity as 'Chief Cryptographer to the War Office'. As a specific example, he was given the task of ascertaining the security value of the 'Stencil Subtractor Frame'* [SSF] *for general communication purposes (not for synoptic weather reports) and when I was at BP the research group under Major Morgan was just completing a rather detailed study of the security afforded by the device.*

The 'Major Morgan' here is no doubt Gerry Morgan, senior officer in the Research group at BP (working upstairs in the Mansion) which Tiltman oversaw, who played an important role in work which led to the breaking of Hagelin and Tunny material among others. See Chapter 4 for reference to the SSF which Tiltman worked on.

In April 1943, in the face of continued Italian resistance, Tiltman presented a report[2] on the state of Italian codebreaking. There were serious problems with the high-grade ciphers and little prospect of reading them (mainly, it would appear, because not enough depth of traffic could be obtained – these were 5-figure additive systems with daily-changing super-encipherment). Tiltman asked whether it should be policy to pursue them, and if not, what to do about continuing lower-grade coverage. The latter were in some cases police codes, and some were not super-enciphered. One ('Genova') was harvested in some quantity and produced worthwhile intelligence, in Tiltman's view. There was also the hope that if Balkan work were to be increased, it might produce enough material to make an attack on the high-grade systems.

The paper is informative of the kinds of cost-benefit thinking necessary throughout BP's time – how best to use limited resources and where to place priorities when choices have to be made. Even in 1943 such decisions are having to be frequently made.

Tiltman had been very much involved with parts of Friedman's visit to Britain at this time. Friedman's diary[3] for 24–25 May shows him meeting Tiltman *inter alia* to help the planning of the visit; Tiltman hosted him for dinner on 27 May.

The fruits of the work done by Tiltman and Tutte could be seen in June and July 1943 on the Russian front. In mid-March the Russians had pushed forward against the Germans, creating a bulge in their front towards Kursk. Hitler determined to eliminate this; the plan became Operation Citadel. Decodes of the Tunny material, sent on the link between Army Group South and Berlin between April and July went to the Russians[4] (probably twice: once in summary form to disguise the source from BP, and again from the Russian spy John Cairncross – working in Hut 3 at BP – perhaps in original form). It enabled the Russians to prepare, and to deliver a pre-emptive air strike[5] just two hours before the start as German units were massing and inflicting damage. The Russians were able to fend off the German effort, and Citadel was called off after less than a fortnight, with serious losses in men and especially tanks. Thereafter (together with the aftermath of the Battle of

Stalingrad earlier) the initiative in the East lay with the Russians. The Tiltman-Tutte success made an important contribution to this.

Personnel and promotion issues also figured in Tiltman's in-tray. At this time he was asked[6] for comment regarding possible promotion for two captains (P.C. Palmer and I.P. Turner). The former was a senior member of the team turning recovered intelligence into signals in the language of the services, a demanding task for accuracy, clarity and promptness. Turner was head of the signals section where efficient distribution in a complex network was vital. It was Turner who gained the recommendation.

In June 1943 there was much discussion[7] about closer linking of cryptography and the W/T (TA) work. Tiltman, with Welchman among others, submitted papers on the subject to management. July 1943 was also a time where the military wing at BP was being considered for reorganisation. In a lengthy memorandum[8] the argument against separation of WT intelligence from cryptography is emphasized, because of the way in which these activities interact and make sense of the other in producing information. The following October[9] the Y-service role and its organisational relationship with others was again under discussion, and again Tiltman was involved. The issue of who controlled different aspects of the process was unclear (e.g. did the cryptographers control the 'Y' service actions? – did the directors of 'Y' control the military work at BP?). Travis's response[10] to Tiltman's concerns shows that he felt the current practice was different from the organisation plan (dating from 1942) and he stressed Tiltman's seniority in all the work of the military wing at BP. MI8 (Military Intelligence at the WO) provided military personnel for BP and 'are the WO authority for providing the "Y" stations.' The discussion reflects the rapid growth of GC&CS as an organisation, with consequent issues of management, change and interaction.

Tiltman's wide range of responsibility emerges in another brief note, this time from Freddie Jacob, in October 1943.[11] Colonel Jacob had been sent earlier (after deputising for Tiltman in the military section) to be director of the Combined Bureau Middle East (CBME), but in late 1942 plans were made to bring him back within the MI6 orbit[12] and he was returned under BP's direct control and in October 1943 was reporting to Tiltman on Romanian codes and ciphers.

Also in October Tiltman paid another visit to the USA, sent as consultant to the British army representatives in Washington. He was a visitor for Laurence Safford, who was now working in naval communications linked to cryptography. Tiltman told him[13] that Safford's prediction about the vulnerability of British Naval Cypher no. 3 had proved to be correct, and that 'our faces are very red'. It had in fact been much earlier in 1943 that the realisation had dawned – perhaps faces were red enough already. Safford, who had been ousted from his work in cryptography, may have derived some satisfaction from this. Safford's talents were to be used again, as his name appears in the 1950 US-UK conference notes (on which see Chapter 10).

An unusual and perhaps sensitive matter[14] fell onto Tiltman's desk in October 1943. The British, including SOE, had been helping the Free French by sending coded messages to the French agents, in codes prepared by the Free French, and decoded versions of these were given to the British to show what was being sent. However the SOE had discovered that the French coded messages contained additional material not covered in the plaintexts supplied. Tiltman was asked to 'put your experts onto it' to check that others were not being 'cheated' in this way!

In February 1944 Tiltman was involved in discussions with MI8 (the signals intelligence section dealing with Y-service – radio interception – matters), regarding likely requirements from Germany when they surrendered.[15] This was a topic looming large a year later when the TICOM missions went to Germany at the close of the war, but would have been pertinent to smaller-scale occasions earlier. A draft of ideas had been drawn up and Tiltman was asked to comment, which he did.

At the same time, he was being consulted over other administrative matters in his role as head of military. Liaison between ever-increasing areas and sections seems to have been a priority issue. He was asked about cooperation between British and Polish SIGINT sections (the latter at Stanmore); and on a more mundane level the organisation of tents and huts for SIGINT outstations at SHAEF and in the Mediterranean.

Tiltman went to the USA[16] in March 1944 as part of the British delegation to a conference at Arlington Hall. With Tiltman were Commander Travis, Edward Crankshaw and Joe Hooper. Crankshaw[17] was by now a lieutenant colonel in the Intelligence Corps, and a leading figure in the management of Traffic Analysis at BP; his previous Russian experience may also have been useful. A formal photograph of the main participants survives in the Arlington archives.

The Director of Military Intelligence at the War Office, Major General Francis Davidson, wrote to Tiltman[18] in April 1944, with appreciation of the work of BP's deputy director. The surviving acknowledgement refers to '[the work] achieved by whole-hearted co-operation between three major sections here and the Intercept stations… and American officers working here.'

D-Day was to see no special contribution from Tiltman recorded at the time. His importance lay in the information which derived from his earlier work. One example can be seen from a decoded Tunny message sent on the 'Jellyfish' link from Berlin to Paris in late April 1944 and detailing a tour of inspection of Panzer units by General Guderian. This gave the dates for his visit, the unit to be inspected, and its location. 2 Panzer group, for example, due to be inspected on April 28, were based at Amiens, while 12 SS Panzer, to be seen the day after, were at Evreux – both within potential range of intervention at Normandy, if transport and communications were functioning. The 155 Reserve (9 Panzer, to be inspected 6 May) was south near Nîmes, the 179 Reserve (116 Panzer, scheduled for 8 May) was just west of Paris and had to be reckoned with. Pinpointing the position of these enemy forces was priceless for the D-Day planners, and the ability, thanks to the legacy of Tiltman's break into Tunny in 1941, Tutte's analysis of the Lorenz structure from this, and the emergence of machines to speed up the analytical process ('Robinson' and 'Colossus') was supremely important in the planning and execution of Operation Overlord.

Tiltman's scrawled letter to Friedman of 28 August 1944[19] shows that by this date his position at BP had changed. He was no longer (in his words) 'commandant' of the GC&CS Military section (his role was taken over by Freddie Jacob); he was now deputy director (DD4), along with Hastings, de Grey and Bradshaw. His promotion and change of role was raised in June 1944. Menzies wrote to Major General Sinclair, then Director of Military Intelligence (DMI), proposing Tiltman's move from management of the military section and to be part of MI6 as chief cryptographer. Sinclair in turn suggested Tiltman's promotion to brigadier on 29 June. Perhaps it was this change of role and promotion that led to him using Room 11 in the 'Mansion' at BP later in 1944, with Professor Vincent (who had been assisting him as cryptography co-ordinator since 1942) next door in room 10.[20]

At the time, Tiltman was in contact with James 'Hamish' Blair-Cunynghame[21] regarding the introduction of a new German army code, which was due to be introduced in August. Blair-Cunynghame had had experience in the field in 1942–3 in the African campaigns and had become O/C to No. 5 Intelligence School.[22] He was now keen to see a research group organized in preparation. As chief cryptanalyst at BP Tiltman was also now involved in the assessment of the American M228 coding machine, working with Gordon Welchman (promoted the previous year from his role in Hut 6 to directorate level, with supervision of machine devices at BP) to assess its security value.

Tiltman's 28 August letter was a reply to Friedman's note[23] of 1 August. Friedman had heard that a group led by Travis was to visit, and asked if Tiltman was to be included. He indeed went[24] with Menzies, Travis and Welchman to the USA again, in September 1944. The purpose of the visit was to consider arrangements for the future and after the war, in particular with regard to the approach to Russian codes, which were apparently being surreptitiously monitored by GC&CS despite Churchill's instruction to cease doing so when Operation Barbarossa began in June 1941 (see below). Wenger[25] in the USA, by now high up in the navy hierarchy, had encouraged the reading of Russian material in 1943, and (perhaps even earlier) Rowlett from the army SIS had likewise pursued some watching of Russian material. Tiltman's earlier expertise on Russian ciphers and their style probably served him well here.

At about this time, Travis and Redman agreed further aspects of exchange of Japanese material, bringing in the British group based at HMS *Anderson* near Colombo. This group had been starved of materials by American reluctance to share but changes in the Japanese JN-25 system had baulked the US navy effort as much as the British. Hugh Alexander, Turing's deputy and later Head of Hut 8 Naval Enigma at BP, was switched from Hut 8 to help and Tiltman was called in to advise in late summer 1944. The result of the consultations was the agreement of October,[26] which further defined the UK-US relationship and ensured participation from the British in the work.

That autumn, Menzies set up a committee to look at aspects of post-war organisation for GC&CS and its relationship with MI6. Along with

Travis, Hinsley and Welchman, Tiltman was a member. This appears to relate to the setting up of the Bland Committee, which was to report on the future of MI6 more widely. The Bland report first draft was submitted in October 1944, so it is not clear how much time GC&CS views had to inform the proceedings. Smith indicates[27] that GC&CS preferred to have close links with MI6 in a single intelligence-producing organisation under Menzies.

Tiltman had his own view on the future. He submitted comments[28] in October 1944 where he stated his belief that there should be a single intelligence body, along the lines of the GC&CS thinking. It should be in MI6 under Menzies.

The Bland Report agreed that MI6 and GC&CS should be under one director, but not that they should be fused. Its final form was submitted in December, to be scrutinized by the Joint Intelligence Committee, which wanted the Services to have more influence, but the outcome was increased separation of MI6 from what became GCHQ in organisational terms, though having much common interest. Tiltman might well have approved of the improved approach to training and recruitment which also emerged from the review.

Tiltman later confessed[29] that he had perhaps misunderstood the nature of the continuing demands and priorities:

> *Travis instituted this conference on post-war organization, and I was in charge of the sub-committee which dealt with cryptanalysis and traffic analysis. Of course, they had all kinds of trouble, because I knew all about cryptanalysis, but traffic analysis… everyone – everybody who gave evidence… traffic analysis was more easy to understand. As far as the organisation was concerned, I think at the end of the war, I completely misunderstood how the emphasis would gradually go over from cryptanalysis to SIGINT as a whole. I mean, my upbringing was younger people would make better cryptanalysts. The rest were just a lot of hangers-on.*

Tiltman was to be proved correct here, as the automation of codebreaking has led to a greater emphasis on matters to do with traffic analysis and the like, towards the tracking and tracing, the metadata analysis, the analytics of the twenty-first century cyber-world. In this respect the post-war work of Welchman in the USA probably represents the next key stage, rather than the brigadier's skills.

The Americans were to have analogous issues regarding their future staffing and organisation, as several memoranda from July 1945 onwards show. In particular, the political leadership was anxious to amalgamate the SIGINT into one body, avoiding the army/navy rivalries of the war and easing both communications and problems of reduced manpower once people left the services. The navy remained concerned about the issue of communications, as opposed to intelligence, not being capable of meeting service-specific requirements; but generally the feelings were positive. It is interesting that in one document[30] written by navy chief Ernest King the phrase 'central intelligence agency' makes an appearance, though in fact the CIA was to be more the successor to the American OSS, while the merger of OP-20-G and Arlington was to lead firstly to AFSA and later the NSA.

There was still practical code-breaking to be done. The German diplomatic 'GEE' system was one target. Of this Tiltman said:[31]

> *I and my Research sections at G.C.H.Q. only joined in at the exploitation stage* [other work being done by the Americans]. *But we did work in this field for three or four months starting in January 1945, our chief contribution being the reconstruction of the first few wheel patterns which led to the solution of a large part of the material passing between Berlin and Tokyo.*
>
> *The system was intended by the Germans to be a one-time system to be used for the most important and secret diplomatic messages, and there is every reason to believe that its vulnerability was never suspected by the German Foreign Office, as it was in use for over ten years, during which reliance was placed on a one-part code (re-edited more than once) and no attempt was made to avoid by bisecting or other means beginning stereotypes* [i.e. formal and repetitive openings, usually a target for code-breaking, were not disguised].

Before the end of the war in 1945, Tiltman, and his bosses, were considering his future. His incomparable skills were not to be lightly confined to history. An interesting personnel card[32] survives from GCHQ showing some features of this. In March 1945 he was considered for the job of Chief Cryptographer for the Civil and Commercial section, a role to begin on 13 May. Meanwhile, in April he was assigned to go as deputy director to a conference in Paris, and three days of accommodation are recorded as being booked. He would meet with General Strong and Colonel Bicher – the former familiar from US intelligence liaison, the latter a high-ranking cryptographer who had been a representative at BP and was involved with, among other things, *Schlusselgeräte* [the machines behind the FISH traffic]. Their 3-day discussions at SHAEF would include looking at French code security (see also Chapter 10); French traffic was to be of great interest to the Americans after the war because of the possible growth of influence of the Communists in France.[33] So before he left it was made clear (on 21 April) that links with France post-war were to be an agenda item. Cooperation 'in Far Eastern and Eastern war and our probable Anglo-French post-war policy' are specifically mentioned,[34] and these are stressed by 'Charlie' – nickname for Churchill. Tiltman was not in fact originally to be part of this group; Commander Wilson, who had been part of the ISCSC and would have been familiar with Tiltman, was due to go but had a clash of events with a Washington[35] meeting, and Tiltman was made the delegation leader in his place.[36]

The conclusion of the war in Europe saw the Target Intelligence Committee (TICOM) go into action. Six teams went to various areas formerly under the Germans, seeking machinery, archives and other information on a host of German secrets and high-level technology, especially in communications. Materials were brought back to Britain and also taken to the USA. William Friedman was sent to work alongside this effort. He records[37] that after a week in late July touring the US-controlled zone in Germany he returned to BP on 28 July, and from 30 July was involved for a week of conferences which included Tiltman as well as Hastings, Dudley-Smith and Hinsley, who was soon to become increasingly involved with discussions with Washington. After a brief visit to London, note is made of further meetings for 9–14 August, and while Tiltman's name is not specifically mentioned here, it is[38] in the notes of conferences from 16–24 August, which are '*as per*' the 9–14 meetings, so his presence is implied. Others such as Travis and Mr Williams (Intercept Control) are mentioned in this context.

Tiltman was thus involved at BP during August at a senior level looking at the results from the TICOM mission. Equipment discovered included codebooks and devices linked to Russian teleprinter coding systems, which could be of use in following what the ex-Allies were up to. These activities also continue to demonstrate the value of the mutual respect between Tiltman and Friedman.

Tiltman also briefed[39] Gerry Morgan, leader of Research, to be prepared to speak about 'electronic machinery'. There were to be meetings about the future. The notes indicate some 'ambitious' developments ('Several of the projects, or more vaguely requirements, need a high speed or instantaneous memory of code groups') as the machinery is pressed into new fields – perhaps indicating at least in part some of the efforts made with Colossus by the Newmanry team at the time.

As chief cryptographer Tiltman's writ continued to range widely. Basil Cottle records Tiltman as giving a talk on 20 July as part of his work on Albanian codes, and another area is described by Rolf Noskwith in his BP Oral History account,[40] in which he says:

> *When the war ended I couldn't tear myself away and was briefly put on Japanese work and possibly Russian as far as I can remember, and then I worked under Brigadier Tiltman on Yugoslav ciphers, and that was fascinating.*

It would seem to bear out Knox's view (and that of others) that there was no need to know much of the actual language of the code you were breaking.

The war now finally over, Tiltman's future was again discussed[41] on 5 October. The idea was that he should leave the army but be retained at GC&CS[42] as a civilian. Tiltman was interested; the personnel card notes that he was 'open to suggestions'. Later in the year (9 December) he was involved in an informal 'Bourbon' meeting, and a further meeting was planned for the 18th. Russia was now a priority.

BOURBON 'was the formally assigned covername for a joint American-British COMINT project to target the Soviet Union after World War II. But it quickly came to be used as a covername for the target country itself.'[43] In other words, Tiltman was to become an important player in the Cold War.

This liaison with the USA over Russian codes brought Tiltman back to territory familiar from before the war. His work in Simla had included study of USSR material, and he had assisted with Comintern code work from 1931 onwards as well as the 'Mask' operation. During the Second World War the British were allowed a small Y-station in Murmansk, ostensibly to monitor U-boats operating from the fjords of Norway.[44] It remained until 1944.

When Operation Barbarossa (the invasion of Russia) began in 1941 Churchill seems to have ordered a cessation of work on Russian codes. It is unclear how quickly this took place. But when was it resumed? Theoretically not until the European war was over, but the evidence suggests much earlier, and later in the war some Y-stations were gradually taking up interception of Russian material, and this was of serious import by 1945 when trust in the USSR had effectively vanished.

The BP Roll of Honour shows certain veterans who were apparently listening to Russian signals by 1945. While some are noted as doing so before the order to desist was given in 1941, army corporal Geoffrey Crossley[45] is listed as doing so in 1945. Though his personal published account[46] of his journey and experience in India does not mention Russia, it appears that this was the target for his Y-skills which had been honed at Shenley. Dennis Jones of the RAF also served in the Far East, listening to a range of material including Russian. In his oral account, Robin Boyd[47] says:

> *I don't think we ever got feedback about our work, we never knew what happened or the result of our work. For example, in the Roll of Honour it shows that in 1943 Bernard Scott broke a Russian code. I got to know him quite well and he never mentioned anything about that, it was a complete surprise to me.*

Hugh Sherdley of the Royal Signals was based at Harpenden and may have been involved with Russian material from 1943; he also went to the Far East to listen in. Rolf Noskwith, apart from the Yugoslavian codes, may have been involved after VE day. Lieutenant Ferdynand Vanke also worked on Russian codes. Another notable in this area was (Ivor) John Croft. A student of Christ Church, Oxford, he came to BP in late 1942[48] and spent about a year (linked to Block F, the 'Testery' which worked on the 'Fish' traffic from the Lorenz machine) before moving to London and the diplomatic section in Berkeley Street. According to Aldrich,[49] Croft worked on Comintern codes transmitted in Europe; later he was to be a senior civil servant and a CBE. It seems that in the late stages of the war, work against Russia was already well underway at GC&CS in spite of the earlier order to desist. The writer Bradley Smith is quoted by Peter Hennessy[50] as saying that while the West may have refrained from major efforts against the Russian codes for the duration of the war, they were working seriously on them as soon as the war ended. Even this assessment (drawing on WO 208/4566) may be too late in placing the start. Michael Smith states[51] simply, 'By the late summer of 1943… British codebreakers were again reading Soviet traffic.'

It seems probable that Tiltman was indeed working on Russian systems in and perhaps well before 1945. According to a report cited in an article by Peterson in his account[52] of the period, Frank Lewis, a US liaison officer with GC&CS, reported that in the UK

> *there are several four-figure systems which are developing into fairly large-scale enterprises, and with the several three-figure systems* [the mixed figure and letter cipher]… *and the 5-figure cipher… which the Brigadier* [presumably John Tiltman] *is studying, a rather clear-cut program seems to be forthcoming.*

It appears that the maestro was still working very much hands-on, and would continue to do so on Russian codes.

This development is perhaps unsurprising. According to Hennessy[53] the British and US governments were highly pragmatic about Russian intentions even before the war ended, and before the end of 1944 were expecting to find Soviet antagonism rather than cooperation. Assessments provided to government took seriously the possibility of further Russian advances beyond agreed frontiers of influence. On 23 May 1945, the day the remaining Nazi government was arrested and imprisoned pending what became the Nuremburg trials, the order was given[54] in Britain that over 600 radios, hitherto used for wartime intercepts, were to be directed towards Russian interception.

The Americans also revealed (in August 1945) the existence of the project which came to be known as 'Venona', the analysis of special Russian codes, and Tiltman was kept informed of progress[55] in his senior position at Eastcote, where he was now based. This extremely secret project,[56] based at Arlington Hall and not even revealed to national leaders at first, began in 1943 with Gene Grabeel, working on hitherto unbroken Soviet 'diplomatic' messages. Boosted indirectly by the defection of Igor Gouzenko in September 1945 – he brought evidence of Soviet espionage in the West – the project gained the young languages professor Meredith

Gardner who became its leading light and began to read scattered messages in 1946. The FBI (in the person of Robert Lamphere) was brought into the project in 1947. The British work on Venona (by now named 'Bride' in the UK) was initiated in 1948, but with a small team. It is not clear at the time of this writing how much Tiltman was linked to them, though it seems unlikely that his expertise was not called upon given his leadership in Russian ciphers. William Bodsworth was in charge of the unit, which numbered less than ten.[57] This work helped the main US effort to reveal codenames of US atomic bomb spies (such as Julius Rosenberg and Klaus Fuchs), and also British spies, notably 'Homer' and 'Stanley', later revealed as Donald Maclean and Kim Philby.

Tiltman would have been affected by the events of 29 October 1948, when the Russians carried out a full-scale synchronized change in security and code procedures. This was clearly in response to awareness that their systems were compromised through 'Venona'. The Soviet agent William Wiesband, who had joined Arlington Hall and had seen some of the Venona material, may have been responsible. Tiltman was again called in to advise and assist in reconstruction.

In January 1946, Tiltman had called a meeting with the American liaison and cryptological staff linked to GC&CS, in which, as head of the Soviet cryptanalytic section, Peterson says[58] he announced the possession of a large cache of Soviet material dating up to 1944, which would prove of use when matched with the TICOM-related materials pertinent to Soviet communications. The value of such intelligence material was demonstrated, for example, in the discovery by the TICOM team of a German report with 4,000 codebook recoveries from a Russian system, half of which matched what the USA already had (thus confirming their work) and the others being as yet unseen (and therefore of future value). The German group captured by Selmer Norland and Major Rushworth,[59] complete with a cache of equipment for reading Russian teleprinter coded material, provided excellent technical knowledge. Codebooks were also found in Saxony and Schleswig.[60] That this kind of TICOM product had value was indeed the case is confirmed some years later in a report for the NSA by Katherine Swift[61] which confirms (in a heavily redacted paper) that even in 1952 some captured keys from TICOM were still being used in the East.

Tiltman was aware of SIGINT issues linked to the Palestinian[62] situation in 1946. The British still held the mandate over Palestine and were trying unsuccessfully to reconcile various Jewish groups regarding future political plans. Some groups, notably Irgum and Haganah, were adopting violent methods to achieve their aims, and Britain attempted to monitor them through message interception as well as 'Humint'. The bombing of the King David Hotel by Irgum in July 1946 killed ninety-one people, including some of those linked to the monitoring and agents. The White Paper published soon after hinted at what the British were up to; in November key Jewish groups changed their cipher systems and it seems that GCHQ and the UK leaders felt the whole thing a lower priority. Tiltman was waiting in the wings to assist, and Ferris thinks the systems could have been cracked, but the effort was ultimately not made.

Chapter 10

The Diplomat – Part Three

As well as with the practicalities of code-breaking, Tiltman had also become engaged after the war with UK-US liaison over continued cooperation – the heart of the 'special relationship'. In this chapter we examine Tiltman's role in this, and how he remained someone to be trusted on all sides.

The Americans were becoming somewhat chary (again) of full disclosure to Britain on a number of matters. They had already withheld information on the atomic bomb,[1] and were to continue to do so in the field of cryptology. The legacy of disagreements with Admiral Redman also raised its head.

Tiltman returned to the USA in October 1945, accompanied[2] by Harry Hinsley, who was to play a role in the forthcoming discussions and conferences as secretary. One of his stopover points in Washington was the navy section receiving intercepts from the US listening station at Wahiawa in Hawaii; he saw the section on 15 October as part of his liaison and fact-finding work.[3] With what seems typical directness, he revealed[4] that British contributions to this joint effort against the Soviets might well be reduced because of losses in personnel (through demobilisation). As it turned out, the Americans were facing a similar problem even though new trainees were coming through.

Tiltman was to attend with Travis at key meetings which foreshadowed the agreements of the following year; the Bourbon cooperation was cited as an example of how well the two sides could (as contrasted with 'would') work together 'in all branches of communications intelligence'. As well as a meeting on 15 October, the meeting of 29 October saw Tiltman alongside Travis, Hinsley and Eric Jones, participating in the joint gathering of the US Army-Navy Communications Intelligence Board and the Army-Navy Communications Intelligence Co-ordinating Committee over drafts of proposed texts in advance of what was to be the 1946 agreement.

The tone of this meeting[5] shows however a rather different quality, and numerous discussions, about terminology and definition of matters for cooperation and sharing, indicate disagreements and reservations. To a British question on extent of full exchange, US members, led by Redman, replied,[6]

> *[America] might have a technique which would not be relevant to a current problem and might even apply to one of our own ciphers. It would not be in the national interest to turn over such a technique to anyone else. [Travis] stated that since British-American collaboration during the war had dealt to a large extent with technical developments, any hindrance to an exchange of techniques would make the agreement impractical… Admiral Redman pointed out that technical exchange with the British in the past had not been entirely satisfactory… and in one case an appeal had to be made to the Admiralty to make the British live up to an agreement.*

When Tiltman pointed out that limitations to exchange were made in the words 'as mutually agreeable in specific instances', Redman flatly replied, 'It is not the intention of ANCIB to allow the British complete access to our intelligence activities.' There seems to have been some support for Travis's and Tiltman's view for maximisation of sharing among the US army members of the group, but Redman and the navy were adamant. Later, discussing the same aspect of the draft, Travis and Tiltman both expressed concerns that the meaning of the wording on exchanges might imply only present and not future developments. Redman's reply 'disagreed with this interpretation, adding that we had worked for the British in the past without receiving all relevant information in every case'. There were disagreements also regarding the British imperial territories and the dominions in particular, America naturally having much interest in the Canadian position.

Clabby[7] describes the effect of this apparent hostility on Tiltman:

> *Redman took the occasion to revisit the difficulties surrounding Enigma, and singled out Tiltman again as in some way responsible. What irritated Tiltman the most was that he knew that Redman was fully aware that it was largely through Tiltman's intervention that the impasse had been broken, in the Americans' favour. Tiltman held his fire during the session, but after it was over he told Travis that he refused to re-enter the room as long as Redman remained in the chair. Every attempt by Travis to calm him down failed, and he withdrew from the negotiating process.*

A draft agreement was nevertheless put forward in November, Hinsley and American secretaries having worked further on the issues from October. Happily Tiltman was fully engaged in the discussions before the establishment of the SIGINT Committee in March 1946.

Tiltman was also concerned with effective use of resources and avoidance of duplicated work between the two sides. Early in 1946[8] he asked, as leader of GCHQ's Soviet section, for a list of the cipher systems being examined by the USA, presumably so that he could prioritize British efforts on others. This initiative did not achieve a response until November, when it was clear that US chiefs (including Wenger from the navy side) were less than enthusiastic about an 'allocation programme', and the result was little more than occasional exchanges of 'current interests' lists.

A draft agreement[9] dated 5 March 1946 was the basis of the next, historic, BRUSA detailed discussions. It provided for exchange of information, how this could be shared (e.g. with the British 'Dominions'), and other broad policies and principles for combined communications intelligence. The ground for the British position had been prepared the previous month by a Commonwealth conference in advance of which Travis had done much negotiation[10] and secured consensus from Commonwealth nations, for whom he could speak at the March meeting. This established the 'Special (intelligence) Relationship', a key element – though not the last word, and by no means set in stone – of British and American security for decades to come.

The participants met on 11 March in London under the chairmanship of Stewart Menzies. US representation included a number of familiar names from cryptography (Corderman, Wenger, Rowlett), and the British names included Travis, 'Joe' Hooper (later Head of GCHQ), Marr-Johnson (who had several roles linked to SIGINT during the war including US liaison and leading the WEC in India) and Tiltman. Tiltman became the British member of the cryptanalysis sub-committee, to be chaired by Rowlett. It reported to the second executive committee (as did other sub-committees), and the minutes state *inter alia* that

> *there was some bewilderment expressed over the phrasing of certain paragraphs, especially paras. 2 and 3. It was agreed to delete the phrase 'groups of systems' from para. 4 since the sense of the phrase was impossible to define.*

– one is tempted to think that technical jargon in cryptography was baffling to non-codebreakers!

Over the meetings of the next fortnight[11] Tiltman is seen intervening from time to time to advise over sensible working practices and best ways forward. His views are taken seriously, if not always accepted, by the committee. On 14 March he was asked by the Executive Committee on the way in which his sub-committee (B) was proposing to circulate reports linked to US draft proposals. Tiltman's reply (ever a practical man) was that sections relevant to different parts of the organisations would go to them but not the whole to everyone – which the Americans, seemingly concerned about too widespread a circulation of information, approved. He is in attendance at the fifth Executive on 21 March, though no comment is recorded in the minutes. He is found in the eighth and final meeting arguing that some tasks are better done with representation from both UK and USA, against the American view that tasks can be divided for economies of manpower (a striking view given the attitude that was to emerge over allocations to either side where the USA wanted involvement in everything). He is present at the final plenary session on 27 March when the documents are given final approval. The resultant BRUSA agreement was to be confirmed by political leaders.

This document[12] goes further than its 1943 predecessor, as it includes the US navy (the STANCIB organisation – State-Army-Navy Communications Intelligence Board – spoke for all) and made clear reference to the British Empire beyond the Dominions (Australia, Canada, New Zealand) as represented by Britain. It is in some ways more secretive: clause 3(a) reads:

> *It will be contrary to this agreement to reveal its existence to any third party whatever.*

It is however somewhat more circumscribed in terms of 'full' exchange, as several clauses indicate that either side can withhold full details of a matter if it is judged prejudicial to national interest – witness clause 4(b) on 'Methods and Techniques', which reads:

> *Such exchange will be unrestricted on all work undertaken, except that upon notification of the other party information may be withheld by either party when its special interests so require. Such notification will include a*

> *description of the information being withheld, sufficient… to convey its significance.*

– in other words, if one side had a new development which it felt unprepared to share, it might be able to avoid disclosure beyond an outline. This is in line with Redman's views (see above) and perhaps the navy generally, though Travis had tried to present the case[13] for 100 per cent collaboration in the November discussions. The dominions are not 'third parties' but London would need to inform the USA about any proposed arrangements with them – and from this root stemmed the 'Five Eyes' working of the next few years; to have worldwide bases for intelligence-gathering clearly suited both Britain and the USA, whatever the latter's feelings about colonial legacies. The channels of communication are clarified as being between STANCIB and the London SIGINT Board (LSIB), avoiding any pitfalls of miscommunications which sometimes interfered during the war.

There were reservations on both main sides in this agreement, which were likely to cause some friction in later years, and amendments to details and appendices were to be made in years to come. Nevertheless the confirmation of a 'Special (and secret) Relationship' post-war, felt by both sides as mutually beneficial in the light of the perceived Soviet threat, was thus achieved, Tiltman playing his part in its establishment.

Tiltman's contributions were recognized in 1946 in America by the award of Officer degree in the US Legion of Merit. The citation[14] for this refers to his

> *exceptionally meritorious and outstanding service for his country and the United States from December 1941 to September 1945. Brigadier Tiltman's exemplary spirit of international co-operation in an extremely technical and specialized field was an exceptionally meritorious contribution to the successful prosecution of the war.*

It was in 1946 that Tiltman retired (again) from the army, and became an assistant director for GCHQ not long after. Achievement of complete cooperation with the USA was not going to be easy. A report dated 24 April 1947 from the US War Department[15] and approved by Thomas Handy shows that when the UK proposed full cooperation regarding development of a new Combined Cipher machine (CCM) to supersede the US SIGABA design, the US wished to withhold information regarding SIGABA and appears to have been a little surprised that the UK were aware of the basic SIGABA technical principles. It appears that the navy had raised objections. The British 'new and revolutionary' ideas for development were thought to be impractical by the US, who instead presented their own suggestions for combined development, to be studied by the British. A proposal by the UK for collaboration on a CCM for lower echelons was also resisted by the US. Instead there was agreement about drawing up a set of combined security regulations which would guide future combined development. Authority to proceed with more open CCM collaboration was to be sought.

In 1949, Tiltman was named[16] a Senior UK Liaison Officer (SUKLO) to the USA and worked in Washington, based at the British embassy there. This was when the Armed Forces Security Agency (AFSA) was established[17] in the USA, reporting to the Joint Chiefs of Staff. It was meant to oversee several areas across the armed forces, including SIGINT, thus hopefully ending the rivalry that had hindered some wartime SIGINT work, but was not established with a clear legal basis and was replaced by the new National Security Agency (NSA) in 1952. It was under this umbrella that further joint discussions and work were carried out. Tiltman's liaison with AFSA and the NSA was to be critical.

In March 1950 there was a less formal opportunity for Tiltman – to present Admiral Stone, who was leading US groups on intelligence – with some antiquarian maps in his honour. Stone had been made head of the Armed Forces Security Agency in 1949. Tiltman was prominent, as SUKLO, in leading this presentation, which was made on 28 March.

Tiltman was now to be involved as SUKLO in a range of conferences, planning meetings and exchanges between 1950 and his retirement in 1954. He was trusted with the most secret information and discussions throughout.

Friedman's report of August 1950[18] shows the planning of the 1950 BRUSA conference. The UK sent Tiltman their list of delegates and proposed dates[19] in September, together with items for discussion and a proposal for 'Exchange of cryptographic principles on a reciprocal basis', but the report indicates US hesitation again on full openness. The British came in September, also wishing to discuss 'a new British cipher machine'. The conference began[20] on 21 September with Friedman, Sinkov, Wenger and Safford on the US side and the British led by T.R.W. Burton-Miller, with Tiltman sitting next to him (an indication of his seniority).

High on the agenda was combined communications and security. The US side presented a new 7-rotor machine (later named 'Brutus'). Both Burton-Miller and Friedman wanted Tiltman, already a member of the executive, seconded to the sub-committee examining this – a tribute to his expertise. A 5-year roll-out was proposed, and disclosure even to UK Commonwealth countries was banned unless both parties agreed. Tiltman's subcommittee also examined and assessed over thirty code devices and systems. Some ('Mercury', 'Rollick', 'Pendragon', 'Hallmark', 'Sorcerer', 'Playfex', 'Linex' – this last the name of a hand cipher devised by Tiltman himself) had their origins in the UK, others ('AFSAM 7', 7-rotor 'BCM', 'ASAX 2', 'ASAY', 'ASAD 1', 'Running Key cipher') were of US origin.

Tiltman was certainly involved as SUKLO in negotiations between 1951 and 1954 between Britain, the USA and France (linking with other NATO countries) regarding security in mutual systems. The founding of the North Atlantic Treaty Organization (NATO) opened a new set of security connections and potential issues. It would appear that concerns were raised in 1951[21] about the effectiveness of some NATO countries' systems. The USA and UK were using systems (CSP 2900; Circuit Mercury) essentially developed by and for themselves (the British in particular had evolved Circuit Mercury), and Britain was interested in sharing some of this with others to raise general standards. As agreement by both UK and USA was needed, an AFSA meeting considered this. This led to an *ad hoc* committee being established under the US Communications Intelligence Board (USCIB).

A surviving report[22] gives the outline of the problem, in which Tiltman became involved. The issue had been discussed as early as 1948 with specific concerns about French systems being penetrated by the Soviets thanks in part to faulty French systems security. At the end of 1950 USCIB designated a representative 'to work out a US/UK position on the matter with Brigadier Tiltman'. A message from the London Signals Intelligence Board (LSIB) arrived in January 1951 proposing a conference to discuss policy.

1 May 1951 saw the US-UK conference in Washington[23] focussed on French communications security, with Admiral Stone in the chair and

Tiltman as one of the British team. He was on the Executive Committee (where he met up with Friedman again), and also on the Technical committee (where he encountered Sinkov once more). Tiltman then helped the preparations[24] for a July UK-US conference. The proposed agenda was being worked on in March,[25] and the focus was on technical matters of equipment and procedures for top-secret communications. He assisted the UK Joint Services Mission,[26] housed in US navy buildings in Washington. In October he helped Friedman with information about various committees[27] in GCHQ, passing on the reply[28] which came from Eric Jones (formerly of Hut 3 and soon to be GCHQ Director).

The BRUSA planning conference[29] of March 1953 again involved Tiltman. The initial meeting took place on 2 March and Tiltman found himself in familiar company. Clive Loehnis led the British delegation; he had been an Admiralty liaison officer with BP (1941–5) and worked with Sandwith on Y-service matters; he joined GCHQ after the war and was to become Director in 1960. Serving in part as secretary was Henry Dryden, whom Tiltman had sent to North Africa in March 1941 after his narrow escape from France ('a month, six weeks at the outside, old boy' – he ended up staying there until May 1944). Bill Millward and Arthur 'Bill' Bonsall from Hut 3 (the latter also a future Director of GCHQ) were also there. On the US side Joseph Wenger led the team. Beneath Loehnis, Tiltman is indicated as 'SBLO', which surely means 'Senior British Liaison Officer'. His role this time seems to have been on the executive committee; his name does not appear on any of the sub-committee lists.

The French question had not been resolved, and in 1953 (by which time the NSA had superseded AFSA) the French made an approach with the desire to get access to American systems, as by then they knew of Circuit Mercury, though they had no knowledge of its technical principles. It was pointed out that NATO security could be improved by such widening of access. The ad hoc committee reported to USCIB at the end of May, not convinced by British or French arguments, and Tiltman was called in to pass the information to Britain,[30] before the June NATO security conference. There is a memo[31] from the US liaison office in London to the NSA indicating that this conference in America should start on 4 or 5 June, with Tiltman present alongside 3–4 others (redacted – one might be Burton-Miller). This UK-US conference on NATO security[32] actually convened on 5 June, chaired by Friedman and including Frank Rowlett. The initial session set up two subcommittees, on intelligence/security and on cryptological aspects. Tiltman (with Friedman, and Navy codebreaker Frank Raven as technical advisor) was part of the latter group. It concluded on 12 June, again with Tiltman present.[33] Disagreement on the French question remained, but measures were taken to stop possible transfer of information or advice, from the US or UK to the Hagelin company (still serving some security needs), which might through Hagelin commercial innovations become available to non-NATO countries – a symptom of the way the US-UK relationship jealously guarded the innermost secrets even from allies.

In November 1953 Tiltman was again to convey to the US the view of the British,[34]

> *and that in particular the proposed approach by the U.K. and U.S. Ambassadors to the French government was still necessary and should be made without further delay to ensure backing at the highest level for French cooperation… I am agreeable that the matter should be discussed by the Combined Working Group and Brigadier Tiltman has been instructed accordingly. He has been urged to do all in his power to secure an early conclusion.*

The matter was reviewed, and initially again the Americans rejected the idea, General Canine (heading the NSA) being particularly unwilling.[35] This was confirmed in a memo of 19 January 1954. The British argued once more in favour and in March 1954 Tiltman was again the conveyor[36] of this viewpoint. He presented the arguments that the risks were outweighed by the benefits of overall higher levels of security for the NATO countries.

The matter was a fairly hot potato – 'Circuit Mercury' was felt by the USA to be 'the best high-grade machine known', and if it were in French hands there was concern about access to it by communists, who were active in French politics (the McCarthy-inspired communist 'witch-hunts' were a feature of US life at the time). Again the USCIB refused to disclose the system to the French.[37] However by 1955 there was more preparedness by the USA to have discussions with Britain and France about communications security, and a conference was prepared for November that year which it was hoped, rather than simply giving the French a very negative rejection, would get the French to initiate positively some ideas of cooperation. These discussions[38] would look at a number of technical issues, including the use by the French of more advanced British Typex machines which had been offered.

Tiltman was therefore a part of some of the most sensitive discussions of the time. He also acted as the liaison over discussions[39] about the loan to West Germany of the ROCKEX cipher system to secure their communications for a foreign ministers' conference in Berlin in January 1954. ROCKEX was a Vernam-type system developed in the later 1940s which became a staple high-grade cipher system in the West and was used in many embassies and for diplomatic traffic;[40] a later capture in 1967 by Communist Red Guards who broke into the British embassy in Beijing was regarded as close to a catastrophic security breach.

The French security issues noted above were a relevant concern here too. Tiltman communicated with Captain Rufus Taylor (USN) to convey the British interest in the ROCKEX loan idea, which seems to have been a response to the USA proposing its own initiative in providing help for the French. He was also to take back the American reply, that (given perhaps the security worries about a conference in Berlin, which makes a political 'statement' about the West but is so close to Soviet activity in the Russian-controlled zone)

> *the Board is unable to perceive what cryptologic advantages are to be gained and would appreciate the U.K. view in that regard. The proposal raises certain questions in the minds of our members, many of which would, no doubt, be answered by a more complete statement of the reasons for this move.*

As with the issue of Circuit Mercury, the Americans remained anxious to guard what the US-UK alliance had, and Tiltman might have to be diplomatic in bringing back another 'negative'. However, at a meeting on 11 January the USCIB, after receiving further information from the British, acceded[41] to the UK suggestion on ROCKEX. Captain Taylor then informed Tiltman orally of the decision and this was followed by a formal response to be cleared by the NSA and State Department. The debate ended up being academic, as by 18 January the West Germans had decided not to use the machine[42] and to focus on books and one-time pads.

In the meantime, the continuing issue of sharing US-UK cryptology with third parties remained, and was discussed[43] on 12 March 1954 by USCIB. The source document is redacted. There were two linked problems, one being the British desire to share and involve French access to cipher developments (see above), the other not specified but linking to 'the Viet Minh' problem – evidently the situation in what was French Indo-China: there was a danger of appearing to be rivals with the UK rather than partners in the Far East. The paper suggests that Tiltman had established a link with a third party in the area during the war which was discreetly continuing, and that under consideration was a more formal recognition of this under the US-UK umbrella.

US doubts about the situation in Vietnam were justified. By early 1954 the French, after several years of mixed guerrilla and more formal warfare in an attempt to prop up their former imperial territory against the northern communists led by Ho Chi Minh, were under pressure. The day after the USCIB meeting began, the Battle of Dien Bien Phu began, and was to end in a decisive French defeat (on the anniversary of VE day), leading to their withdrawal and the establishment of two Vietnams (North and South), with Laos and Cambodia having attained independence the previous year.

The USCIB notes state:

> *[The Chairman] said he would agree to sign a letter to the Chairman, LSIB, on the subject if the content of such a letter would have approval of the Department of State. Mr Armstrong* [US member] *suggested that the matter be put squarely to Brigadier Tiltman and, through him, make arrangements for simultaneous action on the two problems... General Canine agreed to discuss the matter with Brigadier Tiltman at the same time that he informs him of the Board's decision on the Viet Minh problem.*

Again, Tiltman's status in handling sensitive matters is recognized. On this occasion however, the meeting changed its mind later and decided on a (for the time being) more informal approach.

In retrospect, it was highly fortunate that there was someone in place for these talks in the early 1950s, in the form of John Tiltman, who combined extraordinary expertise in the fundamentals of cryptology, the experience of developing mechanisation of SIGINT, the skills of diplomacy and the personal integrity that helped to smooth the exchange of information and dialogue so essential to the running of a 'special relationship'. It must be remembered that these events took place against the background, in 1950–51, of the defections of Burgess and MacLean, and the revelations about Klaus Fuchs and his betrayal of atomic secrets to the Russians – both of which events damaged British security standing with the USA.

Fuchs,[44] an atomic bomb scientist, had been identified in part from 'Venona' decrypts which referred to a British scientist 'Charles' and 'Rest' and incidental references which fitted him. From autumn 1949 he was closely watched, hoping for other evidence, as revealing 'Venona' in open court was a security non-starter. After several interrogations he confessed in January 1950. The USA, and particularly the FBI, was furious that British vetting had failed to bring out his weaknesses, and faith in the special relationship was shaken. In April 1951 an already bad situation worsened. Donald MacLean (former first secretary in Washington and latterly with the Cairo diplomatic mission) and Guy Burgess (who had been working with both MI6 and MI5 in his time and was now with the FO), two of the 'Magnificent Five' Cambridge spies, fled to Moscow. They were helped in part by 'Third Man' Kim Philby (MI6 representative in Washington) who was privy to Venona evidence identifying MacLean as the coded 'Homer'. The association with Burgess cost Philby his job, but he was not to flee until 1963 when evidence against him, previously circumstantial and by association, became clear.

While the Americans continued to express their reservations about their Allies in general, there is no indication of doubts about Tiltman; on the contrary, he is someone to whom things can 'be put squarely' and with whom a straightforward conversation could be had. His record of experience, directness and above all integrity made him the ideal person for these tasks at this time, even if others might have been capable of the work too.

According to *The Carthusian*,[45] in 1950 Tiltman was made First Secretary to the British Embassy in Washington. He held the post until 1954. The task of a 'secretary' in such a position has more recently been defined[46] as 'to monitor and report on developments in [the country] and to advise on British policy'. If such was Tiltman's role, then his experience, particularly over Russia and the information emerging from cryptography, would have been useful, as well as his many contacts with US intelligence. It would be a measure of the trust that the US had in him, inasmuch as this was a post previously held by Donald MacLean. It is less clear however if this reference represents simply another description of his role as SUKLO; the Foreign Office was generally hesitant about having people with links to secret services intruding on their areas of interest or holding diplomatic status.[47]

Tiltman's authority and knowledge were sometimes consulted for less technical matters. There seems to have been an interest in recording the history of recent events on both sides of the Atlantic. Friedman[48] contacted Tiltman in May 1952 regarding the 'histories' written at the end of the war at BP for each main section of the organisation, and he refers to a previous message dating from late 1950. It looks as though Tiltman responded positively, for in September 1952 Captain Leigh, USN, acting Chief of Staff, wrote to Tiltman[49] asking whether, in view of his provision of previous material, he could find any other volumes of SIGINT history relevant to the navy, and whether any other accounts by Frank Birch, who post-war compiled several volumes of history, were available. Tiltman's response is not (to date) recorded but it seems likely that things were sent; in March 1953 Friedman sent an acknowledgement[50] to Tiltman that he had received photographs sent of some of the key people at BP. Tiltman (perhaps modestly) had omitted to send one of himself. Friedman followed this up[51] at the end of 1954 enquiring through Tiltman's successor Freddie Jacob as SUKLO to see if further histories were yet available.

Chapter 11

Later Years

Tiltman retired in 1954. However, things were not to move at once in that direction.

By April 1954 the Americans were working on 'succession planning' for his departure. A memorandum[1] dated 16 April shows USCIB circulating a (redacted) CIA proposal to board members asking for votes, 'with the view to making it possible to discuss it with Brigadier Tiltman before his departure if an affirmative response is received'. Another memo ten days later confirms approval of the matter, and again Tiltman was to be informed. Even at this late stage, his personal authority was influential.

Tiltman's official retirement from GCHQ should have been when he reached the 'mandatory' retiring age of 60. Tiltman had been warned some while back that his pension status was doubtful, and according to Currier[2] he had not accrued sufficient pensionable time from GCHQ:

> *He retired from GCHQ - retired's* [sic] *the wrong word. He has a small... or did have, at least, a small army pension and he - I've forgotten exactly when the situation was, but I think that he didn't work a sufficient number of years for GCHQ to get an actual pension. He took – I believe he took severance pay, but I may have it wrong. I don't think he did, and I'm pretty certain that he gets no pension from GCHQ, but he does still have, and continues to get, a small army pension.*

However, this was not to be. As a special arrangement he was to continue with GCHQ. This period seems to have included some time in the USA, at least from 1958. The diaries of Friedman's appointments[3] in 1954–5 show meetings booked with Tiltman for 10 February and 29 April 1954 – no subject is defined for these.

Tiltman's professional and historical interests were linked in April 1954 by the recent publication by Michael Ventris and John Chadwick (the latter a codebreaker at BP during the war when he was involved with Japanese messages) of a solution to the 'Linear B' language from the Mediterranean (it proved to be an archaic form of Greek).[4] Tiltman sent a copy of the article to John von Neumann[5] who informed Friedman, with the latter's historical interests in mind, of its arrival. It is possible that the techniques used by Ventris attracted him; Ventris had created tables ('grids' he called them) of rows and columns that were shuffled up and down, back and forth, in a manner not unlike trying to align a depth in code-breaking.

In 1954 Tiltman was honoured by being made a Companion of the Order of St Michael and St George – CMG. There seems to be little in the public domain at the time of this writing about his work with GCHQ in later years. It is likely that, as he seems to have done later in America (see below), his expertise in analysing diverse hand-ciphers around the world continued to be used.

Tiltman's interest in breaking ciphers was not limited to his professional career. He became interested in the puzzle that was the Voynich manuscript. The Voynich manuscript is a booklet dating from perhaps the early fifteenth century unearthed by Wilfred Voynich in 1912. It was donated to a Yale University library in 1969 after attempts to sell it at auction failed. It is written in a strange and still unsolved script, perhaps not all by the same hand and perhaps not all in the same 'language'. There are illustrations through it, suggesting that the subject matter is natural science – herbal matters, pharmaceuticals, as well as astronomical and cosmological matters. In the 1940s William Friedman became interested in the Voynich manuscript and analysed some of the lettering. He was part of a team which attempted to solve the mystery in the 1950s. It was here that Friedman brought in Tiltman, who says:[6]

> *In 1950 I was introduced to the manuscript by my friend, Mr William F. Friedman, who gave me photostats of a few of the pages to work on, chiefly the unillustrated pages at the end. From these pages I made a preliminary analysis of the text.*

Tiltman made comparisons with other herbals of Renaissance times and after, but concluded:

> *After reading my report, Mr Friedman disclosed to me his belief that the basis of the script was a very primitive form of synthetic universal language such as was developed in the form of a philosophical classification*

of ideas by Bishop Wilkins in 1667 and Dalgarno a little later. It was clear that the productions of these two men were much too systematic, and anything of the kind would have been almost instantly recognisable. My analysis seemed to me to reveal a cumbersome mixture of different kinds of substitution.

In January 1961 Alastair Denniston passed away. The news of this was brought to William Friedman (and others) by Tiltman[7] in America. He wrote back with sadness at the loss. It is indicative of Tiltman's long friendship with Denniston; they had shared Christmases together[8] and their wives were friends too. Tiltman wrote[9] to Denniston's son Robin: 'I had a great respect for your father... and remember him as a very good director and personal friend.' Tiltman also expressed sympathy for Denniston and his treatment when he was 'ousted' from BP in 1942, feeling it was unfair.

In 1963 there was a conference in the USA which Tiltman attended. Among other attendees were William Friedman and Josh Cooper, former head of the Air Section at BP. The three were photographed[10] together.

His 'final' retirement from GCHQ in 1964 saw him move to the USA to be nearer his daughter. Here[11] he became a consultant to the NSA and was particularly concerned with a range of hand ciphers in use worldwide. It is tempting to think of the veteran codebreaker jumping at a chance to use his skills once more, after what appears to have been several years of diplomacy and administration.

Lutwiniak describes Tiltman's work, and his own first meeting[12] with 'The Brig'. In 1974 he had become responsible for the area which included Tiltman's research, and his account outlines what Tiltman would have been doing during his consultancy with the NSA:

I had been on the job a few days when [Tiltman] *dropped in to see me... He explained that he was under contract to NSA on a yearly basis, that he was to conduct cryptanalytic studies of certain cipher systems to be agreed upon, that he was to write a report monthly on his activities, and produce an annual report summing up the year's work... He then asked what I would like him to do. I asked him if he would mind very much just carrying on as before. He simply said, 'Thank you', and left.*

I consulted the files and found out that the arrangement had been going on since the end of 1964 and that there was a thick folder of monthly and

> *annual reports from him. I leisurely browsed through these and discovered that the Brig had done a superb job of diagnosing, and in many cases solving* [detail here redacted]... *The monthly reports are a fascinating mixture of handwritten notes, worksheets, machine runs, diagrams, and other cryptologic* [material]. *There is, for instance, a superb handwritten report on the solution of* [detail redacted] - *an outstanding piece of cryptanalysis. It was during a time when the Brig's health was poor, and he had apologized to me (too) often for 'missed days'.*

According to Currier,[13] Tiltman's engagement by the NSA and work for the USA did not cause any problems for security:

> *I'm sure that the fact that we were about to offer him a contract was made known to them, I'm sure, because we are... we're very close, and I'm sure there was nothing held back – nothing withheld on either side, and I'm just as certain that they were in complete accord, and there was... no problem at all.*

In 1966, partly through his continuing links with GCHQ and the NSA, Tiltman became involved with the work of David Kahn, who was preparing a book about codebreaking. According to Clabby,[14] GCHQ was concerned about references to itself (there were equal concerns in the USA about what might emerge there), and Tiltman brought his diplomatic experience to negotiations with Kahn about leaving out references of concern. The resulting book was acceptable in the UK. Kahn later wanted to speak to Tiltman about other matters of cryptology, but Tiltman refused, citing his oath of secrecy over his codebreaking work and career.

Tiltman had by now begun to write articles for the *NSA Technical Journal*. In 1961 he explained something of the background to the 'Tunny machine' (nowadays referred to as the 'Lorenz' SZ40 machine) which encrypted teleprinter messages. The term 'Tunny' was applied by the British to the machine decoding output from the networks of the German *Heer* – army – which used it for high-command messages.

His 'A cryptological fairytale', recounting some of his work in breaking and making transposition systems, appeared in 1962. He contributed 'Some reminiscences' to the 1966 summer edition, in which he gave an account of his early work in Russia and India and his 'induction' to code-breaking, and his views on the Voynich manuscript appeared in summer of 1967. He was to complete 'Experiences', written in 1972, which gave a detailed account of his efforts to counter the Russian code systems in the 1920s.

He wrote 'Some principles of cryptographic security' for the journal in 1974, in which he expounded his thinking about methodology and underlying ideas which pervade the whole field. He highlights the need to balance security with practicality; he warns of weaknesses in transposition and substitution systems; he stresses the fallibility of the human element, especially if aspects of the process are too complex.

These articles give something of a picture of the depth of thinking of which Tiltman was so capable, and of the extent of his technique and powers of analysis. At the same time, the technical side was so valuable and relevant that large parts of the articles, when they were declassified and published by the NSA early in the twenty-first century, were redacted, presumably because the skills described within them remained of use.

The appearance of Winterbotham's book *The Ultra Secret* in 1974 made known to the British public for the first time some aspects of the codebreaking work during the war. There had been some concern about what might be in it, but probably the publication the previous year in France of Bertrand's book about Enigma[15] made possible this work, which (apparently by agreement) contained virtually no detail about cryptanalysis, machinery, mathematics or any other reference to methods.

Tiltman was invited to review it in 1975, which he did for the NSA in *Cryptolog* in December.[16] His views demonstrate his directness which occasionally irritated others:

> *The book is poorly written and very inaccurate in some areas where I know the facts. The references to the early history of Enigma solution and to the activities of the staff of Hut 6 (who performed the cryptanalytic part of the enterprise) are hopelessly wrong. It is difficult to understand how the author who had considerable responsibilities for the organisation and distribution of Enigma intelligence could have been so completely ignorant of the technical side of the operation. He doesn't know the difference between the Enigma (a rotor machine), other German ciphers, the Japanese high-grade diplomatic machine (the 'Purple', a totally different kind of machine), and the Japanese Fleet general cipher (a codebook and additive hand system). His remarks about the 'Bronze Goddess' appear to be a complete invention*

– though this 'invention' might well be Winterbotham's attempt at an analogy for something held in awe by most who saw but did not understand.

Most damning is the simple sentence:

> *In view of its general inaccuracy, especially when touching on technical matters, I believe the book, taken by itself, does no harm.*

But most significant perhaps, and typical of his attitude to loyalty and integrity, is the statement:

> *I hold the view that everyone who worked in Bletchley Park is still under a moral obligation not to disclose secrets not previously published without official permission and, I would have thought, is aware of this obligation.*

See below for his more emotional private reaction to the book.

His interest in the Voynich manuscript continued. Studying it in detail, he gave a lecture on the subject[17] and in consequence was a guest of honour the following year at an august gathering in Washington under the guidance of Mary D'Imperio at which one of the leading speakers was Prescott Currier, he of the Sinkov mission over three decades previously.

In April 1977, Tiltman linked up once more with Telford Taylor, presenting an outline talk[18] before Taylor's main account of work at BP. The gathering followed an earlier seminar led by David Kahn, who had written some years before on the topic. Tiltman, now in his eighties, set the scene for Taylor's lecture:

> *General Taylor called to mind the use of ULTRA in various cover plans and his strong conviction that if it had not been for ULTRA intelligence the Battle of the Atlantic might have been a much closer thing than it was.*

Tiltman was at last persuaded to undertake some Oral History interviews in 1978. He finally gave four extended interviews about all aspects of his work from his earliest days until the end of the Second World War (he deemed it inadvisable to speak about post-war work, much of which was classified). It would be impossible to write about much of what he did without this resource.

John Tiltman died in 1982 on 10 August at the age of 88, two years after his final retirement from work with the NSA. On retirement he had moved to Hawaii, to be near his family.

He was inducted into the NSA 'Hall of Honor' in 2004. The notes there state:

From 1964–1980 he was a consultant and researcher at NSA, spending in all 60 years at the cutting edge of SIGINT. John Tiltman made the transition from the manual ciphers of the early twentieth century to the sophisticated machine systems of the latter half of the century. 'The Brig', as he was affectionately known in both countries, compiled a lengthy record of high achievement. His efforts at training and his attention to all the many facets that make up cryptology inspired the best in all who encountered him.

In his tribute, William Lutwiniak said of him:

The Brig was a modest man. No matter how great the accomplishment, he would deprecate, or give the credit to others, or speak of luck, good fortune, or a fluke. Praise embarrassed him; I think it made him physically uncomfortable… The Brig was a shy man, but warm and generous in his friendship. He couldn't do enough for friends… The Brig was a man of many parts - orchids, weaving, bookbinding; literature, music, art; name it, and he was in it or knew much of it. His inquiring mind and keen intellect had him always acquiring knowledge, seeking answers.

Such a description is probably indicative of the sentiments of many regarding Tiltman, for whom there seems to be hardly anything but good in the accounts of those who recall him.

Only once, it seems, was his ire openly aroused. Lutwiniak says:

The Brig was a gentleman. He never raised his voice. It is hard to recall him being angry and I can only recall hearing him use an unprintable word on one occasion. That was the time he came to see me after reading F.W. Winterbotham's The Ultra Secret. *He was obviously upset and spoke to the effect that there were so many who could have written the book, and deserved to, and could have done it so much better, and yet 'that **** Winterbotham does it, and so atrociously that he thinks ULTRA is the **** ENIGMA and even has the Japanese using it in the Pacific because there is ULTRA end product there, and if the end product is ULTRA they must be using the machine.' This all came out in a rush of words, very untypical of the Brig; I think I was the first person he discussed the book with, for subsequently he was his usual gentle, controlled self.*

Bradley Smith and Stephen Budiansky describe him[19] warmly. Smith sums him up as a 'cheerful and agreeable man' who was 'the embodiment of British eccentric brilliance' who more than any other made the US-UK liaison work. Budiansky sees him of the 'old school' and compares him with the characters in Edgar Allen Poe or Sherlock Holmes – 'more a detective'. His ability to follow an idea or 'hunch' for long periods of time was a valuable quality. He comments on Tiltman's ability to pick up aspects of languages. He refers to a 'Colonel Blimp exterior' – the archetypal old-fashioned mellowed soldier who was perhaps not too bright – but with an 'extraordinarily supple mind' beneath the 'Teddy Bear' exterior (to borrow Leo Marks' image), as well as being someone who, as we have seen, sometimes ignored too rigid an interpretation of military regulation in favour of a softer – and more humane – approach.

Ronald Lewin wrote of him in an obituary,[20] 'a private and at times abrasive personality' – perhaps indicative of trying in vain to extract information from him for a book about the Pacific war – and commented on Tiltman's commitment to security. He admits, however, that in time the 'warm humanity which won him so many friends' showed through. It may be surmised that Tiltman, especially in the 1970s when secrets were beginning to emerge – and after his encounters with Kahn and the experience of Winterbotham's book – was cautious of enquiries about secrets which were matters of honour. Lewin describes him as a 'father figure' in his later years, which seems apt.

His colleague Prescott Currier put it[21] this way:

> *There is no doubt in my mind that he has an innate talent which he exercises with great skill and that has probably done more, not only in producing end product, but in encouraging others to work and be a part of the organization. This is one of his great contributions, really, because everyone that I've ever known who had known John Tiltman at any time in his life, particularly the younger people… they all looked up to him… and no matter what they did and how they developed in their future lives, they always looked to him as their original mentor and feel that he is really one of the greats.*

In 1954 the British government purchased about 100 acres of land near Harrogate, to become an RAF base soon to be known as RAF Menwith Hill Station. The base became a site for NSA surveillance in the 1960s and has expanded to become one of the largest. Nearly forty 'radomes' ('golf balls') protecting surveillance and aerial equipment which monitor satellite and other transmissions now stand on the site, linking into a worldwide system. The close security around it is one reason for local controversy about its use, which some claim[22] to include the use of drones for remote 'strikes'. In 2012 a new facility was completed at Menwith Hill. Originally the 'Phoenix' project, part of it has been named after Brigadier John Tiltman. His portrait[23] now hangs there, painted by his daughter Tempe Denzer. The spirit of the 'Brig' continues to oversee UK-US cryptology and security to this day.

Tiltman was, in this writer's view, unique in his combination of qualities – of innate talent, technical skill, perseverance and problem-solving skills on the one hand; and deep and lasting humanity, kindness and consideration for all kinds of people on the other. He was a man of character, capable of high achievement without showmanship, prepared to lead by example, and ready with a helping hand whenever needed.

He was not super-human: he expected high standards from those working with him and could be impatient when this was lacking, as comments about French codebreakers or Agnes Driscoll showed; he was not immune to stress and pressure: his letter to the WO in 1936 and his need for a sick note to cover his holiday in 1944 reveal that. There were people (such as Colonel Jeffrey or Admiral Redman) with whom it took him time to see eye to eye, but these were few.

When his country needed him he was there. He did some things which perhaps no-one else could have done, to help save his country, win a war, and maintain peace.

He was, simply, a very great man.

Afterword

This account is, of course, not the last word on the 'Brig'.

There may be more information about Tiltman's early life. David King and Mark Lubienski (linked to Bletchley Park) are at the time of this writing working on material concerning his earlier years and perhaps more personal background, and may have access to new material. We await any publication that may come.

There may well be more information to be gleaned from the National Archives, and there is no reason for future enthusiasts not to examine further documents to fill in some of the gaps.

Future declassifications may also help to fill out the picture, especially with regard to the later years and his work with GCHQ and the NSA.

What matters most is that due honour and wider recognition should be given to a remarkable man. This writer hopes that at least something has been achieved in this direction, and would welcome further development which might contribute to the picture.

With thanks to:

David King, academic, colleague and schools guide at Bletchley Park, who suggested that this work should be taken further, kindly read the early drafts, and gave valuable and corrective advice.

Mike Chapman, Bletchley guide and expert on BP history, who likewise read and advised in valuable detail on the publication.

Bletchley Park archives, especially Guy Revell, former archivist, and Dean Annison, current archivist at the time of this writing.

Dr David Kenyon, Research Historian, Bletchley Park Trust, who read the text at an advanced stage and advised on many corrections and changes (always for the better); if I have occasionally departed from his ideas on matters of uncertainty, structure or order, then where there is error the fault is not his and the blame is mine.

A number of colleagues at Bletchley Park who, along with the author, work or volunteer at Bletchley, including Dr Tom Cheetham, Research Officer at Bletchley Park, Karen Lewis, and Chris Northcott, all of whom have provided useful 'snippets' of information at various times; in the case of Dr Cheetham, additional comment and advice on ways to improve the overall nature of the book.

Fiona Jenkins, Curator at Bletchley Park Trust, who kindly assisted with illustrations for the book and gave valuable advice on them, as well as liaison with GCHQ.

Bletchley Park Trust, who have cooperated warmly with the author in granting permission to quote, access resources and use illustrations and material from their extensive collection.

The National Security Agency (USA), and the National Cryptological Museum, which generously make available historic archives including oral histories, photographs and volumes of declassified papers on the subject of signals intelligence and cryptography. These include the papers of William Friedman.

The National Museum of Computing, which houses the Colossus rebuild, the work of the late Tony Sale and the team, as well as exhibits and information about the history of computers.

The National Archive, Kew, which has provided access, as well as permission to reproduce illustrations and to quote from materials.

Henry Wilson, of Pen & Sword, who has given his encouragement to me from when the project was first mooted, and continued to advise and guide from then on. Also Barnaby Blacker and Matthew Jones at Pen & Sword, for their patient work on editing the manuscript, correcting my errors and bringing the product to fruition.

The many volunteer stewards, archive workers and guides at Bletchley Park who have inspired me to persevere with this work.

Any errors in the text are solely the responsibility of the author.

Appendices

Chronology of the life of John Hessell Tiltman

		Tiltman events	World events
1894	25 March	Born in London, younger son of an architect	
1907		Admitted to Charterhouse	
		Offered place at Oxford University; has to be declined later because of financial issues	
1910		Death of Alfred Tiltman (father)	
1911		Began teaching career (Fulham, Hastings, Bognor)	
1914		Teaching in Bognor; enlisted in KOSB	Outbreak of war
1915		His unit sent to France	
1916		His unit involved in Somme battles (Bazentin, Delville Wood)	
1917	May	Involved in Battle of Arras; seriously wounded; awarded MC	Russian revolution
1918			Armistice
1919		Sent to Russia, to work as translator, Irkutsk	
		Hospitalized in Vladivostok; returns to UK	GC&CS established
1920	Aug	Takes Russian course, passes as 'interpreter'	
		Sent to GC&CS, London, initially two weeks, begins translating codes	
		Posting extended to one year	
1921		Posted to Simla, handling Russian diplomatic codes	
		Begins visits to Baghdad, studying range of codes and signals techniques	
1923		Messages from Indian interception probably help UK government reveal Soviet espionage	
1925		Retires from army; remains in post as civilian	
1926		Marries Tempe Robinson	General Strike

		Tiltman events	World events
1927		ARCOS raid disrupts code work when codes are changed as a result of publication of decodes	
1928		Birth of daughter Tempe	
1929			Stock market crash
1930		Became head of Military Section of GC&CS (remaining civilian), main focus, Russian and Comintern codes	
		Rank of captain restored	
		Created OBE	
1931		Works on Russian Comintern codes; success in breaking their systems	'Asche' begins passing information on Enigma to French
		First of three visits to Berlin concerning Russian codes and intelligence	Japan occupies part of Manchuria
1932		Visits France; first contact with Bertrand	
1933		Broke Japanese military attaché code	
		Visits France; exchanges of code information	
1934		Resumes work against Comintern codes; worked on the 'Mask' operation	Polish codebreakers secretly begin reading Enigma
1935		Helps establish first military unit at Hong Kong (alongside navy section); Begins learning Japanese	Italy invades Abyssinia
1936		Analysis of Enigma indicator system by Tiltman	
1937		To Hong Kong, tries to get section to take on further army work, but hindered by lack of trained people	
	July		Main attack on China by Japan

		Tiltman events	World events
1938	March		Anschluss – takeover of Austria by Germany
	Sept	Requests more Enigma information from French; joins move to BP as part of 'Captain Ridley's shooting party'	Munich crisis
		Broke Japanese military code	
	Nov	Meeting with Bertrand in London; exchange of code information	Germany upgrades Enigma systems
1939	Jan	To Paris (9-10 Jan) with Denniston *et al* to meet Poles for first Enigma meeting; involved in London training courses for 'men of the professor type'	
	Mar	Training new codebreakers, including Welchman, Turing *et al*	
	July	To Hong Kong, organizes army codebreaking to be done 'on the spot'; visits India	
	Aug	GC&CS begins move to Bletchley Park	
	Sept	Breaks German police codes as Germany attacks Poland	Outbreak of world war
		Breaks 'system' of the earlier version of JN-25 Japanese	
	Sept	Made lieutenant colonel	
	Nov	Further liaison with French secret services	
1940	Jan	To France liaising with Bertrand	
		Visits Finland; is given information on Russian codes	GC&CS makes first breaks into Enigma
	March	Return from visit to Finland; helps with Russian additive systems; appointed chief recruiting officer for GC&CS.	
		Makes initial breaks into German Railway Enigma	

		Tiltman events	World events
	May	In France; receives assurances from Bertrand	Churchill becomes Prime Minister
	June	Advising committee on changing British codes after Dunkirk	Dunkirk evacuation
	Aug-Sep	Breaks 'Barbarameldung' code system	
	Nov	Advising on Free French and Polish codes	
1941			
	Feb	Meets Sinkov mission at BP; persuades his superiors to reveal Enigma success to US visitors	
	March	Escorts Sinkov mission to Scotland for their return to USA; further visit to Finland	
	April	Returns to UK; Research Section set up at BP, Tiltman in overall charge	
		Creates cryptanalytical 'school' in Bedford for training new recruits to BP	
	June	His Research Section analyses the Hagelin C-38 system	Germany invades Russia
	Sept	Decodes 'Tunny' messages sent by mistake in depth; allows the coding layer to be identified leading to Tutte's work analysing structure of Lorenz machine	
		Breaks German-Spanish Kryha code?	
		Involved in breaking Railway Enigma	
	Oct	Considered for visit to India to supervise development and expansion of WEC	
	Dec		Japanese attack Pearl Harbor; USA enters war
1942	Jan		British retreat to Singapore
	Feb	Involved with reorganisation of Hut 3; Tiltman named C/O all army personnel at BP; sets up Japanese courses for BP codebreakers in Bedford, with Captain Oswald Tuck RN	Japan takes Singapore; 4-rotor U-boat Enigma shuts out Bletchley codebreakers.

		Tiltman events	World events
	March	Visits USA; two months liaison and negotiation about exchange of information	
	Oct	Persuades UK to reveal Shark 'blackout' to USA	
		Is kept informed of 'Holden' agreement with USA which gives them dominance in Far East code work	
	Nov		Operation Torch; Allied landings in N. Africa
	Dec	Visits USA to confirm arrangements for full exchange; finds disagreement and barriers from Strong and especially from US navy.	Bletchley breaks back into U-boat Enigma
1943	Jan	Meeting with Strong allays many US concerns; urges cooperation when he finds out about US Bombe plans	
		Assists with negotiations on security exchange agreement	
		Attends conference in Canada between US, UK and Canada regarding mutual intelligence work	
	March	First draft of BRUSA agreement prepared	
	April	Organizes conference on army codes at BP; visit to BP by Friedman; two-month stay, helped by Tiltman	Admiral Yamamoto shot down thanks largely to breaking JN-25 message
	May	Involved in conference at BP finalising fields of interest and primacy of work between US army and UK	
	July		Battle of Kursk won with aid of Tunny material
	Oct	In Washington as consultant to British section; meets Safford	

		Tiltman events	World events
	Dec	Responsible for design of new navy code system to improve on ones read by Germans (1942); in full use by end of year	
1944	Jan	Breaks Japanese Army Air code 3366	
	March	Created CBE	
	June	Visits USA, discussing Japanese codes and others	D-Day Normandy landings
		Made Deputy Director at BP. Becomes brigadier	
	Sept	Called in to advise following JN-25 code changes by Japanese; discussions on US-UK sharing of material	
		Part of Menzies' committee discussing future of GC&CS	Liberation of Paris
		Visits USA with Menzies' group for UK-US discussions on future	
1945	April	Visits France for 3-day conference with Allies	
	May		Victory in Europe
	July	Involved with UK-US conferences (including Friedman), partly linked to TICOM mission returns	New Labour government in UK
	August	Continues TICOM discussions, including focus on Russian codes monitored by Germans; is informed about 'Venona' project in USA against Russian codes	Atomic bombs dropped on Japan
	Oct	Visits USA with Hinsley	
		In USA with Travis for US-UK talks; attacked by Redman and withdraws from further proceedings	
	Dec	Involved in informal talks with USA on 'Bourbon' work, dealing with Russian codes at start of Cold War	
1946	January	Is head of the Russian cryptology section at GCHQ	

		Tiltman events	World events
	March	Takes part in SIGINT committee inaugural meetings and cryptological discussions, leading to BRUSA agreement	GC&CS leaves Bletchley Park
		Received USA Legion of Merit	
1947		Retires from army. Made Assistant Director, GCHQ	
1948		Tiltman made aware of 'Venona' project and early decrypts	Start of Berlin airlift
	Oct	Russians change major code systems; Tiltman brought in as advisor	
1949		Attends UK-US-Canada conference on security	Founding of AFSA
		Made UK-US liaison officer	'Venona' identifies Fuchs as traitor
1950		Involved with BRUSA conference (as liaison officer and expert)	
		Introduced to Voynich topic by Friedman	
1951	April		Burgess and MacLean flee to USSR
	May	Involved in London UK-US conference; liaising between GCHQ and Washington on administrative details	
1952		Is asked to provide historical materials for US research	Creation of National Security Agency NSA
		Liaison with USA regarding concerns about NATO communications security and British ideas on sharing of expertise, especially with French	
1953	March	Attends Canadian conference as SUKLO	
		Preparation for BRUSA planning conference	
		Attends BRUSA conference	
	May	Continuing COMSEC liaison	

		Tiltman events	World events
	June	Attends US-UK conference on NATO security	
	Nov	Involved with US-UK security conference and negotiations over support for French	
		Acts as liaison regarding French access to 'Circuit Mercury'	
1954		Liaison with USA over possible British ROCKEX cipher equipment loan to West Germany	
		Reaches official GCHQ retirement age but is asked to continue	
		Receives CMG	
1958		While working for GCHQ, is embedded with NSA for joint work	
1961		Begins to write articles for *NSA Technical Journal*	
		Writes to Robin Denniston following the death of his father, former head of GC&CS	
1963		Attends US conference with Friedman and Cooper	
1964		Finally retires from GCHQ; is engaged by NSA as consultant	
		Moves to USA to be closer to daughter	
1966		Is approached by Kahn to assist with information on code work; refuses except for aspects of Voynich work	
1973			Bertrand writes *Enigma*
1974		Reacts angrily to publication of Winterbotham's book revealing code-breaking story for first time in UK	*The ULTRA Secret* published in UK
1975		Gives lecture on aspects of Voynich manuscript	
1976		Guest of Honour at Voynich conference	
1977	Nov	Participates in American Historical Association seminar on codebreaking and intelligence (with Telford Taylor)	

		Tiltman events	World events
1978		Participates in four US NSA oral history interviews	
1980		Finally retires from NSA; moves to Hawaii (near family)	
1982		Death of Tiltman (10 August)	
2004		Inducted into NSA Hall of Honor, first non-US member	
2012		Opening of John Tiltman facility at RAF Menwith Hill	

Copyright information

Text

Quotations from *The Secrets of Station X* (Michael Smith) and *The Codebreakers of Bletchley Park* (Smith and Erskine eds) by kind permission of Biteback publications, represented by Lucy Stewardson.

Materials from the NSA

'Unless a copyright or trademark is indicated, information on the National Security Agency Web site is in the public domain and may be reproduced, published or otherwise used without the National Security Agency's permission. We request only that the National Security Agency be cited as the source of information and that any photo credits or bylines be similarly credited to the photographer or author or NSA, as appropriate.' (nsa.gov/terms-of-use/#terms).

All such materials by kind permission of NSA and the National Cryptologic Museum Foundation.

Materials from Bletchley Park

Quotations from the BP Roll of Honour, photographs of BP equipment and buildings and quotations from BP library documents are reproduced by kind permission of Bletchley Park Trust (represented by Rebecca Foy).

Materials from The National Archives

Crown copyright. All references or quotations from this source are under Open Government Licence; contains public sector information licensed under the Open Government Licence v3.0. See also nationalarchives.gov.uk/doc/open-government-licence/version/3/.

Pictures (apart from those in sources listed above)

Torrington Square, by kind permission of Sally Williams and Londons Garden Trust.

The ECM/SIGABA machine, by kind permission of the San Francisco Maritime National Park Association (maritime.org) represented by Richard Pekelney.

Ardour House, Bedford, by kind permission of Nick Cooke.

Charterhouse School, by kind permission of the school, represented by archivist Ms C. Smith.

Colossus computer, reconstruction led by the late Tony Sale, from the National Museum of Computing, Bletchley, by kind permission of the Museum, represented by Jacqui Garrad.

Every effort has been made to ensure that copyright guidance has been observed; if there remain any issues then the author expresses apologies and will undertake to correct them urgently in any further printing.

Example of the Vigenere coding square

One way to use the square with a keyword, the letters of the keyword are used in order (repeating the keyword as often as the message length needs) one at a time to select the column, and the plaintext letter is found from the side letters. The intersection letter of the line and column is the cipher letter. So if the Key is 'PARK' and the message is 'Bletchley' then:

- Column P and line B gives Q
- Column A and line L gives L
- Column R and line E gives V
  – and so on to give 'QLVDRHCON'.

The same process works with a 'running key', which would often use the same columns more than once, but in a less obvious order than a single or short keyword.

	A	B	C	D	E	F	G	H	I	J	K	L	M	N	O	P	Q	R	S	T	U	V	W	X	Y	Z
A	A	B	C	D	E	F	G	H	I	J	K	L	M	N	O	P	Q	R	S	T	U	V	W	X	Y	Z
B	B	C	D	E	F	G	H	I	J	K	L	M	N	O	P	Q	R	S	T	U	V	W	X	Y	Z	A
C	C	D	E	F	G	H	I	J	K	L	M	N	O	P	Q	R	S	T	U	V	W	X	Y	Z	A	B
D	D	E	F	G	H	I	J	K	L	M	N	O	P	Q	R	S	T	U	V	W	X	Y	Z	A	B	C
E	E	F	G	H	I	J	K	L	M	N	O	P	Q	R	S	T	U	V	W	X	Y	Z	A	B	C	D
F	F	G	H	I	J	K	L	M	N	O	P	Q	R	S	T	U	V	W	X	Y	Z	A	B	C	D	E
G	G	H	I	J	K	L	M	N	O	P	Q	R	S	T	U	V	W	X	Y	Z	A	B	C	D	E	F
H	H	I	J	K	L	M	N	O	P	Q	R	S	T	U	V	W	X	Y	Z	A	B	C	D	E	F	G
I	I	J	K	L	M	N	O	P	Q	R	S	T	U	V	W	X	Y	Z	A	B	C	D	E	F	G	H
J	J	K	L	M	N	O	P	Q	R	S	T	U	V	W	X	Y	Z	A	B	C	D	E	F	G	H	I
K	K	L	M	N	O	P	Q	R	S	T	U	V	W	X	Y	Z	A	B	C	D	E	F	G	H	I	J
L	L	M	N	O	P	Q	R	S	T	U	V	W	X	Y	Z	A	B	C	D	E	F	G	H	I	J	K
M	M	N	O	P	Q	R	S	T	U	V	W	X	Y	Z	A	B	C	D	E	F	G	H	I	J	K	L
N	N	O	P	Q	R	S	T	U	V	W	X	Y	Z	A	B	C	D	E	F	G	H	I	J	K	L	M
O	O	P	Q	R	S	T	U	V	W	X	Y	Z	A	B	C	D	E	F	G	H	I	J	K	L	M	N
P	P	Q	R	S	T	U	V	W	X	Y	Z	A	B	C	D	E	F	G	H	I	J	K	L	M	N	O
Q	Q	R	S	T	U	V	W	X	Y	Z	A	B	C	D	E	F	G	H	I	J	K	L	M	N	O	P
R	R	S	T	U	V	W	X	Y	Z	A	B	C	D	E	F	G	H	I	J	K	L	M	N	O	P	Q
S	S	T	U	V	W	X	Y	Z	A	B	C	D	E	F	G	H	I	J	K	L	M	N	O	P	Q	R
T	T	U	V	W	X	Y	Z	A	B	C	D	E	F	G	H	I	J	K	L	M	N	O	P	Q	R	S
U	U	V	W	X	Y	Z	A	B	C	D	E	F	G	H	I	J	K	L	M	N	O	P	Q	R	S	T
V	V	W	X	Y	Z	A	B	C	D	E	F	G	H	I	J	K	L	M	N	O	P	Q	R	S	T	U
W	W	X	Y	Z	A	B	C	D	E	F	G	H	I	J	K	L	M	N	O	P	Q	R	S	T	U	V
X	X	Y	Z	A	B	C	D	E	F	G	H	I	J	K	L	M	N	O	P	Q	R	S	T	U	V	W
Y	Y	Z	A	B	C	D	E	F	G	H	I	J	K	L	M	N	O	P	Q	R	S	T	U	V	W	X
Z	Z	A	B	C	D	E	F	G	H	I	J	K	L	M	N	O	P	Q	R	S	T	U	V	W	X	Y

The Teleprinter 'addition' square (for use with teleprinter systems such as the Lorenz cipher attachment)

To 'add' any two teleprinter code letters (or subtract one from the other), find the row of one letter on the left, and the column headed by the other letter. Where row and column intersect is the 'total', the code-letter for the two with their mark-space patterns combined. Thus for example:

looking along line 'R' to column 'P' produces 'M'

(Murray code *X*X* plus *XX*X gives **XXX)

Line 'G' and column 'F' produce 'Q'

(Murray code *X*XX plus X*XX* gives XXX*X); and so on.

/	/	9	H	T	O	M	N	3	R	C	V	G	L	P	I	4	A	U	Q	W	5	8	K	J	D	F	X	B	Z	Y	S	E
/	/	9	H	T	O	M	N	3	R	C	V	G	L	P	I	4	A	U	Q	W	5	8	K	J	D	F	X	B	Z	Y	S	E
9	9	/	T	H	M	O	3	N	C	R	G	V	P	L	4	I	U	A	W	Q	8	5	J	K	F	D	B	X	Y	Z	E	S
H	H	T	/	9	N	3	O	M	V	G	R	C	I	4	L	P	Q	W	A	U	K	J	5	8	X	B	D	F	S	E	Z	Y
T	T	H	9	/	3	N	M	O	G	V	C	R	4	I	P	L	W	Q	U	A	J	K	8	5	B	X	F	D	E	S	Y	Z
O	O	M	N	3	/	9	H	T	L	P	I	4	R	C	V	G	5	8	K	J	A	U	Q	W	Z	Y	S	E	D	F	X	B
M	M	O	3	N	9	/	T	H	P	L	4	I	C	R	G	V	8	5	J	K	U	A	W	Q	Y	Z	E	S	F	D	B	X
N	N	3	O	M	H	T	/	9	I	4	L	P	V	G	R	C	K	J	5	8	Q	W	A	U	S	E	Z	Y	X	B	D	F
3	3	N	M	O	T	H	9	/	4	I	P	L	G	V	C	R	J	K	8	5	W	Q	U	A	E	S	Y	Z	B	X	F	D
R	R	C	V	G	L	P	I	4	/	9	H	T	O	M	N	3	D	F	X	B	Z	Y	S	E	A	U	Q	W	5	8	K	J
C	C	R	G	V	P	L	4	I	9	/	T	H	M	O	3	N	F	D	B	X	Y	Z	E	S	U	A	W	Q	8	5	J	K
V	V	G	R	C	I	4	L	P	H	T	/	9	N	3	O	M	X	B	D	F	S	E	Z	Y	Q	W	A	U	K	J	5	8
G	G	V	C	R	4	I	P	L	T	H	9	/	3	N	M	O	B	X	F	D	E	S	Y	Z	W	Q	U	A	J	K	8	5
L	L	P	I	4	R	C	V	G	O	M	N	3	/	9	H	T	Z	Y	S	E	D	F	X	B	5	8	K	J	A	U	Q	W
P	P	L	4	I	C	R	G	V	M	O	3	N	9	/	T	H	Y	Z	E	S	F	D	B	X	8	5	J	K	U	A	W	Q
I	I	4	L	P	V	G	R	C	N	3	O	M	H	T	/	9	S	E	Z	Y	X	B	D	F	K	J	5	8	Q	W	A	U
4	4	I	P	L	G	V	C	R	3	N	M	O	T	H	9	/	E	S	Y	Z	B	X	F	D	J	K	8	5	W	Q	U	A
A	A	U	Q	W	5	8	K	J	D	F	X	B	Z	Y	S	E	/	9	H	T	O	M	N	3	R	C	V	G	L	P	I	4
U	U	A	W	Q	8	5	J	K	F	D	B	X	Y	Z	E	S	9	/	T	H	M	O	3	N	C	R	G	V	P	L	4	I
G	Q	W	A	U	K	J	5	8	X	B	D	F	S	E	Z	Y	H	T	/	9	N	3	O	M	V	G	R	C	I	4	L	P
W	W	Q	U	A	J	K	8	5	B	X	F	D	E	S	Y	Z	T	H	9	/	3	N	M	O	G	V	C	R	4	I	P	L
5	5	8	K	J	A	U	Q	W	Z	Y	S	E	D	F	X	B	O	M	N	3	/	9	H	T	L	P	I	4	R	C	V	G
8	8	5	J	K	U	A	W	Q	Y	Z	E	S	F	D	B	X	M	O	3	N	9	/	T	H	P	L	4	I	C	R	G	V
K	K	J	5	8	Q	W	A	U	S	E	Z	Y	X	B	D	F	N	3	O	M	H	T	/	9	I	4	L	P	V	G	R	C
J	J	K	8	5	W	Q	U	A	E	S	Y	Z	B	X	F	D	3	N	M	O	T	H	9	/	4	I	P	L	G	V	C	R
D	D	F	X	B	Z	Y	S	E	A	U	Q	W	5	8	K	J	R	C	V	G	L	P	I	4	/	9	H	T	O	M	N	3
F	F	D	B	X	Y	Z	E	S	U	A	W	Q	8	5	J	K	C	R	G	V	P	L	4	I	9	/	T	H	M	O	3	N
X	X	B	D	F	S	E	Z	Y	Q	W	A	U	K	J	5	8	V	G	R	C	I	4	L	P	H	T	/	9	N	3	O	M
B	B	X	F	D	E	S	Y	Z	W	Q	U	A	J	K	8	5	G	V	C	R	4	I	P	L	T	H	9	/	3	N	M	O
Z	Z	Y	S	E	D	F	X	B	5	8	K	J	A	U	Q	W	L	P	I	4	R	C	V	G	O	M	N	3	/	9	H	T
Y	Y	Z	E	S	F	D	B	X	8	5	J	K	U	A	W	Q	P	L	4	I	C	R	G	V	M	O	3	N	9	/	T	H
S	S	E	Z	Y	X	B	D	F	K	J	5	8	Q	W	A	U	I	4	L	P	V	G	R	C	N	3	O	M	H	T	/	9
E	E	S	Y	Z	B	X	F	D	J	K	8	5	W	Q	U	A	4	I	P	L	G	V	C	R	3	N	M	O	T	H	9	/

Adding two identical letters produces ***** – a 'blank'.

Notes

Chapter 1

1. There may be much more to learn about Tiltman's early life than is currently available. Tiltman's direct descendants live in Hawaii at the time of this writing, and colleagues David King and Mark Lubienski are in touch with them. Access to work and materials relating to Tiltman's earlier life are retained within these interests, and we await the outcome of further research in due course.
2. scottisharchitects.org.uk.
3. 1871 census records.
4. At the time of writing no definite link can be found between Brigadier John Hessell Tiltman and the Hessell-Tiltman literary prize. The prize was named for Marjorie, an author and wife of Hubert (Hugh) Hessell Tiltman, a journalist and writer born in 1897, son of Frank Tiltman (born c.1859) who grew up in Rye, East Sussex. Frank's mother Mary was born c.1823 but her husband is not named in the census records. Alfred's father Thomas, and his mother Mary, both born in 1822, were from Sussex and there seem to be Tiltmans linked to both Sussex generally and Rye in particular. Future writers may be able to solve this one.
5. 1891 census records.
6. *Dictionary of National Biography* 'Tiltman, John Hessell' (2004).
7. hatfield-herts.co.uk/aviation
8. Carthusian obituary of Tiltman
9. Clabby (2007)
10. Smith, M., lecture given at Bletchley Park, c.2013.
11. *DNB*
12. forces-war-records.co.uk/records/10206054/colonel-john-hessell-Tiltman
13. theroyalscots.co.uk/823-2. A number of the details in this part of the narrative draw on this source.
14. Simkins, Jukes, Hickey (2003), especially pp. 122–33
15. See https://www.forces-war-records.co.uk/maps/units/772/kings-own-scottish-borderers?battalionName=6th-service-battalion
16. Anecdotal comment from Mr D. King, Bletchley Park, who had connections with the family.
17. Ferris (2020)
18. Ferris p.61
19. discovery.nationalarchives.gov.uk/details/r/D8458371

Chapter 2

1. NSA (1975), Tiltman-Currier interview, seminar for members of Cryptanalysis Field, NSA, Fort Meade, p.30
2. Clabby, p.8

3. Tiltman, 'Experiences 1920–1939', in NSA archive 3868631 (declassified 2007), p.1
4. *DNB*, 'Denniston, Alexander Guthrie [Alastair]'.
5. Cf. e.g. Greenberg (2017), p. 84 ff.
6. Oral History interview with Tiltman on his early years in codebreaking, NSA archive, doc 4235147 (1978), OH-05-78, p.9
7. Ibid. p.9.
8. Ibid. p. 14.
9. West, 1986, p. 115.
10. Tiltman, 'Some reminiscences', NSA archive, doc 3838686, p.3
11. West, p.114
12. Erskine and Smith (2011), p.18
13. The Great Soviet Encyclopedia
14. Tiltman, 'Experiences 1920–1939', NSA archive 3868631, p.8.
15. Oral History interview with Tiltman, NSA archive 4235147 (1978), OH-05-78, pp. 15ff.
16. Clabby, p.8
17. NSA archive, document A72447; memo from American embassy to Arlington, 20 May 1943 describing Chinese area of Diplomatic Section.
18. Jeffrey (2010), 228ff.
19. *The sailor in room 53 – has never, it's true, been to sea – but though not in a boat, he has served afloat – in a bath at the Admiralty*.
20. Oral History interview with Tiltman, NSA archive 4235147, p.28
21. TNA HW 62/19 memo, 8/12/1927.
22. TNA HW 62/19.

Chapter 3

1. TNA HW 62/19/13a.
2. West (1986), 117.
3. Peterson, 'Before Bourbon', NSA doc 3863634.
4. Oral History interview with Tiltman, NSA doc 4235147 (1978).
5. Ibid.
6. Oral History interview with Tiltman, NSA doc 4236467 (1978), p.1
7. Oral History interview with Tiltman, NSA doc 4236153 (1978), p.4
8. Bletchley Park Roll of Honour
9. TNA 14/2/5 Letter from Kenworthy 5/11/1939 to Colonel Butler.
10. Bletchley Park Roll of Honour
11. Mask, p.5
12. Smith and Erskine op. cit.
13. West (2005), 41ff. This and subsequent examples are cited from this invaluable source for easier reference, though all are publicly available at TNA.
14. West, p.127
15. The Mask messages consistently spell Harry Pollitt's name with one 't' instead of two.
16. Batey (2009) p.50
17. Turing (2018) p.64
18. NSA archive, doc 4236153, p.15
19. Ferris (2020), 102ff

20. TNA HW 62/20/11b memo 12/2/35 signed by Cptn. Tiltman
21. TNA HW 62/20/11a letter to Lt. Col. Carr at MI 1(b), War Office, 13 Feb 1935
22. TNA HW 62/20/12a Notes on conference held at GC & CS 11/4/35
23. NSA archive, doc 3838686, 'Some reminiscences', article by Tiltman, p.5: NSA archive, doc 4236153 (1978), OH-06-78, p.8
24. Smith, M. (2010), 47ff.
25. TNA HW 12/191/060421 1 May 1935 and 060454 4 May 1935
26. Smith, M. (2010), 37ff.
27. Ibid. 38ff.
28. NSA archive, doc 3838686
29. NSA archive, doc 3838686, p.5
30. West (1986), p.150
31. TNA HW 62/20 report on half-year to June 30th 1935, dated 11 July
32. TNA HW 62/20 memorandum dated 22/11 1935 'French Military and Air ciphers'
33. Greenberg (2017), p.93
34. TNA HW 62/20/13a appendix to draft document of the working of the Military Section, 1/5/25
35. TNA HW 62/20 Italian codes chart dated 13/6/35 with addenda, November 1935
36. TNA HW 62/20/1A dated 28/4/1936, 'Survey of the work of the Military Section of the GC&CS'
37. TNA HW 62/20/2A – letter of May 1936 to Tiltman from Colonel ?Allen.
38. TNA HW 62/20/4A, handwritten letter signed by Tiltman dated 10/07/36 to Allen
39. TNA HW 26/20 nos. 17A, 18A, Nov 1936, exchanges of correspondence between Allen, Tiltman and others.
40. NSA doc 4236467 (1978) archive OH-07-78, interview with Benson, p.2
41. TNA 62/21, proposal dated 14 June 1938 asking for two additional clerks for the Italian work; Tiltman writes comments 15 June.
42. TNA 62/21, letter 11 May 1938
43. TNA 62/21 Report on GC&CS Military Section July 1938, signed by Tiltman, to Col Allen.
44. TNA 62/21 to Denniston dated 30 August 1938.
45. Tiltman, 'Some reminiscences', NSA archive, doc 3838686, p.9
46. TNA HW 62/20/5, August 1936
47. Batey (2009), 66–7
48. TNA HW 62/21/10
49. TNA 62/21, two-page letter requesting information, copy indicates Tiltman was author.
50. TNA 62/21
51. Turing (2018), p.90
52. TNA HW 25/10, account of early Enigma work, dating from 1949, by Hugh Foss, quoted in Erskine (2011), 38ff.
53. TNA HW 62/21 Jan 1939, detailed programme of training course – the author is not named but Tiltman looks the likely organiser.
54. See Greenberg (2014), p.11
55. TNA HW 62/21 memorandum dated 3 January 1939
56. NSA archive, doc 4236467 (1978), OH-07-78, oral history interview with Tiltman, p.14

Chapter 4

1. Tiltman's own note of codes worked on; unpublished MS (NSA archive).
2. Oral history interview with Tiltman, NSA archive, doc 4235147, p.9
3. Conveniently demonstrated on practicalcryptography.com/ciphers/running-key-cipher
4. NSA archive 3868631, p.5
5. Tiltman, 'Some principles of cryptographic security', NSA document 3838697, *NSA Technical Journal* vol. 19, no.3 (1974), p.17
6. There is an interesting message in the 'Mask' traffic (West 2005 p.63) which shows that a Russian sender had been reusing these cut-up books instead of one-timing them; the British message complained about the risk.
7. NSA archive, doc 3838686, p.5
8. M. Smith (2010) p.47
9. NSA archive, doc 4236153, 4ff.
10. Hinsley and Stripp (1993), p.298
11. M. Smith (2010), appendix 1
12. Dryden in Hinsley and Stripp, 1993, p.197
13. M. Smith (2010), p.58
14. NSA archive, doc 4236153, p.5.
15. Duffy (2017), p.64
16. NSA archive, doc 4236153, 5–6
17. See his account in Hinsley and Stripp, p.209
18. David (1994), and Friedman (1938), 77ff available online at nsa.gov
19. See his account in Hinsley and Stripp (1993), 211 ff. Also David, esp. 34–5.
20. NSA archive, doc 4236467, oral history interview with Tiltman, p.6
21. NSA archive, doc 3838686, 'Some reminiscences', p.16
22. Erskine and Smith (2011), p.61.
23. Hinsley and Stripp, p.116
24. [5–67] NSA 4157007, nsa.gov/Portals/70/documents/news-features/declassified-documents/history-today-articles/22_June_2009.pdf
25. See Hanyok, p.26
26. Jackson (2014), p.363
27. See Wilkinson in Hinsley and Stripp, p.64
28. See his account in Copeland (2010), appendix 4, 352ff.
29. Tutte in Copeland, p.353
30. See Mowry, D (2014); 'German cipher machines of World War 2'; NSA publication; p. 16
31. Copeland, p.353
32. Bletchley Park Roll of Honour, oral history record by Sylvia Godden (Kaufmann).
33. A process of using bundles of 'rods', with sequences of letters matching various wheel patterns from the machine, which could be used to trace possible decodes of letters through a set of wheels.
34. Tordella (1974).
35. Gannon (2006), 35ff.
36. Gannon, p.38
37. See his chapter in Copeland, appendix 5 (p.370)
38. 'General Report on Tunny', ch. 41, alanturing.net. See also Gannon, p.142
39. In a lecture given in 1960 to the Crypto-Mathematical Institute later published in *Cryptologia*.

40. NSA archive, doc 4236153, 1–2
41. NSA oral history interview with Tiltman, OH-06-78, p.8ff.
42. NSA 41781389082044 traffic enciphered using KRYHA, p.2. See also Cheetham, T.; 'Pocket-sized puzzle', article in Bletchley Park's *ULTRA Magazine*, issue 15 (summer 2021); p.8.
43. NSA archive, doc 4236153, p.5
44. See Wiles' account in Hinsley and Stripp, p.284.
45. p.297–8
46. p.297–8
47. M. Smith, 247ff.
48. Owen (1946), 121ff.
49. See Bletchley Park Roll of Honour at bletchleypark.org.uk
50. See Bletchley Park Roll of Honour
51. See illustrations and also Tiltman (1967) NSA archive, doc 3838686, 'Some reminiscences', p.32
52. NSA 3838686
53. See Tiltman, 'A cryptological fairytale', *NSA Technical Journals* 1962, vol. 7, no. 2, p.21ff
54. NSA 3838686, pp. 3–4
55. Op. cit. p.45
56. NSA archive, doc 3838686, p.15.
57. C. Andrew, Defence of the Realm (2009)
58. Hinsley and Stripp, p.198
59. NSA 3838697 (1973), 'Some principles of cryptographic security'
60. BP Roll of honour, 2032, Jean Nissan (Lewis). 2032 is the index place on the roll.

Chapter 5

1. Op. cit. p. 14
2. NSA archive, doc 4236153 (1978), OH-06-78, oral history interview with Tiltman, p.16 ff.
3. Tiltman (1967) NSA archive, doc 3838686, 'Some reminiscences', p.8
4. NSA archive, doc 4236153, p.6 ff.
5. GCHQ and Bletchley Park Trust (2009), p.25
6. In Erskine and Smith, p.31
7. NSA archive, doc 4236467 (1978); OH-07-78, oral history interview with Tiltman, p.6ff
8. TNA HW 14/4 March-April 1940, Tiltman reports on Finnish visit and promise of SIGINT equipment.
9. See Smith in Erskine and Smith, p.31
10. NSA 3838697 (1973), 'Some principles of cryptographic security', p.18
11. NSA archive, document 4235410, OH-17-82 (1982), interview with Solomon Kullback, p.50
12. Ibid. p.65

Chapter 6

1. See his chapter in Hinsley and Stripp, p.277
2. See Peter Donovan in *Cryptologia* Vol. 33, p.56
3. Information from a lecture at BP by Karen Lewis from TNA research, 16 Oct 2019, and personal information from her on subsequent research, August 2021. There

seems to be evidence that chauffeurs, who slept in the Mansion, were provided for other MI6 personnel but not for GC&CS people, and similar feelings of being 'lesser mortals' may have prompted Denniston to write to Menzies – see TNA HW 14/1 – expressing concerns. Tiltman's billet in Leighton Buzzard (the Swan Hotel) also had MI6 people in residence, and if the latter and not the former had access to transport it might have led to 'issues'.
4. M. Smith, lecture given at BP, c.2013.
5. NSA 41768289080739 William Friedman diary of visit to UK May-June 1943.
6. Information kindly supplied by the owner at the time of this writing, Geoff Banbury.
7. GCHQ and Bletchley Park Trust (2009), p.10
8. Ibid, pp. 27ff, Bletchley Park archives document BLEPK 0108.3.22 listing rooms of numbers of senior people and activities.
9. McKay (2010), p.31
10. Quoted in Greenberg (2017), p.111
11. Information on display at Bletchley Park, May 2021, in 'Early Days' exhibition (by courtesy of Dr Cheetham, Research Officer, Bletchley Park)
12. Here and for following personnel, information also from Bletchley Roll of Honour.
13. Not to be confused with Emily Anderson, who also handled Italian and worked in the Military Section, but was a veteran from WW1 and was reckoned by Ferris (op. cit.) to be one of the finest female codebreakers of her time – alongside Elizebeth Friedman. Before the war she headed the Italian Section but allowed herself to be sent to Cairo in 1940 for several years before returning to diplomatic work. She was also a musicological authority.
14. See Ferris (2020), 91ff.
15. TNA 14//2 memo unsigned, 'Investigation of German Military ciphers; Progress report', dated 7 Nov 1939, stamped IS.4
16. See Erskine and Smith (2011), p.31
17. TNA 14/2/21 memo to Spencer (replying to query of the 18th) about sharing information.
18. TNA 14/2/2 memo 18/12–39
19. TNA 14/2/2 typed and written letter in French to Denniston
20. TNA 14/3 'Memento (codes generals)', 27 Feb 1940
21. TNA HW 14/4, March 1940
22. See NSA oral history OH-25-82 (1982), interview with Wilma Davis, p.17
23. In Hinsley and Stripp, 198ff.
24. TNA HW 14/5/9, May 1940, WO asked Denniston to agree 13/5/40, Denniston replied positive but concerned about duplication of work 18/5/40.
25. TNA 14/5/20, dated 17 May 1940, memo in French (author's translation) on outcomes from Tiltman's visit exchanging information on various codes.
26. TNA 14/5/10 memorandum from Saunders 15/5/40 on organisation of 'Intelligence' room and central sorting officer.
27. TNA 14/5/16 handwritten response from Tiltman to the Saunders memo of 15 May, dated 17 May.
28. TNA 14/5/19 and 26 – memo confirming establishment and agenda of first meeting.
29. NSA archive, doc 4236153, p.8 ff.
30. TNA 14/5/10 memo to Director, Military Intelligence and Air Ministry Signals, regarding ciphers, dated 6/6/40.

31. TNA HW 14/8; memo regarding cipher support for de Gaulle
32. NSA archive, doc 4236153, p.24
33. TNA HW 14/11, GC&CS report for 1940; quoted in Greenberg (2017) p.134
34. Greenberg (2017), p.125
35. See Benson, R., in NSA Cryptologic Spectrum.
36. See e.g. Budiansky in Erskine and Smith (2011), p.202
37. NSA archive, doc 4234882 (1978), oral history interview with Tiltman, OH-04-78, p.9.
38. NSA oral history OH-02-79 with Abraham Sinkov.
39. NSA oral history OH-38-80, interview with Prescott Currier 1980, p. 68
40. Sherman (2016), p.29
41. Sherman (2016), pp. 33 and 38.
42. Gannon (2006), 85ff
43. Kenyon (2019), p.43
44. See his chapter in Hinsley and Stripp (1993), p.209
45. Roberts (2017), 70ff.
46. Tiltman, (1962), p.29
47. TNA HW 14/22, Tiltman consults with Norwegian expert on Hagelin, also information on Finland, November 1941.
48. TNA 14/22/70 report 15/11/41 to Denniston passed to Tiltman for information.
49. bletchleypark.org.uk
50. Hinsley, British Intelligence, p.182
51. L.P. Wilkinson in Hinsley and Stripp p.64
52. Tiltman, 'The Tunny machine', p.3
53. See the 'General report on Tunny', ch. 41, alanturing.net
54. TNA HW 65/7, passim
55. TNA 14/22/19
56. For Lucas, TNA HW 3/119, History of Hut 3. For Bennett, see Hinsley and Stripp p.31. Bennett worked for much of the war in Hut 3 and related sections, and later published a key book about Ultra and its impact on the Western war before and after D-Day not long after the decodes were first made available in public records.
57. NSA archive, doc 4236467 (1978), OH-07-78, oral history interview with Tiltman, pp.21ff.
58. Greenberg, p.172
59. TNA HW 14/59, November 1942
60. *DNB*, 'Travis, Sir Edward Wilfred Harry'
61. NSA archive, doc 4236153, p.12
62. NSA 41779359081846 undated list of key committees
63. TNA HW 14/28, January 1942
64. M. Smith (2010), p.119
65. Ibid. p.45.
66. See his chapter in Hinsley and Stripp 1993
67. See Loewe's chapter in Hinsley and Stripp
68. NSA archive, doc 4234882, p.38
69. TNA HW 14/46/27 Tiltman's report on visit, 25 March-26 April 1942
70. Agnes Driscoll had been highly successful working on Japanese codes including JN-25 for many years with OP-20-G, before Safford moved her to a new section to work on Enigma. It appears she gravely underestimated the difficulty and nature

of the machine, but even then declined Denniston's help when he visited in August 1941. Safford's move and Wenger's arrival to lead at OP-20-G saw more liaison with the British over Enigma, and the decision to develop US bombe capacity, as well as Driscoll's move back to Japanese work. It is possible that ill-feeling or frustration played a role in the encounter as well as the natural concern about lack of naval Enigma material at the time.

71. TNA HW 14/55, exchanges 15 October
72. TNA 14/54 Memo dated 4 October 1942 from de Grey to 'C'
73. TNA HW 41/54 message 2 October 1942 from CBME
74. Ibid.
75. TNA HW 14/59/22 WTC/HP/17 unsigned proposals for re-organisation November 1942
76. TNA HW 14/58/9 document dated 11 November 1942 by Lewis and Welchman
77. TNA HW 14/58/297 memo dated 14 November 1942
78. TNA HW 14/61, letter 15 December to MI-8

Chapter 7

1. NSA archive 41784989082401, news article from *The Star*, 12 Oct 1955
2. See airandspace.si.edu/stories/editorial/tizard-mission-%E2%80%93-75-years-anglo-american-technical-alliance
3. NSA archive, doc 4234882, p.3
4. NSA archive, doc 4236467, p.6
5. Sherman (2016), p.29
6. In M. Smith, *The secrets of Station X*, p.150
7. M. Smith, *The Emperor's codes*, pp. 78–9
8. Sherman, p.37
9. NSA (1975), Tiltman-Currier interview, seminar for members of Cryptanalysis Field, NSA, Fort Meade, p. 28
10. Sherman, p.34
11. NSA 41779169081825 10 Sept 1941 Denniston to Friedman
12. Budiansky refers to this in Erskine and Smith, p.196, politely not naming Stevens; but see Budiansky (2000), p.296.
13. NSA doc 4229014, oral history report on interview with Elizebeth Smith Friedman, OH-1976-22.
14. NSA 41778239081732 undated, Denniston to Friedman
15. TNA HW 14/46, various documents and reports
16. TNA 14/46 note 5 Feb from Denniston to Menzies, and Menzies' reply. Denniston pointed out that more than half of the US liaison was to do with diplomatic traffic (which he was supposed to be taking over shortly), with Captain Hastings as liaison officer in the USA.
17. TNA HW 14/46 Hastings letter (via Stevens)
18. NSA archive, doc 4236467, p.8
19. TNA HW14/46 memorandum from Denniston to Tiltman listing a range of materials to carry to the USA, dated 8 March. The breaking of Floradora owed a great deal to Patricia Bartley, named by Ferris as one of the four finest female codebreakers of her time. She worked in the GC&CS Diplomatic section during the war, at BP and then in Berkeley Street; see Smith's *Guardian* obituary, May 2021.
20. Aldrich (2010), p.44

21. TNA HW 14/47, assorted cables between USA and Britain 14–18 April 1942
22. NSA archive 41777859081694; unsigned from GC&CS to US War Dept.
23. Erskine and Smith, p.207
24. TNA HW 14/46/9a Memo 1/4/42 Tiltman to Travis listing further US wish-list items.
25. maritime.org/tech/ecm2.htm
26. NSA archive 41771849081093, US War Department memo outlining the terms of collaboration and the limits
27. NSA archive 41773049081213, memorandum by Friedman (1949) on background to ECM and its replacements
28. TNA HW 14/46, various documents and reports
29. NSA archive 41777839081692, letter Friedman to Tiltman
30. M. Smith, lecture given at Bletchley Park, c.2013.
31. NSA archive 41776739081583, Tiltman's letter of thanks to Friedman, 29 May.
32. TNA HW 14/47/49, report of 4 June 1942, Tiltman consulted for advice.
33. NSA archive 41776859081594, Friedman's letter to Tiltman.
34. NSA archive 41776989081607 memo of 31 May 1942 listing technical training materials and other items (sent by Lt. Kaye for Tiltman).
35. NSA 1338 American cryptology during the cold war, p.14
36. NSA archive 41778859081794 Denniston to Friedman 22 July 1942
37. NSA 19420709 PreNSA Doc 398408, memo for General Marshall 9 July 42
38. TNA HW 14/47, report late July, Stevens to Tiltman
39. NSA archive 41698649073798, correspondence on Friedman's reprimand and subsequent restriction from communicating with British and others
40. NSA archive 41776619081569, note from Tiltman to liaison officer Stevens 4 Nov.
41. See Budiansky in Erskine and Smith, p.208
42. See Sebag-Montefiore (2011), p.253
43. TNA HW 14/54, messages from Travis to Tiltman and others, early October 1942.
44. TNA HW 14/54/58
45. Sherman (2016), p.29
46. See Benson (1997), p.71
47. There appears to be evidence that Redman was involved with mis-analysis of the information in advance of the critical battle of Midway but subsequently claimed credit, and supported Rudy Fabian in the Far East who withheld US-found information from other Allies.
48. NSA archive, doc 4234882, p.14
49. NSA archive, doc 4236467, p.9
50. 'Madame X, Agnes in twilight', NSA document 3575741, Cryptologic Almanac Feb 2003.
51. For Agnes Driscoll, see note 70, chapter 6.
52. See NSA 'Early_papers_1940–1944 concerning US-UK agreements'. This valuable collection is fundamental for the events of this time and vital for the details of the entire section.
53. NSA 'Early_papers…', passim.
54. Telford Taylor NSA-OH-01-85-taylor, p.26, available on www.nsa.gov
55. Benson (1997), p.107
56. NSA 'Early_papers'

57. Ibid.
58. Ibid.
59. Ibid.
60. NSA 41743689078291, descriptions of analytical machines, 1954, pp. 38ff
61. See Budiansky in Erskine and Smith, p.210
62. NSA archive, doc 4234882, p.18ff
63. NSA 'Early_papers', passim
64. NSA archive, doc 4234882, p.21
65. NSA 'Early_papers'
66. NSA 19430610_PreNSA_Doc_3678774
67. See nsa.gov/Portals/70/documents/news-features/declassified-documents/ukusa/spec_int_10jun43.pdf
68. See Greenberg (2017), p.189
69. Benson (1997), p.107
70. See Erskine and Smith, p.123
71. Erskine and Smith, p.122
72. NSA archive 41784409082346 dated 8 July 1943 outline report by Friedman on visit to Britain, p.9
73. NSA 41768289080739 William Friedman diary of visit May-June 1943 to UK
74. This section owes much to Friedman's account; there is much less detail in Tiltman's oral history.
75. NSA 41751439079062 Friedman memo visit UK June 1943, 'Random notes', p.8
76. NSA oral history, nsa-OH-01-85, with Telford Taylor, p.43
77. NSA archive 41775129081420 letter Tiltman to Friedman 25 July 1943
78. See Liberty, H (2020) 'USA essays' for this much higher figure than is usually quoted; it includes the 6812 contingent at Eastcote and the 6811 at Hall Park, Bexley, early in 1945
79. NSA archive 41774699081379 Friedman to Tiltman 1 August 1944
80. NSA archive 41774789081387 Tiltman to Friedman 28 August 1944
81. NSA archive, doc 4236467, oral History interview with Tiltman, p.26
82. Ibid. p.16
83. M. Smith (2010)), 148ff, 155ff.

Chapter 8

1. Copeland (2010), p.53
2. Greenberg (2014), p.18ff
3. Welchman (1982), p.43 (online pagination)
4. Clabby, p.28
5. E.g. Smith M, *Station X.*
6. Clabby (2007), p.29
7. Recounted in Stripp (1995), p.16
8. To Tiltman from R.W. Forsyth of Regent Street, October 1939, Bletchley Park archives
9. Greenberg (2014), p.36
10. Hinsley and Stripp, ch.22
11. Lutwiniak (2004)
12. Batey (2009), p.144
13. Clabby (2007), p.22

14. Marks (2007), chapters 19 and 20.
15. NSA archive, doc 4234882 (1978), oral history interview with Tiltman, OH-04-78, p.34
16. BP Roll of Honour 1964, account of Arthur Maddocks, BP oral history project.
17. Smith (2011), p.91
18. BP Roll of Honour
19. Smith (2011), p.251
20. BP Roll of Honour
21. Smith (2010), 159ff.
22. Ibid. p,257
23. NSA oral history nsa-oh-17-82-Kullback interview, p. 50
24. NSA Tiltman interview 1 nsa_OH_05_78 p.13
25. NSA doc 3067796 oral history interview NSA-OH-14-83 with Cmdr. Howard Campaigne, pp.106ff.
26. See NSA oral history, nsa-oh-1994-32 Juanita Moody, p.5, document 4310433
27. See her account in NSA oral history OH-25-82 interview with Wilma Davis, p.16
28. Erskine and Smith, 2011, p.196
29. NSA 41776989081607, 31 May 1942 memo to Friedman listing contents of despatch; A275347
30. NSA 41775189081427, August 1943, letter from Friedman to Tiltman, A275303
31. Friedman's diary for 1 June 1943, NSA 41768289080739
32. NSA 41774699081379 Friedman to Brigadier Tiltman 1 Aug 1944
33. TNA HW 14/46/27 Tiltman's report on visit, 25 March-26 April 1942
34. E.g. nsa.gov/Portals/70/documents/resources/everyone/digital-media-center/video-audio/historical-audio/nsa-60th/nsa-60th-1960s/audio/19600901_Tiltman.mp3 (discussing the Tunny machine) – or nsa.gov/Portals/70/documents/resources/everyone/digital-media-center/video-audio/historical-audio/voices-from-the-past/audio/OH-2011-66-Capt.Currier_Lecture-122minutes.MP3 – accessed March 2021 (joint talk with Prescott Currier).
35. Simpson's chapter in Erskine and Smith, 2011, pp. 138 ff and Appendix VI.
36. See Jackson (2014), p. 233
37. NSA archive, doc 4236153 (1978), OH-06-78, oral history interview with Tiltman, p. 30
38. NSA Currier and Tiltman interview 1975, p.32
39. See Bletchley Park oral history for Michael Loewe.
40. Ferris, p. 174
41. Simpson's chapter in Erskine and Smith, p.142
42. NSA archive, doc 4236467 (1978), OH-07-78, oral history interview with Tiltman, p. 24
43. NSA archive NSA-OH-38-80, interview with Prescott Currier 1980, pp.118ff.

Chapter 9

1. NSA 41751439079062 Friedman memo visit UK June 1943, 'Random notes', p.1
2. TNA HW 14/73 report memo 16 April on Italian military ciphers
3. NSA 41768289080739 William Friedman diary of visit May-June 1943 to UK, p.38
4. Smith (2011), 234ff.
5. Gilbert (1990), 441ff.

6. TNA HW 14/83, undated memo, probably c. 25 July, detailing qualities of two promotion candidates.
7. TNA HW 14/80, copies of papers 25 June
8. TNA HW 14/83 memorandum 25 July, 'Remarks on "Y" at GC&CS and the reorganisation of the Military Wing'.
9. TNA HW 14/89, October 1943, Col Sayer to EWT 30 Sept-3 Oct on WO paper of 21 Sept on SIGINT and duties of MI-8 and DD (Y), comments by EWT to Col Tiltman of Military Wing BP.
10. TNA HW14/89/25, 8 October
11. TNA HW 14/90, 19 October 1943, Jacob reports to Tiltman on Romanian police traffic.
12. TNA HW 14/55 October 1942
13. Parrish (1986), p.159
14. TNA HW 65/7, memo dated 6/10/1943 to Tiltman from ACSS
15. TNA HW 14/97, Feb 1944, MI-8 to Col Tiltman at BP 2 Feb with draft of Allied signals requirements from Germans under Armistice terms, asking for Tiltman's comments, reply 8 Feb.
16. Greenberg (2014), p.104
17. See BP Roll of Honour
18. TNA HW 14/102, DD 1 to DMI 16 Apr thanking him for complimentary memo to Col Tiltman of 13 April
19. NSA 41774789081387, 28 Aug 44, Tiltman to Friedman
20. TNA HW 14/106 memoranda late June 1944; BP archives document BLEPK 0108.3.22 showing room listings for Drama group information circulation, dated December 1944
21. TNA HW 14/106 memoranda late June 1944
22. See also BP Roll of Honour
23. NSA 41774699081379 Friedman to Tiltman
24. McKay (2010), p.279
25. NSA 3853634; Peterson, 'Before Bourbon', p.9
26. 19441023_PreNSA_Doc_3678776_Agreement 23 Oct 1944 between GC&CS and NEGAT
27. Smith, Station X, p.173
28. See TNA HW 3/130, referenced in Greenberg (2017), p.210
29. NSA archive, doc 4234882 (1978), oral history interview with Tiltman, p.33
30. NSA 19451108_PreNSA_Doc_3983912_Memorandum Admiral Ernest King, 8 Nov 1945
31. NSA document 'The Gee System – 1', introduction by Tiltman.
32. Personnel card from GCHQ archives; on exhibition at BP at the time of this writing, GCHQ history section
33. Aldrich, p.53
34. TNA HW 14/126/123 memo 21 April 1945
35. TNA HW 14/125/82, 14 April 1945 from Wilson
36. TNA HW 14/125, April 1945, Brig Tiltman from BP to lead party with Lt Cdr Dudley-Smith and Major Edwards from BP and Cdr G Bull from CPB, party could leave UK Apr 26.
37. NSA 41698549073788 Friedman Copy of Orders Account of Movements and Duty on Trip July-Sep 1945, p.8

38. Ibid.
39. TNA HW 14/132 handwritten note 31/7/45 for Travis from Morgan
40. See the account at bletchleypark.org.uk/roll-of-honour/6738
41. Personnel card on display at Bletchley Park in GCHQ exhibition 2019–20
42. It was still being referred to as GC&CS at this stage, though GCHQ was increasingly encountered.
43. NSA doc 3853634, Peterson (2011), p.1
44. Ibid. p.13
45. See BP Roll of Honour
46. See bbc.co.uk/history/ww2peopleswar/stories/25/a3454625.shtml
47. See https://bletchleypark.org.uk/
48. BP Roll of Honour
49. Aldrich (2010), p.37
50. Hennessy (2002), p.15
51. Erskine and Smith, p.34
52. Peterson, 'Bourbon to Black Friday', p.48
53. Hennessy (2002), p.14
54. Peterson, 'Before Bourbon', p.13
55. Aldrich, p.78
56. See Benson, *The Venona Story*
57. Aldrich, pp. 80ff
58. Peterson, 'Bourbon to Black Friday', p.75
59. NSA-OH-20-80-norland-OH-1 4279643, oral history of Selmer Norland, pp. 88ff.
60. Benson, *The Venona Story*, p.9
61. NSA 41755459079461 A66702 'Value of TICOM documents in western area sections', 21 Feb 1951
62. Ferris, 'Behind the Enigma', 572 ff.

Chapter 10

1. Direct cooperation ended with the McMahon Act of 1946, the last British scientists leaving in early 1947.
2. NSA archive 41780349081942, Friedman to Travis 19 Sept 1945
3. Peterson 'Bourbon to Black Friday', p.50
4. p.55
5. See NSA ANCIB-ANCICC joint_meeting_29 Oct 45, minutes of discussion.
6. Ibid. p4.
7. Clabby, p.58
8. Peterson 'Bourbon to Black Friday', p.169
9. NSA archive 19460305_PreNSA_Doc_3678942 5 Mar 1946 US-UK agreement; Minutes of the Inauguration Meeting British Signal Intelligence Conference, 11–27 March 1946
10. Aldrich, 92ff
11. NSA 2959299 inauguration meeting March 1946 UK-USA SIGINT agreement
12. See nsa.gov/Portals/70/documents/news-features/declassified-documents/ukusa/agreement_outline_5mar46.pdf?ver=-qlDQi02-MBbEm2KltWA3g%3d%3d, UKUSA 1946
13. Ibid.

14. TNA WO 373-148-720 copy of citation
15. NAS archive 41772989081207, US War Department summary on US and British collaboration on Combined Cipher Machine development.
16. Clabby, p. 57
17. W.T. Smith, *Encyclopedia of the CIA*.
18. NSA archive 41757599079673, Memorandum on BRUSA Comsec Conference planning, 24 August 1950, by Friedman.
19. From NSA archive 41757629079676US memo, August 1950, redacted.
20. NSA archive 41756329079550 October 1950 minutes of UK-US security conference.
21. NSA 41712769075207 June 1952 AFSA Security conference A517089
22. NSA 41775419081451 USCIB meeting on French security 1951 and previous history, A522787
23. NSA 41774819081390, 1 May 1951 UKUS conference on French comms security Tiltman involved A522618.
24. NSA archive 41756719079586 memo to Tiltman 15 Mar 1951 concerning July dates.
25. NSA 41756699079584, 13 March 1951 memo for comments on agenda and committees.
26. NSA 41717609075690, ID A71749, Reply from Friedman to Tiltman 18 October 1951 thanking him for GCHQ committee lists.
27. NSA 41718129075742 Oct 1951 Jones reply to Tiltman concerning members and TOR of committees at GCHQ.
28. NSA A71763 letter from Tiltman to Friedman 17 October 1951 forwarding memo from GCHQ.
29. TNA HW 80/10, BRUSA Planning Conference, 2–19 March.
30. NSA 41714079075338 June 1953 USCIB meeting accepting ad hoc committee report to Tiltman for liaison A517222.
31. NSA 41714349075365 May 1953 arrangements for conference A517348.
32. NSA 41721499076076 June 1953 US-UK conference on NATO security and French issues A58630.
33. NSA 41721439076070-1 June 1953 US-UK conference on NATO security final session A58616
34. NSA 41785929082494 1955 USCIB Comms Security conference A4045873, p.197
35. Ibid. p.185
36. Ibid. p.151
37. NSA 41783709082275 April 1954 USCIB meeting includes rejection of 'Mercury' for French and Tiltman involved A67997
38. NSA 41785929082494 1955 USCIB Comms Security conference A4045873, p.11
39. NSA 41731679077091, 7 Jan 1954 Discussion of ROCKEX use at Berlin conference A61238
40. See Easter, 'Protecting secrets' (2018)
41. NSA 41730949077018, 11 Jan 1954 USCIB approves Rockex use in Berlin A61202
42. NSA A61179 Memo to Tiltman 18 Jan 1954
43. NSA 41775419081451 USCIB meeting on French security 1951 and previous history, A522787
44. Andrew (2009), 384ff, 420 ff; Macintyre (2014), 146 ff.
45. Obituary of Tiltman

46. See, for example, article in *The Guardian* by Tom Drew theguardian.com/society/2003/mar/20/10
47. See for example Jeffrey (2010), 676ff.
48. NSA A68425, 9 May 1952 memo from Friedman to Tiltman
49. NSA A68048, 12 Sept 1952 From Leigh to Tiltman, NSA doc. 41787529082653
50. NSA A67276 25 March 1953 Friedman memo to Tiltman
51. NSA A64263 memo to SUKLO (name redacted) Dec 1954

Chapter 11

1. NSA 41722559076182 Memo for USCIB, A59014
2. NSA archive NSA-OH-38-80, interview with Prescott Currier 1980, p.122
3. NSA archive 41698459073779 Friedman's appointments 1954–5
4. Ventris and Chadwick, 'Evidence for Greek Dialect in the Mycenaean Archives', *Journal of Hellenic Studies* (1953)
5. NSA 41709219074855, correspondence over a conference about General Purpose Flexible Analytic equipment, A70291
6. Tiltman, J., 'The Voynich Manuscript'
7. See Greenberg (2017), p. 216
8. p.138
9. p.226
10. NSA A4046187 photo of Tiltman, Friedman and Cooper, c.1963
11. Clabby, p.58
12. Lutwiniak (2004)
13. NSA archive NSA-OH-38-80, interview with Prescott Currier 1980, p.112ff.
14. Clabby p.58
15. Gustave Bertrand, *Enigma: the Greatest Enigma of the War*
16. See http://cryptome.org/2013/03/cryptolog_15.pdf,pp.3ff. Information kindly supplied by Mike Chapman.
17. https://www.nsa.gov/Portals/70/documents/news-features/declassified-documents/voynich/proceedings-of-a-seminar-30-november-1976.pdf
18. NSA nsa-OH-1977-10, Taylor-Tiltman talks to the American Historical Association.
19. Copeland et al (2010), p.53
20. Written for *The Times*, quoted in *The Carthusian*.
21. NSA archive NSA-OH-38-80 interview with Prescott Currier, p.119
22. theguardian.com/world/2012/mar/01/menwith-hill-eavesdropping-base-expansion, and theintercept.com/2016/09/06/nsa-menwith-hill-targeted-killing-surveillance/
23. 'Station Break', June 2012; article kindly provided by the Denzer family from Menwith Hill station magazine.

Bibliography

In connection with the books and texts listed below, three vital archive sources need to be mentioned:

THE NATIONAL ARCHIVES (TNA) contain many papers relevant to the life of Tiltman. The HW series in particular hold the papers relevant to GC&CS/GCHQ. Included also are the 'Mask' documents 1934–37, reports from the Military Section of which Tiltman was the head, and a wide range of administration papers.

THE NSA (National Security Agency) archives, which hold, among other valuable sources:

- the oral history interviews with Tiltman: OH-04-78, OH-05-78, OH-06-78, OH-07-78
- the papers of William Friedman, chief cryptologist for the US army
- oral history interview with other main players (Kullback, Taylor, Norland etc)
- official USA reports of conferences, meetings etc, including documents relevant to the UK/USA agreements on intelligence.

The Bletchley Park Roll of Honour, which contains the names of women and men who worked at BP 1938–46; an official employee list does not appear to have survived, but the Roll is available online.

Aldrich, R., *Intelligence and the war against Japan*, Cambridge University Press (2000)
Aldrich, R., *GCHQ*, Harper Collins (2010)
Andrew, C., *Defence of the realm*, Allen Lane (2009)
Batey, M., *Dilly, the man who broke Enigma*, Biteback (2009)
Benson, R., *A history of US Communications Intelligence during WW2*, NSA (1997)
Benson, R., 'Origin of US-British Communications Intelligence Co-operation' in *NSA Cryptologic Spectrum*, Part 1, Autumn 1977
Benson, R., *The Venona Story*, NSA publication
Bertrand, Gustave, *Enigma: the Greatest Enigma of the War of 1939–45* (1973)
Budiansky, S., *Battle of Wits*, Simon and Schuster (2000)
Clabby, J., *Brigadier John Tiltman; a giant among cryptanalysts*, NSA (2007).
Copeland, J. et al., *Colossus – the secret of Bletchley Park's Codebreaking Computers*, Oxford (2010)
David, C., *A World War II German cipher and how we broke it*, NSA (1994)
Donovan, Peter, 'The thought behind high-level cryptological discovery' in *Cryptologia* Vol. 33 (2014 – 01), p.56, available at nsa.gov
Duffy, D., *The secret codebreakers of Central Bureau*, Scribe (2017)
Easter, D., 'Protecting secrets, British diplomatic cipher machines in the early Cold War', KCL (2018)

Erskine R. and Smith M., 'Brigadier John Tiltman, one of Britain's finest cryptologists', *Cryptologia* vol. 27, issue 4 (2003).
Erskine R. and Smith M. (eds), *The Bletchley Park Codebreakers*, Biteback (2011)
Ferris, P., *Behind the Enigma*, Bloomsbury (2020)
Friedman, W., *Military Cryptanalysis*, Part 1, (1938)
Gannon, P., *Colossus; Bletchley Park's Greatest Secret*, Atlantic (2006)
GCHQ and Bletchley Park Trust, *History of Bletchley Park huts and blocks, 1939–1945*, Royal Holloway (2009)
Gilbert, M., *The Second World War*, Fontana/Collins (1990)
Greenberg, J., *Gordon Welchman; Bletchley Park's architect of ULTRA intelligence*, Frontline (2014)
Greenberg, J., *Alastair Denniston*, Frontline (2017)
Hanyok, R., *Eavesdropping on Hell*, NSA (2005)
Hennessy, P., *The Secret State*, Allen Lane (2002)
Hinsley, F. and Stripp, A. (eds), *Codebreakers, the inside story of Bletchley Park*, Oxford (1993)
Hinsley, F., *British Intelligence in the Second World War*, HMSO (1993, one-volume edition)
Jackson, J. (ed), *Solving Enigma's Secrets*, Booktower (2014)
Jeffrey, K., *MI6, the History of the Secret Intelligence Service*, Bloomsbury (2010)
Kenyon, D., *Bletchley Park and D-Day*, Yale University Press (2019)
Liberty, H., 'USA essays', unpublished research pamphlet for Bletchley Park (2020)
Lutwiniak, W., 'John H Tiltman, a reminiscence', NSA paper for the induction of Tiltman to the Hall of Honor (2004)
Macintyre, B., *A Spy among Friends*, Bloomsbury (2014)
Marks, L., *Between Silk and Cyanide,* The History Press (2007)
McKay, S., *The Secret Life of Bletchley Park*, Aurum (2010)
Mowry, D., *German Cipher Machines of World War 2*, NSA (2014)
Owen, Lt. Col. F., *The Campaign in Burma*, HMSO (1946)
Parrish, T., *American Codebreakers*, Scarborough House (1986)
Peterson, M., 'Before Bourbon, American and British COMINT efforts against Russia and the Soviet Union', declassified NSA document (2011)
Peterson M., 'Bourbon to Black Friday', volume 2 of series on 'Bourbon', NSA document 4314365 (1995)
Roberts, G., *Lorenz; breaking Hitler's top secret code at Bletchley Park,* History Press (2017)
Sebag-Montefiore, H., *Enigma, the Battle for the Code*, Phoenix (2011)
Sherman, D., *The first Americans*, NSA (2016)
Simkins, P., Jukes, G. and Hickey M., *The First World War*, Osprey (2003).
Smith, B., *The Ultra-Magic deals*, Airlife (1993)
Smith, M., *Station X*, Channel 4 books (1998)
Smith, M., *The Emperor's Codes*, Dialogue (2010)
Smith, M., *The secrets of Station X*, Biteback (2011)
Smith, M. and Erskine, R. (eds.), *The Bletchley Park Codebreakers*, Biteback (2001)
Smith, W.T., *Encyclopedia of the Central Intelligence Agency*, Facts on File (2003)
Stripp, A., *Codebreaker in the Far East*, Oxford paperbacks (1995)
Tiltman, J., 'The Tunny machine and its solution', *NSA Technical Journal* vol. 6, no.2 (1961)
Tiltman, J., 'A cryptological fairytale', *NSA Technical Journal* (1962)

Tiltman, J., 'Some reminiscences', *NSA Technical Journal* vol. 11, no.3 (1966)
Tiltman, J., 'The Voynich manuscript; the most mysterious manuscript in the world', *NSA Technical Journal* vol. 13, no.3 (1967)
Tiltman, J., 'Experiences 1920–39', *NSA Technical Journal* vol.17, no.3 (1972)
Tiltman, J., 'Some principles of cryptographic security', *NSA Technical Journal* vol. 19, no.3 (1974)
Tordella, L., 'Select SIGINT intelligence highlights', *NSA Technical Journal*, vol. 19, no. 4 (1974)
Turing, D., *X, Y and Z*, The History Press (2018)
Welchman, G., *The Hut Six Story*, Allen Lane and McGraw Hill (1982)
West, N., *SIGINT Secrets*, Weidenfeld and Nicholson (1986)
West, N., *GCHQ*, Coronet (1986)
West, N., *Mask*, Routledge (2005)
West, N., *GCHQ, The Secret Wireless War*, Coronet (1986)
The Great Soviet Encyclopedia, 3rd Edition (1970–79), Gale (2010)

Index